Studies in Public Communications

THE IMAGE DECADE:

Television Documentary:
1965–1975

STUDIES IN PUBLIC COMMUNICATION

THE IMAGE DECADE:

Television Documentary:
1965—1975

by

CHARLES MONTGOMERY HAMMOND, JR.

COMMUNICATION ARTS BOOKS

HASTINGS HOUSE · PUBLISHERS

New York, N.Y. 10016

Library of Congress Cataloging in Publication
Hammond, Charles Montgomery.   The image decade.

   (Studies in public communication) (Communication arts books)
   Bibliography: p.
   Includes index.
   1. Television broadcasting of news—United States.
2. Documentary television programs—United States.
I. Title.
PN4888.T4H36   1981   070.1'9   80-28488
ISBN 0-8038-3431-4
ISBN 0-8038-3432-2 (pbk.)

Published simultaneously in Canada by
Copp Clark Ltd., Toronto

Printed in the United States of America

for Mary

The beginnings and endings of all human undertakings are untidy.
— John Galsworthy

(Quoted by CBS news correspondent John Hart on the CBS News Special: *A Television Album*, broadcast Sunday, December 29, 1974, 9:30–10:30 p.m. EST, p. 17.)

CONTENTS

Part Three
Reporters

Part Four
Events

INTRODUCTION: WHAT THIS BOOK IS ALL ABOUT

TO WRITE THIS BOOK I went through the decade 1965–1975 three times, first with NBC News, then CBS News and finally ABC News. To understand what happened in TV documentary at each network, I felt I had to travel through each network news department's output for the decade. I also spent a summer screening TV documentaries. I interviewed key administrators and producers. I tallied innumerable reviews and clippings about TV documentaries, mostly from major eastern newspapers, national news weeklies and the broadcast trade and consumer press. I carefully read books about documentary and nonfiction film.

All this took four years. Throughout the period since January, 1975, I've been haunted (believe me, the word fits) as to just how to present the enormous collective effort put into TV documentary between 1965 and 1975. Researching this output was relatively simple to do; writing about each network's news work also was easy. What was bothersome was how to relieve you, my reader, of the tedium of also traveling through the decade three times in order to understand and appreciate what had happened during those years at NBC News, CBS News and ABC News.

Therefore, I decided to ignore chronology wherever necessary, respecting it only as it helped me deal directly with the art and practice of TV documentary in terms of concepts, programs, producers, reporters and events. In short, to credit representative figures and archetypal reportage in TV documentary of the decade.

Thus, the book is organized as follows: Part I, Television News and Theme Documentary, is about the evolution of TV documentary from 1965 to

1975; Parts II and III isolate only those producers and reporters who I believe did innovative or representative work during the era under study; Part IV, Events, concentrates on three areas: social confrontations, war and Washington. Each discussion will tell you what TV news and theme documentaries accomplished when they turned to look at the emergence of minorities and women, at the American family, education, urban life, Vietnam, or Washington — nexus of the decade's basic conflicts: conflicts between government and the press, conflicts between government and political dissenters, and internal upheavals within the federal power structure proper.

Another determinant of this book's structure was the need to recognize the volume and quality of work done during the decade at each network. One can say I've been outrageously unfair in giving CBS News by far the most attention. I've allotted percentages which run something like this: CBS News, 60 percent; NBC News, 30 percent; ABC News, 10 percent. On the surface, these figures do appear blatantly unfair. But remember, this study is only about news and theme documentaries — not the networks themselves or even their respective total news operations. Seen in this way, CBS News can't help but dominate a survey of TV documentary from 1965 to 1975. Edward R. Murrow and Fred W. Friendly, both of CBS News, invented TV documentary. Despite deep inroads into CBS News's prestige and leadership made by Fred Freed of NBC News in the sixties and early seventies and by Av Westin and the ABC News's *Close-up* series in 1973–1974, CBS News consistently aired a remarkably competent number of pertinent and informative documentaries. Moreover, as TV documentary evolved into other news forms, CBS News usually managed to pioneer or appropriate such forms advantageously. *60 Minutes* is an outstanding example.

THE ABSENCE OF PUBLIC TELEVISION

As I said at the start, this book is about commercial network television news. Therefore, except for an occasional reference, public television documentaries and their progenitors are absent from this study. Why, when so many wonderful documentaries have been aired by public television stations since 1967? That question answers itself: public television has screened more theater and traditional documentaries than has any of the commercial networks since 1967 (but this cannot be said of public TV's news presentations, especially live news specials, which are rarely seen on PBS). PBS experimented for a time with news documentaries on its Public Broadcast Laboratory series. It has been a bountiful haven for the theme documentary. Many of its documentary series, such as *Nova, Civilization* and *The Ascent of Man,* are some of the best cultural programs ever presented on TV. Finally, public TV has shown us the important work of Fredrick Wiseman, the Maysles, Nan Cox and numerous others working in the vérité genre.

Aside from the sheer quantity and scope of documentary presentations on public TV since 1967, which really call for their own distinctive analysis and study, I feel public TV still is an alternative broadcasting service which is quite different in most respects from ABC, CBS and NBC. It does not sell time as do the commercial networks. To me, it resembles a free circulation publication competing against paid circulation magazines. Because public television programming sustains itself via public appropriations and private contributions, it is based on the premise: give them what they need to know, not what they want, the latter of which is at the heart of all commercial network programming. As a result, public TV audiences, though very small, are demographically elitist.

But public TV documentary is absent here for another reason — a reason that overrides all the foregoing. Consider a market with four television stations: three commercial and one public. Such a broadcast market is typical. For the public station to be considered in the same light as the commercial stations, which, let us say, are each affiliated with one of the three commercial networks, it must earn at least 25 percent of the audience in its market. That is the onus that the commercial stations face. If three stations are in a market, each must win at least 33⅓ percent of the general audience if each is to have a commercial rate card that is competitive and potentially profitable. PBS stations don't face these pressures even though they may face numerous financial, personnel and programming difficulties. But commercial stations do, as do the networks with which they are affiliated. Hence, the necessity to cast aside the pear, PBS, to concentrate on three apples — ABC, CBS and NBC.

To keep this study directed solely toward commercial network documentary, other important avenues of TV documentary also had to be shunted aside, such as the work of the Group W stations, documentary on the local-station level, theater documentary, and vérité programs. Still, whenever necessary, I do refer to these categories.

THE EMERGENCE OF TELEVISION NEWS

This study will say over and over again that whenever people in commercial network television decided to speak the truth during 1965–1975, they used the TV documentary as the best means to do it. We have to go back to 1965 to understand this. TV documentary in 1965 was a highly respectable news form because network executives deliberately used it to refurbish their public image with audiences, advertisers and government regulators after the debacle of the Van Doren quiz scandal. Truth-telling, via TV documentaries, was used to overcome widespread disgruntlement about question-rigging and quiz participants pretending they were honestly struggling to get correct answers when, all the time, having been previously coached, they knew the answers.

In the process, the networks discovered they could make money broadcasting the truth. So the lid came off newscasts as a particular programming category with results that continue to spill about even today.

Meanwhile, throughout the period 1965–1975, events both beneficial and tragic — but made to order for TV news — began breaking here and abroad, and newsgathering became the one essential public service offered by the TV commercial networks. TV documentary, in turn, embellished that service by evolving into a new form of journalism, a new, visual expression of history.

Cazenovia, New York   Charles Montgomery Hammond, Jr.
June, 1979

ACKNOWLEDGMENTS

I OWE A PERSONAL DEBT of gratitude for their extensive help to three people: my wife, Mary Klysa Hammond; Mrs. A. William Bluem; and Dr. Louis Salomon, whose pertinent criticism and good advice were most welcome.

To the late Ben Semmel, to Howard and Bash Bernstein and Editor Russ Neale, my personal thanks.

I also thank:

At Morrisville College: typist Debbie Snyder; librarians Hewlett Fagan and Michael Gieryic; Journalism Department Chairman Gerald A. Leone; Division Chairman Lawrence Baker; and Vice President John Stewart, either for their active assistance or generous cooperation and counsel.

At Washington State University, Pullman, Washington, where I was visiting professor of communications, 1975–1976: the late Humphrey Leynse, professor of cinema studies, the Edward R. Murrow Communications Center; and Mrs. Deborah Lisser, my teaching assistant.

At CBS News: Burton Benjamin and John Sharnik; Marcia Ratcliff, director, and Roberta Hadley, assistant director, CBS News Library; Deborah Richardson and Allen L. Maraynes, CBS News archives; and Ellen Ehrlich, CBS News press relations. At NBC News: Al Perlmutter, Robert ("Shad") Northshield, Eliot Frankel and George Hoover, NBC News press relations. At ABC News: Av Westin, Stephen Fleischman, Paul Altmeyer and Catherine Lynch, librarian, ABC's general reference library.

In addition: Richard D. Heffner, Ford Foundation; Mary Ahern, curator, The Museum of Broadcasting, New York City; and David Maysles; critics such

15

as Larry Lichty, John J. O'Connor, Jack Gould, Harriet Van Horne, Bob Williams, John Horn and Kay Gardella, among others, for their magazine and newspaper reviews, which collectively represent a prime source about TV documentary in America from 1965 to 1975; the many anonymous writers of *Broadcasting* magazine; such by-liners as the late Bill Greeley of *Variety*; and the various authors of pieces on TV documentary to appear in *Television Quarterly* — a magazine founded, by the way, by the late A. William Bluem, to whom I owe my deepest appreciation and gratitude.

June, 1979   C.M.H., Jr.

Part One / TELEVISION NEWS AND THEME DOCUMENTARY

1 / Evolution of the Television News Documentary

INTRODUCTION

THE LATE A. WILLIAM BLUEM'S seminal study, *Documentary in American Television,* surveyed the roots of documentary in modern America and demonstrated how that particular form of mass communications developed out of kindred technical and cultural expressions in photography, film, broadcasting and theater. It revealed, too, how documentary went on to find its most efficacious helpmate — television.

"Television" and "Documentary." Electronic sight-and-sound transmissions linked to a film art form which pioneer documentarist John Grierson once described as "the creative use of actuality." And the "television documentary"? What is that? If we must define it, it is a news program that ignores fantasy and fiction for facts by using clusters of edited film or videotape actualities to reflect, comment on or interrelate current problems or realities.

Bluem enunciated three versions of television documentary in his text. I shall review them shortly. My point in mentioning them now is that Bluem left us with a critical method that I've done my best to apply here. Still, if I have taken off into new avenues, it's only because the decade under study was a time of high contrarieties. American television moved into areas where it never had been before simply because the country itself moved into such areas. The decade 1965 to 1975 was a time of advances in medicine, space probes and international accommodation via economics, jet travel and satellite communications. It endured the morass in Vietnam, widespread revulsion over the spoilage of our cities and countryside, and remained heedless as vast amounts of monies were appropriated for armaments. The decade witnessed the breakdown

of repressive sexual patterns and saw the emergence of minorities and women
into the mainstream of American life. Yet, simultaneously, a continuous *angst*
afflicted the young, now the nation's largest age group, who felt they were
destined to live senselessly in a world where most people were helpless to fend
off exploitation by hitherto respected social forces, such as church, school,
family and government. The decade was a time of triumph as well as turmoil.

ACTUALITY

Actuality is the heart of present-day news operations on TV. It is present,
unblemished and cogent, in nearly every newscast and television news magazine segment or is an integral part of news and (some) theme documentaries.

In fact, it has to be present for any of these forms of broadcast news to
reflect the genuine properties of film or videotape. Film, in the generic sense,
is protean: film records so much so easily, it's difficult to organize it in any
orderly fashion. Film depicts riots, vistas, interiors, micro- and macro-actions,
whether man-made or natural. Film has compositional qualities reflecting internal states of mind and emotions which the people behind the camera may feel
at the time they focus on their subject. In short, film is not just a recording of
reality; it is a record of intangibles as well.

Actuality is important because it is the mold that most often retains and
shapes these filmic qualities.

But does this mean you do as one NBC staffer has put it: ''The customary
way to present two or more sides of a question in a documentary was first to
interview the persons involved, then pare the interviews down to essential statements, and finally to 'shotgun' the statements throughout the program.''[1] No.
People should not be used as mere ''word banks'' — talking heads mouthing
dreary facts. The words can be there — must be there — but they should support the filmic qualities of actuality, not impair or obscure them. Words sup-
plement visual elements; words used to caption footage or tape shouldn't interfere with what the film already is showing. Also, judgments and opinions
should emanate from sources, not from the narrator-reporter. It's far easier to
let the correspondent say something about the problem or theme being described, and such situations are far too prevalent in most TV documentaries,
but actuality doesn't depend upon someone telling you what's happened.

Actuality tries to resurrect what has happened in mostly filmic terms so
that it appears to be happening again. Its cardinal characteristic is vivid immediacy.

Actuality, then, is a film episode meeting five conditions:

1. It is a recorded series of brief but real visual experiences.
2. It uses natural, spontaneous materials which transmit a self-contained

[1] Footnotes are arranged by chapter in a special section, Sources, at the end of this book beginning
on page 253.

meaning, or intrinsic emotion, to the viewer without the need on the viewer's part for conscious rearrangement.

3. It surveys the real, seeking the character behind people's actions and the essence of things as they are. It accepts; it never directs.
4. It tends to be factual rather than poetic; but can be either or both.
5. It expresses viewpoints, attitudes, feelings — sometimes those of its producers alone, but often also those common to all mankind.

The handicap we face when writing about actuality is that we often fail to convey the volume of information which only sight and sound, working together, convey. But let us try, using an excerpt from the work of CBS News producer John Sharnik:

> I think it's perfectly true that sometimes the most dramatic things on television are tight shots of somebody telling you some marvelously revelatory experience. The distinction is between the abstract or the factual. I don't necessarily try to avoid talking heads. I do try to avoid abstractions, cliché questions, asking people opinions about something. I try to zero in on people telling about their own experience: 'Tell me what happened to you.'[2]

Sharnik likes to have people in familiar situations acting familiarly. A good example is near the end of his *CBS Reports: "The Germans,"* an hour-long show broadcast on September 27, 1967, at 10:00 p.m. EDT. It was about the character of West German society in the late sixties.

Sharnik had picked a man named Hamburger to represent the last remnants of the Nuremberg Jewish community; Nuremberg had been selected because it was so typically German, especially to the Germans themselves. Hamburger had come back to Germany after the war, after having been in Israel. Sharnik wanted Hamburger's reactions as to what life was like for Jews, especially in a city with unpleasant overtones still lingering from past racial laws. Sharnik had researched his man carefully. He had found out that Hamburger was a passionate lover of soccer. An athletic type, still in his late thirties, Hamburger also was a coach of the local Jewish soccer team. The team had a big upcoming game with a German team from Hamburg. Sharnik decided to interview his man during the game on the sidelines. While Sharnik stood by, directing the sequence between Hamburger and CBS Correspondent Hughes Rudd, the show's narrator, a Mr. Mandel, representing the elderly Jewish generation, nosed in:

Rudd: What is it like being a Jew in Germany today? Don't you feel uncomfortable being in this country?
Hamburger: No I don't feel uncomfortable. You know and I know, and my children go to school here, and they feel perfectly at ease, much more at ease than I personally feel because — I mean, we are burned, my generation. I was exactly ten years old when Hitler came into power — I mean,

Mr. Mandel knows me from childhood on more or less, and so, of course, I very often have got a funny feeling in my stomach, especially if I hear things like "Dachau," myself. I go out very often, very frequently to have discussions with the German public, and I try to explain to them what we are. I mean, most of the younger generation doesn't know; they don't know a Jew. They haven't seen a Jew.

Rudd: And you, Mr. Mandel?

Mandel: I wouldn't say uncomfortable, because I am very proud that I am a Jew. I live here. You know I am in the Bavarian Senate, speaking for all the Bavarian Jews here, and I wouldn't say that I feel uncomfortable. I got used to living here, and I get back friends, and then I took part in the social life of the community, and so forth, and so I always find another reason to stay here.

Rudd: Do you notice much anti-Semitism in Germany now?

Hamburger: No, I don't, not at all.

Rudd: Mr. Mandel, do you detect much anti-Semitism in Germany?

Mandel: I wouldn't say very much, but there is still — there is still. One hundred years ago we had the ghetto still — and fifty years ago 'til the last world war we had a *geistiges* ghetto.

Hamburger: A spiritual ghetto.

Mandel: A spiritual ghetto here still — and this we have still. And you have people, living people from this time here, what brings all those ideas, that a Jew cannot be a general — they have not the same rights. And this doesn't happen in other countries, in the Western countries.

Hamburger: Oh, you wouldn't say that if you start from history — what happened in Spain, what happened in Russia, what happened in Poland, for heaven sake.

Mandel: It makes the thing a lot better.

Hamburger: Oh, no.

Mandel: It makes —

Hamburger: No, but . . . but this isn't an argument, Mr. Mandel.

Mandel: This is a big argument.

Hamburger: Excuse me, I don't think this is the place — No, no my life is over there.

Rudd: On the football field.

Hamburger: Sure.[3]

The viewer saw Hamburger preoccupied by things — the game taking place on the soccer field — so that he couldn't fully concentrate on what he was saying to Rudd and Mandel, but still he was concentrating enough to give what he said a feeling of life, of what I call actuality.

Until recently, actuality always was part of documentary proper, and because it was, it remained unnoticed. Only since the growth in variant forms of television news has actuality, as a distinctive kind of visual language, clearly become independent enough to stand by itself. Moreover, it was the newscast, not the documentary, that was the garden in which actuality thrived. It began as a visual story alone or as a story crudely told in visual terms and overly explained by voice-over narration. But it eventually ended up as an entity.

THE NATURE OF NEWS

Because so much that has happened between 1965 and 1975 has been related to a vast audience via journalistic channels, I have concentrated considerable attention on the commercial network use of television news.

News never is reality. It's never the thing it reports. "News is by definition a construct of what happened today. Yesterday's newspaper is used to wrap fish, and yesterday's broadcast does not exist at all."[4]

Yet some concrete quality is at work in the presentation of the day's news. It may not be literal reality but *something is there*. "Network news is resented because it told us the truth. It is resented by people who wanted to hide the truth and by people who didn't want to know the truth because the truth was depressing."[5]

Still the question remains: What kind of truth does TV news tell?

Essentially, television is an optical phenomenon; it magnifies what it sees. It also is limited in what it sees. But that very limitation also leads to another magnification of sorts, for if TV news cannot cover everything, what it does cover is given a tacit expansion in importance by the very fact that it is on the air. Public statements tend to be believed simply because they are public statements.

TV news is simplistic. It undoubtedly leaves out too much, and it seldom repeats itself. In a sense, it censors — either by publicizing what it does cover or by deemphasizing what it ignores or has abandoned. No one sinks faster and deeper into oblivion than the TV candidate failing to win a primary, a political event largely significant because network news chiefs think it is and consequently send their top news people to cover it.

TV news, in the long run, has a debilitating effect on the individual because it keeps showing him how ineffectual and powerless he is: how prone to accident or death; how susceptible to financial loss; how exposed to exploitation. Often TV news is worthless to the viewer because it points out dangers and troubles besetting only a small segment of the audience. Police-blotter accidents and petty crimes are good examples. What real meaning do they offer most people to justify the attention they receive?

Aside from the limitations of news in general, TV newscasting in particular has its own limitations which though they may appear to be obvious, are nonetheless worth noting. For instance, there is the fact that everything you hear and see comes from what might be called an electronic billboard or an electronic front page, depending upon the message. What has been chosen for you to see, you see exclusively. No browsing on your part, no ambling from headline to headline, page to page, selecting topics. They already have been picked. And each selection is complete, a unified narrative in pictures and words with a beginning, middle and end. Let your mind wander, and you are in trouble. The selection isn't repeated. One *must* understand a TV news story (documentary) at its first and only "reading."

Oddly enough, the range of selection for TV news stories is nearly limitless. Messages from transmitting equipment on the Moon or Mars are available to TV as is the conventional studio interview. The technology of TV is complex and expansive, exactly the opposite of its capabilities as a diurnal scanner of news.

TV news lacks perspective. Despite a new commentator's weeknight essays, TV cannot place events in context as well as print media can. This role, I suppose, is allotted to the viewer and, if the information being offered comes out of the tube too quickly or with too great an emotional bang, then TV news is perennially doomed to remain simplistic, a crude, rudimentary news service. Because TV news has all the hallmarks of good conversation, or should have, it never can do well presenting discursive lectures.

This enforced elementary level of presentation is partly choice, partly due to high costs and partly because of time and talent limitations. However, it mainly occurs because the TV picture tube is an optical purveyor of information, not a coded source.

NEWS, THEME AND VÉRITÉ DOCUMENTARY

This emphasis on news links my study directly to Bluem's. Bluem's versions of American television documentary ran along three lines: the television documentary as a news program; as the extremely cohesive presentation of a theme about a person or a place or an event; and as a predominantly visual report.

Television news documentary is a mixture of art and reportage. It subordinates the visual to the subject at hand. A choice is offered: either the program recites facts that are hinged to some kind of news lead or facts are expressed directly through the reproductive power of the film to recreate "what happened" without much help from the reporter. Still, the reporter's presence in a news documentary is strongly prominent since he introduces, interconnects and signs off the several actualities being successively shown. The degree of dominance of these two — reportage and film craft — is determined by the content of the program; in effect, by the content of the several actualities. Nothing should be allowed to interfere with that. Sometimes the film will benefit from the knowledgeable intervention of the reporter or program presenter who sets the scene and gives us a verbal reconstruction of the essentials of an event. The reporter lends credibility to the story. He gives it editorial approval in the sense that he is there on the screen talking about it. Yet, what always works best in terms of telling you "what happened" *is what the film or video-*

tape reveals. We must remember that what is at work in the television news documentary is not only the presentation of news (facts) but also the presentation of interpretation (background content). There's also a third ingredient at work: *the news program's overall ability to put the viewer back into the course of the story just as it once occurred.* Too often this quality is stinted or fails to come off at all because the visual treatment is too scant in visual information, too often looks at wrong aspects of the story or, by omitting key scenes, is too fragmented altogether.

CBS Reports: "A Night in Jail, a Day in Court," broadcast on January 27, 1972, at 10:00 p.m. EST, had all the attributes of a news documentary. It was a detailed account of the experiences of two young men accused of crime and their encounters with our judicial system. It was filmed in the jails and courts of Indianapolis. It was produced, written and — to some extent — reported by John Sharnik, but was narrated mostly by someone familiar to the audience, CBS News National Correspondent Eric Sevareid.

This example, however, is broad. We shall later examine news documentary in detail.

The television theme documentary is more complicated than the news documentary. It provides for more amplitude than the television news documentary and it lacks the haphazard, yet harsh, dreamlike qualities of the vérité approach. Where the television news documentary tends to control the artistic treatment by sticking closely to an analysis of a particular news event, the television theme documentary tries to control the "life." TV theme documentary sets up artistic credos for its subjects, then proceeds to explain them subjectively, even personally. Such programs make no attempts to be objective, as do news shows. The rule dividing the two forms would appear to be: if you build your actualities around a news lead, you end up with a TV news documentary. But if you build your program around a theme — a point of view — then you have created a theme television documentary.

According to Bluem, three production methods are available to the theme documentarian:

1. *Compilation,* which equally employs cinematic, narrative and musical techniques. Director, film editor, writer, narrator and composer — each makes his distinctive contribution.
2. *Biographical,* which depicts the exertions of one person's will to surmount or to be overcome by a series of private or public confrontations, or both. To relate such encounters, the biographical theme documentary uses all the talents just listed under *compilation,* but concentrates on the person being scanned with their collective eye rather than undertaking the broader scope that compilation documentary ordinarily offers.
3. *Dramatic television theme documentary, or docudrama,* frankly imitates fiction television programs by dressing up facts and circumstances in the garb of a story line of some sort. It sacrifices what it can of actuality to

gain emotional — "intellectual" is perhaps a better word — involvement, and strives to capture attention with dramatic techniques unabashedly stolen from the stage.

A documentary that certainly combines these methods was filmmaker Bud Greenspan's *The Glory of Their Times* (1969), which was based on a book by New York University professor Lawrence S. Ritter. Ritter had used taped interviews to recapture the memories of baseball players of the vintage of John J. McGraw and Christy Mathewson. Greenspan also used taped interviews as well as old photos and early films to capture what baseball — and the country — was like between 1900 and World War I. The Hughes Sports Network had put up $45,000 to finance *The Glory of Their Times,* but later, after seeing the final result, allowed Greenspan to buy it so that he could sell it on his own. Greenspan used as his narrator the peripatetic Alexander Scourby, whose rich voice is a part of so many theme documentaries. At one point, Scourby praised baseball players as "giants who walked the earth when the earth was still." But later the players mentioned Ty Cobb's "rotten disposition" and complained about having to put up with the hard-drinking spitball artist Bug Raymond: "You don't spit on the ball, you blow your breath on it and the ball comes up drunk."[6]

An example of biographical theme documentary was the CBS News Special half-hour study of Richard Cardinal Cushing, broadcast on June 11, 1968, at 10:30 p.m. EDT. Reporter Harry Reasoner described the Cardinal, then Archbishop of Boston and a close spiritual advisor to the Kennedys, as "a model of Catholic power." The program showed him presiding over a confirmation at the Cathedral of the Holy Cross, visiting the aged in St. Joseph's Home, delivering an all-faiths memorial address for Dr. Martin Luther King, Jr., and in interviews with Reasoner. While at St. Joseph's he danced an Irish jig and said, "Keep living. You'll be dead long enough." Then he passed out tiny bottles of Seagrams, which he said were "just a little holy water."[7]

Bluem's third category, vérité televison documentary, is light years away from the others because it is directionless. It is a predominantly visual expression wherein the camera is the only true reporter. If sound assists, it does so only because sounds occur as the camera roams about, giving us maybe some kind of random talk as well. Thus, vérité is not subservient to a script, to a particular theme, to a plotted narrative, to anything, in fact, but the naked unfolding of several connected events. Musical background, the omniscient off-camera narrator, or the on-the-spot interviewer — all are abandoned or at least minimized.

Salesman, the 1967 cinema vérité theater documentary produced by Al and David Maysles and edited by Charlotte Zwerin, is a 90-minute saga of a Bible salesman who no longer can sell. Paul Brennan, 50 years old, separated from his wife, sucking nervously on a cigarette, is one of four salesmen the Maysles follow as the four make their calls around Boston and, later, Florida, and as they partake in their company's national sales meeting in Chicago. Each salesman has a nickname: Paul Brennan is "The Badger"; Charlie McDevitt, "The Gipper"; James Baker, "The Rabbit"; and Ray Martos, "The Bull." Ken Turner, the company sales manager who oversees their efforts, is alternately easygoing then tough. But he shares a confident belief in himself and his sales abilities with Charlie, James, and Ray. Their sales records, as the documentary unfolds, disclose this. Each steadily racks up anywhere from one to three sales daily. Each attacks his prospects directly, putting all of his efforts into the sale, letting up only when the four gather together in a motel room to rehash the day's work. They have a job and they do it.

Paul is different. Gradually we realize he has played out his string.

Paul: Not much time to work with and, you know, if you're not familiar with the territory, no matter how good a man you are, if you're not familiar with the territory, it's difficult, you know?
Ken: Permit me to offer my own alibi. (Everybody laughs, especially Paul.) Any man that's not good at sellin' should be able . . . should be good at makin' excuses. (Everybody laughs.)
Charlie: Any man not good at sellin' should be good at findin' territory.
Paul: Findin' territory. (Laughs) [8]

The documentary doesn't dwell on anyone but Paul except to show them either selling or being sold. Ken makes a successful practice pitch to the Rabbit: The Rabbit, in turn, along with the Gipper and the Bull, is shown completing orders for Bibles. Even Dr. Melbourne I. Feltman, Ph.D., "the world's greatest salesman of the world's best seller," successfully revs up the company pitchmen at a Chicago sales meeting.

Watching everyone else in the film, you are fascinated with the ease with which an expensive Bible can be sold door-to-door. You come to believe those aspirations expressed in Chicago about making $50,000 a year.

This euphoria disappears quickly, however, when the camera centers on Paul. Nothing works for him, not his prospects, not the exhortations of Dr. Feltman or Sales Manager Turner, not even the ministrations of his fellows who take him along on a call.

Charlie: We place it in the home for as little as forty-nine ninety-five, complete. Isn't that amazing?
Man: Now, this will all be changed pretty soon, won't it?
Charlie: No. Are you with the Knights of the Holy Name?
Woman: No, he's not a Catholic.
Man: I'm not a Catholic.
Woman: But I mean he follows me right along and all that.
Charlie: Well, I'll tell you. You know what I appreciate, honest to gosh. When you go to a home and it's a mixed marriage . . . we find this in many cases — the husband is much more enthused often times than we even as cradle Catholics.
Woman: I wish you were selling a children's encyclopedia instead of this.

(Paul plays with the little boy, waltzing a toy car through the air as Charlie talks.)

Charlie: Yeah, let me put it this way. None — none of your chilren would ever get a sunburn or they'd never get a cold unless they were exposed to a draft. They'd never get a sunburn unless they were exposed to the sun. The mere fact that they've been exposed to it, they're going to — they're going to receive so many benefits from it. They have to, you know, because see if it never does them any good, it'll never do them any harm.

Man: It's kind of a fancy Bible for a child, isn't it?

Woman: Yeah.

Charlie: What do you mean, Mister? Uh — ?

Woman: I mean, they're kinda young but . . .

Man: You were saying that they'll be exposed to this.

Charlie: Right. Uh-huh.

Man: In what manner? Looking at it or . . .

Paul: (aggressively) May I interject to say one thing. The hand that rocks the cradle rules the world. Is that right? The woman behind great . . . there's a great woman . . . Now she spends, according to the *Reader's Digest,* about eighty-five percent with the children. Now whatever she is and what she imparts to them is how those children are going to grow up and this is the age when they need it. Because if your house doesn't have a foundation you've got no kind of house. Does that make sense?

Man: That's just . . . well . . .

Paul: (cutting him off) There we are. There we are.

Man: That's exactly what . . .

Paul: (pontificating vehemently) There we are! And we have that in white and red. And we can give it in any color that you might like. And that's another thing, too . . . the Bible is the heritage of life. And so, when you come right down, I know the price is something that doesn't enter in at all. It's the utility of it. And believe you me, I think you both have to agree that you have the utility there. Is that true or isn't it?

Woman: Well . . .

Paul: That's all we have to say.

Charlie: It's the way anything is designed as to what effect you — we — get from it.

Woman: I just feel sorry with all your work and demonstration I mean . . . but we . . .

Charlie: (packing up hastily) No, listen . . . I tell you I was running a little stale anyway. And I had to — this is why I'm taking Mr. Brennan out tonight to see if I can sort of spark him up a little. He's, uh . . .

(Paul, who knows he has lost the sale, stands with his lips pressed thin and his eyes tracing the floor.)

Man: You need practice?

Charlie: He's been droppin' away down . . .

Woman: I really appreciate the uh . . .

Charlie: (mocking Paul) He — he used to — he used to write. If I can recall one time, Paul, in your prime, you were writing twelve a week? Right? He dropped way down to three. He says, what's the matter, Mr. McDevitt? And I says, well, Paul, I . . . I think you're a little negative. You're negative and I think somebody should take you out and spark you up and show you how the people will acquire this. (chuckling) I'm not doing this to embarrass you, Paul, believe me.

Paul: (with grim humor) Well, sometimes it isn't a spark. You need an explosion. (Laughs with strain) With that I think we'll say good adieu.

(They leave.)

Charlie: Thank you very much.

Man: Okay.

Woman: Thank you very much now.[9]

What exactly is Paul's problem? And why don't the others, so much like him, have it? Paul no longer knows how to handle himself in a sales situation because his feelings run counter to those called for in selling. Where a canned delivery, or even an aimless diatribe lauding the Bible, would probably work, Paul offers only his uncertain emotions.

Salesman is about an ethnic demise, the disintegration of an identity. Paul Brennan's Irishness is being misplaced. He is an ethnic fish out of water, guilt-ridden by what he does for a living, and thus he violates his Irishness by bandying it about when it does him the least good.

Paul: (drifts into a self-mocking Irish brogue) Be you selling anything? Naw, we're not selling anything. The Irish fighting with the English. When it comes right down to it makes no difference to me. 'Case the English are not payin' me bills an' the Irish are takin' away from me. Yup! Ah, here's another one here that's an old biltzy. Jeez, I got some beauts today. Gippo, the infarmer. I'm infarmin' you that I'm here.[10]

Television generally clings to news and theme formats; vérité is almost nonexistent on commercial TV, and appears only infrequently on PBS. Vérité usually appears on commercial television as various vérité witnesses — street gamins, killers, distraught mothers and other inarticulate observers.

ALL NEWS IS DOCUMENTARY

Bluem had another idea that is basic to this study: he believed that all television news was documentary; that there were small- and big-D documentaries; that you could find evidences of them in news stories, in so-called mini-docs and in the set pieces done regularly on the TV news magazine shows.

He once described his idea:

We all are aware that somewhere between the purely "objective" instructional film designed to transmit operational skills or elicit imitative behavior and the purely "subjective" films of the experimental and "expanded cinema" filmmakers lies a broad range of filmed, "live" and videotaped presentation of useful socio-cultural information which deserves to be called "documentary communication." Whether they exist (1) as independent "set pieces," which formally are called documentaries; (2) as informational programs of a kind carried in broadcasting long before the notion of separate genre of "documentary" was established; or (3) as one of a variety of lesser, shorter journalistic "pieces" — all tend to combine in some way those properties and characteristics traditionally assigned to the documentary idea. All of them offer a "creative interpretation of fact" in service of either the social interdependence established by Grierson or the vision of men in harmony with the universe which was Flaherty's.

It is time, however, that we began to consider the separate existence of "big-D Documentary" and "small-d documentary." The former can remain as whatever the definer thinks it should be. The latter ought to embrace all . . . the various styles, approaches and techniques which it really represents. This kind of mind-stretching has not been easy to promote in the past, but with few exceptions most observers recognize that television, which has changed all other things, has also changed the meaning of documentary communication, of the "small-d" variety with which I am concerned.

The fact is that any kind of informational programming intended for the public or "mass" audience becomes a documentary the moment those processes which will bring it to the *screen* are initiated. Every definition out of the past suggests the introduction of a "sight-sound-motion" technique and a "public" target audience casts a communication into a documentary role. In television, then, the old "big-D Documentary" is to "small-d documentary" communication as the novel is to literature. While novels represented the major thrust of all literature by offering the great "set pieces" — literature in all times and places has also included essays, short stories, poetry, drama, histories, biographies and many other forms.

I would therefore propose that we begin to include any and all public affairs-based informational programs under the "documentary" classification. The word "programs" is a specific designation for an organized content in which there is a beginning, middle and an end. The specific exception to such definition might come in those "hard-news" programs in which various items are presented episodically — in capsules arranged in time according to their journalistic significance. But even within this kind of "hard-news" program there are various shorter reports which are in effect "mini-documentaries," because they represent — in design, intent and execution — that effort to give creative interpretation to fact which has always been the hallmark of documentary communication.

I am unwilling, therefore, to except the "hard-news" program from the "small-d" documentary definition, even to spare the feelings of hard-bitten newsmen who recoil in horror at the suggestion that they are engaged in a kind of "poetic" communication. All news programming, including every known variety and species of television public affairs program — interviews, discussions, "in-depth" reports, actuality coverage and all cultural and "aesthetic-appeal" types of programs — fall within the broader definition I propose.[11]

Some of the fun in studying TV documentary comes about when you seek out snippets of one or another of these production techniques. It's good to recognize, for example, that the camera's ability to reproduce actuality at its own pace and proportions allows, in turn, the producer to integrate into a program effects that could not have been achieved by rigidly adhering to one particular format. This is due partly to the immediacy of the actuality and partly to the versatility of a camera to record speeds, angles and various focuses. Repeated slow-motion sequences, to take one example, first used by Riefenstahl in the diving sequence of *Olympiad* (1936), reappear with the slow-motion shots of a pole vaulter in the second program of the theme documentary series, *The Ascent of Man* (PBS, 1974).

Or take the consistent use of interviews on the TV news magazine series, *60 Minutes*. Interviews, as we all know, can be dreary and dull. But when they are spiced up with talking heads, as practiced on this brilliant CBS News series, encounters result. By merely keeping the camera on a man after he had been asked whether he thinks his life is in danger because of his role in an Arizona real estate escapade, the producer created unbearable tension as the viewer waited to see what the man would say, his face a map of conflicting feelings, as he finally numbly agreed: "Yes, maybe my life is in danger."

Other than studying the use of such techniques in TV documentaries, there are textual aspects worth one's attention. Probably the most important of these is the question: Why was this documentary made? The documentarian is much like an Elizabethan poet seeking a rich patron. Once he or she obtains such assistance, the patron rarely allows the producer the privilege of filming anything unless the person, regime or organization sponsoring the project approves. That's why we should be aware that the backdrop against which the documentarian must work often is dotted with powerful figures who have okayed what it is the forthcoming program intends to say.

For this reason alone, television documentary can never be considered as being objective but must always be recognized as being in the service of one contender or another. Sometimes the propaganda of the documentary is liberal, sometimes establishment. Sometimes, once created, it is destroyed, bowdlerized or otherwise censored. Despite always being held in captivity, however, the documentary, by its very nature, is not a hapless creature.

2 / Environment for Television News Documentary

THE TRADITIONAL FORMAT GETS INTO TROUBLE

IT'S MONDAY, March 28th, 1977, at 10:00 p.m.

NBC is telecasting the NCAA finals; ABC, the Academy Awards; PBS, *The Pallisers,* a BBC-TV series based on Trollope's parliamentary novels, to be followed in turn, by another series, *Soundstage*.

And what is on CBS? A 60-minute news documentary about Rhodesia's racial/political problems at that time.

Is this evening a representative night for American TV programming? No.

For one thing, it is exceptionally rich in programming splendors. It is a high-interest night. What with the Academy Awards on ABC capturing most of the nation's attention, the other networks have counterprogrammed to pick up those people who don't want to watch the movie industry pat itself on the back.

When winning at least a third of the mass audience becomes impossible for a major network, then programmers of that network resign themselves to minuscule pickings by paradoxically offering the public really good programs. Such was the case this particular night.

CBS was presenting an hour-long news documentary, a program exactly representative of other hour-long news documentaries which we had long been getting from all the networks during the mid-sixties and early seventies.

Producer Irv Drasnin's documentary on Rhodesia, one of CBS News's famous *CBS Reports,* was edited down from as much as 70,000 feet of film, probably cost around $250,000 to produce, ran 55 minutes in length and had

33

employed a producer-reporter and his crew on location for a period of from three to six months. It used actualities to treat people or places as they were or are, ignoring fictional reconstructions to interpret, instead, through edited film, some kind of reality relevant to the events portrayed.

Drasnin's documentary was about human rights being violated. It showed a soon-to-be-imprisoned Roman Catholic priest speaking out in behalf of fair treatment for the Rhodesian black minority. It showed examples of racism in schools, homes, parks, jobs.

The viewer was left with the impression that Rhodesia was a nasty place in 1977. All in all, it was a carefully crafted, clearly expressed statement about a crucial public issue.

Yet its effects upon the American public were practically nil.

Why?

Well, for one thing, nine-tenths of the potential audience were watching something else. (But we must realize that CBS already accepted this situation by showing the Drasnin documentary in the first place.) Another reason for its failure was its format. Sixty-minute news programs no longer can be just a series of reconstructed actualities strung out along a single story line. Hour-long news documentaries devoted to one solid topic just don't hold audiences any longer.

There undoubtedly are other reasons for the demise of the traditional news documentary. Family viewing, fairness concepts and token appeals to minorities are all partly responsible, but the need to reach everybody between the ages of 18 and 49 is why most popular shows have pushed most *public affairs* programs right off the tube.

Popular programs appeal to those who least prefer documentaries. Documentaries are news. News, hopefully, will continue to be about reality. People watching popular programs, however, seek escape from, not information about, reality.

So we end up with tinsel issues, comic-strip programs, happy talk news. Accenting soft news becomes a habit and avoiding ugly issues, powerful ideas and disturbing developments, a way of life.

PRODUCING A NETWORK DOCUMENTARY

An hour-long documentary costs between $150,000 and $250,000, and the length of time on average to produce it runs from three months to a year. The lead time — that is, knowing exactly what is prepared and scheduled — is only six months in advance of the show's projected broadcast date. These dates usually are firmly fixed for such-and-such a documentary to appear as scheduled, but the networks freely move different documentary programs or titles around, substituting one for another. You can expect to see a documentary on Tuesday at 10:00 p.m., just as the schedule calls for, but because of news or topical exigencies, its title may be changed.[1]

Of course, series documentaries are a different matter. Shows such as

Close-up, CBS Reports and *60 Minutes* have regular time slots. Their formats, whether primarily "talking heads" or library film, also determine how long it will take to produce individual shows.

The selection of documentary subjects is often the key as to whether or not the documentaries themselves will be any good.

By controlling money allocations as well as the jobs of those possessing the talent to produce such documentaries, top network management obviously has a final say about subject matter. TV documentarists often feel privileged, as they should, to work with the most compelling and persuasive communications format ever conceived. They also must realize, however, that theirs is an environment in which they not only exist but in which they also must survive.

Even when top management commits itself to documentaries, other factors are at work to mitigate that commitment, because a network is selling time, the value of which is determined by the size of the audience who views —in a sense, shares — that time.

Av Westin:

> The networks, all networks, put aside at the beginning of the year a certain amount of money for news operations, and they almost always say, "We're going to lose it all." And a certain amount of that money is put aside for documentaries, and they almost always say, "We're going to lose it all." At ABC News, whether the documentaries are sold or not sold, they go on the air. I don't even know whether a show is sponsored or not. I leave six one-minute holes in a show, and either a commercial goes in them, or a promotional announcement plugging some other ABC show, or some local station will insert its own commercials. Okay. Let's talk money. If you produce a documentary and it costs a hundred and fifty thousand dollars, it probably will not be sold for much more than that to a sponsor. So there's no profit. If it costs more than a hundred and fifty thousand, there can be even more of a loss. If they are going to sell it to the XYZ company, they'll sell it for twenty-five thousand dollars a minute. Six times twenty-five thousand is a hundred and fifty thousand. No profit, right? And that doesn't include line charges to distribute it.[2]

Westin says scheduling is controlled by the network, not by ABC News. *Close-up,* under his tutelage, was committed once a month to prime time but the network determined when that once a month was. He also said that none of his documentaries were ever produced to appeal to a clear-cut demographic breakdown. (Example: designing a John Denver entertainment special to reach the young and young marrieds.) Once a documentary has been telecast, inside network reaction is always predictably uniform: its ratings always are too low and, aside from the momentary glory, it's upsetting to know the show hasn't produced a thin dime.

The network can make a contract with a sponsor that only allows the network to preempt so many times annually, usually only twice. If the network exercises this right to preempt, then it will install big, glittering entertainment specials, such as *The Missiles of October,* not a *bona fide* documentary, which would siphon off the high ratings the regular show — say the *Streets of San Francisco* series — ordinarily generated weekly.

Time and money are wider aspects of TV documentary making. Once such management problems have been solved, what does a network news unit do to produce its documentaries?

At CBS News in 1975, Bill Leonard was vice president for documentaries, reporting to Richard S. Salant, CBS News president.

Under Leonard were John Sharnik, Perry Wolff and Les Midgley — respectively dealing with news specials or straight documentary, the investigative *CBS Reports* and pure newsgathering.

John Sharnik:

> Documentary ideas must originate with the executive producers; that is, two or three people whip up ideas, put a paragraph or two on paper, and present them to Leonard. I'm sure Salant is involved; that is, Salant can veto an idea, but I think pretty much he gives Leonard his head nowadays.[3]

At CBS News, a five-page statement, much like an article outline, suffices to get a documentary topic off the ground and flying. But where does the topic originate?

John Sharnik:

> I remember about a year-and-a-half ago, one of the producers working for me then came to me. He was not a very journalistically oriented guy, so I was kind of surprised when he said, "Listen, just look at all these little clips I have been picking out of the paper. Obviously, these suggest to me a large story, one that's going to inundate us in a few months. They suggest to me that the whole world is about to undergo some kind of crisis in relation to food supply that's different from our traditional concern for over-population. There's some crisis in agriculture going on and the United States is right in the middle of it, and the role of the United States is somehow going to change drastically. The United States is going to be the breadbasket of the world, not the arsenal of the world, not the manufactory of the world. It's going to be the breadbasket. Maybe we're going to revert to some other scheme." Well, it seemed to me to be a large enough idea — a documentary has to be a large idea or else a very human small idea that has large suggestions, implications. This seemed to be such a large idea, it intrigued the hell out of me, and I put this guy to work along with a couple of other people researching it. He came back in two months and said, "All right, here's what it is."[4]

Developing a documentary subject is a more formal procedure at ABC News. Picking up an idea, a researcher, or sometimes a correspondent, develops it in about three months given over completely to research trips. On return, the researcher sits down and turns out what ABC News calls a position paper, which states exactly what the contents of the proposed documentary will cover.

The 11 producers on the ABC News staff in 1975 were assigned to any one of the several series then in active production except the *Action-Biography* series, which was handled by two producers fully familiar with the series' format. Even their associate producers, film editors and others were interchanged from show to show.

Finally, several structural techniques are open to the TV documentarist:

1. The narrator-reporter introduces the topic. Then the story line is taken out of the studio, via film or tape, to cover scenes consisting of people and action at one or more sites.
2. The narrator-reporter stays in the studio and interviews his subjects, or goes to an outside site and carries out his interviews with several persons. This is the shotgun or cross-cut approach. Numerous subjects are recorded. Then these interview takes are rearranged for a clear story line, maximum exposure of certain viewpoints and a narrative balance.
3. The narrator-reporter conducts a portraiture interview, which emphasizes the subject's uniqueness and newsworthiness but is severely limited in the use of strong pictorial values, advantages which the first two approaches readily provide.

These are the more common approaches. Many times, however, structure isn't what's important. In-depth reporting, succinct yet smooth coverage or on-the-spot explication — these qualities may override how a program is put together. So we next should see how they are created and perfected.

THREE MODES: INVESTIGATIVE, MAGAZINE, NEWS SPECIALS

After 1967, television news documentaries began to evolve into three major formats. What we consider to be the traditional television news documentary is an hour-long program dominated by a narrator of at least correspondent status and produced by an experienced team that had worked on the program for at least six months. Cost for such a project ran from $100,000 to $300,000, depending on what year in the decade the documentary was produced.

The first change in format, evolution of the traditional television news documentary into the investigative mode, was the least drastic. The format remained intact; only the emphasis changed as more and more news documentaries asked why and how a hard news event took place. Examples are the *Close-up* series at ABC News, several three-hour NBC News *White Papers*, the *NBC Reports* and *CBS Reports,* some of which will be reviewed later in detail.

The second change was the development of the television news magazine wherein the documentary was used to entertain, not inform. Soft news, that is, topics of high interest but of low importance, often populate these programs. The Public Broadcast Laboratory takes credit for the rise of this format since PBL originated *The Great American Dream Machine* series in 1967. Commercial examples of this same format are *60 Minutes, Weekend* and the defunct *First Tuesday*.

The third specialty to evolve out of the traditional television news documentary was the News Special, a documentary made up of hard-news actualities strung together into a coherent narrative.

News Specials followed one of two forms:

1. The compilation of short takes photographed or taped at the scene of the event. Most often the news event was about death, destruction, achievements, ceremonies or rituals. These takes are edited at a later time for presentation as a special — that is, a one-time program. Sometimes they can be interview recapitulations which have delved into the circumstances of a hard-news story.
2. The presentation of live news, breaking as it unfolds, without either the participating producers or news teams knowing exactly what its outcome will be. Sometimes, such unedited reportage is presented at a later hour but still *without editing*. Haphazard conditions reign over this kind of News Special. Usually the reporting is live, too, or is taped at the scene amid gross special events-coverage problems. Voice-over commentary is completely ad-libbed.

Each form of the News Special, compared to the traditional television news documentary, is unique, often unexpected and wildly erratic in content and quality. Reason: News Specials are documentaries spawned by news events and brought into play because of the inability of series documentaries or even newscasts to handle such events in terms of meeting deadlines, providing ENG (Electronic News Gathering) coverage or offering sufficient background information.

THE INVESTIGATIVE MODE

When we discuss evolution in TV news documentaries, we are talking about the growth of both present station and network broadcasting facilities as they have been used down through the years for gathering the news. We should be especially aware as to how that growth was affected by the early, crude unions between film and news reporting. For that is where what we are calling TV news documentary came from. It began back when documentary with a capital ''D'' still was being shown only in the movie houses and it continues today with the countless small-d documentaries aired nationwide to millions of American homes.

The changes, moreover, are not just in program content. Not only have conditions under which a particular program was viewed changed drastically, but also the makeup of the audience has vastly changed. More people see a TV documentary in an evening than would have seen an early newsreel or theater documentary in a whole year of showings. Also, the control or sponsorship of documentary production has altered from a movement of artisans working for the federal government or for private motion picture firms to journalists working in clusters at complex network production units. These units are formally organized to present well-planned, well-researched documentaries on a regular basis, sometimes even as prime time series earning more than creditable commercial ratings.

Nonetheless, television documentaries attracted an audience in 1965 of usually only half the share of a sports event or popular Hollywood movie. The closer their subject matter was to fictional programs, the higher the rating. During the years 1963 to 1967, reality films were watched extensively. "Hits" won an audience share ranging from more than 50 percent of the sets in use to 30 percent; successful documentaries won an audience share ranging from below 30 percent down to 19, while modest successes and "flops" won a share of 18 percent down to about 8.[5]

The main ingredient up to 1967 to win a better rating was what Reuven Frank, veteran NBC News executive and documentarist, called drama. "You cannot interest people unless you tell stories. Usually in a good story there's a protagonist, a conflict and a resolution."[6]

This formula worked for a while, but as the decade progressed, viewers saw more and more news stories on such volatile subjects as the Vietnam war, Watergate, inflation, energy, pollution, land use, land order, urban decay, minorities — even about television journalism itself. Moreover, these were headache stories. None were headliners exactly, to be played up big for a day or a week, then dropped. They were topics demanding nearly continuous explanation. To supply it, network television news became what ABC News Documentary Chief Av Westin called "a three-stool affair, that is, special events, evening news and documentaries."[7]

Only one strong similarity between the old documentaries and the news remains: the fact that they were and are controlled by network men and women devoted to earning money by entertaining audiences, not by informing them. Even though documentary today on television is inspired and produced by network news staffs, the play-dates for these staffs' efforts are not determined by them but by people who control the entertainment side of television network programming.

It was a condition that Edward R. Murrow and Fred W. Friendly had to live with, too. Despite this condition, what's more important is that without Murrow and Friendly, it is difficult to envisage when TV news documentary would have appeared.

Up to 1954, documentary proper had no news format. The nearest thing to it was the compilation film, made up mostly of old World War II footage. Documentary's role was customarily that of an alternative, albeit a powerful one on occasion, to the fiction film.

Fortunately, however, thanks to Murrow and Friendly, their documentaries were very different from those produced in the past, including the master works of Flaherty and of John Grierson and his fellow producers in Australia, Canada and Great Britain. As CBS News Executive Producer Burton ("Bud") Benjamin has said, "Grierson once defined his purpose as making 'dramas from the ordinary.' The word 'drama' would have driven Murrow and Friendly up the wall."[8]

Murrow and Friendly did for documentary what the progenitors of earlier linkups between film and news failed to do: namely, they reported not only what was happening but also *what was wrong with what was happening*. They also set up guidelines — technical, creative and moralistic — which are still with us. They understood that the documentarian's function was to explain changes in society. They knew they were only successful when they really managed to do so. They also knew that actuality was an end product — a visual experience that sometimes was plain happenstance — and that when it did occur, one must be discerning enough to know it.

What Murrow and Friendly were after with their CBS News *See It Now* series was the exposure of injustice. They were muckrakers. If there was a theme in their collective work, it was a belief that a set of rules exists for keeping society fair and equitable; when a person, such as Senator McCarthy, or an event, such as the Korean war, assaulted these rules, then proper attention must be paid, via public exposure to redressing or eliminating such acts.

Murrow's particular favorite of all the superb *See It Now* series was the Milo Radulovich story, "Guilt by Association" (1953). Murrow introduced the program as the story of an Air Force officer who is "no special hero, no martyr." He went on to tell how Radulovich was threatened with dismissal from the Air Force as a security risk. A board of three colonels had recommended Radulovich be separated from the service — although there was no question of his loyalty — because he had maintained a close relationship with persons suspected of Communist associations, namely his father and sister.

Murrow and reporter Joseph Wershba interviewed the Radulovich family; the people of Dexter, Michigan; the Radulovich lawyer and others. A burly beer-truck driver said he didn't know Radulovich but "if the Air Corps gets away with the purging . . . then they can do it to anyone." The father's union steward said he had known John Radulovich for years and worked by his side and never heard a Communist word.

Five weeks later, as a result of Murrow's crusading journalism, Air Force Secretary Harold E. Talbot announced he had overruled the colonels.[9]

Of course, not all television documentary is investigative, but those shows that are usually turn out to be the best. For one thing, more time is taken to produce them than other categories — and time and depth of effort are inextricably interlinked. Investigative reporting is the most difficult to do well. The *Selling of the Pentagon,* for instance, took 51 weeks to produce. Often, a single hour isn't long enough to pour in all the information necessary to cover the subject, and a second show is required. The muckracking documentary thrives on facts — lengthy, richly conceived details. It is the one form of documentary that must be immaculately documented — a wearisome condition on TV. But dreary details can be compensated for by the excitement — even danger — involved.

CBS News documentarist Jay McMullen, producer of *Biography of a Bookie Joint,* said: [10]

> It is a real problem in the investigative area, protecting your sources. . . . We need the public's help, and it is the individual who makes these broadcasts possible. They are the ones who had their necks out. They're the ones who accuse and they are the ones who face the boomerang. And without that kind of individual, without those people who are willing to stand up and take a position, we really cannot do very much nor can any investigative reporter. We must lean on those sources.

TELEVISION NEWS MAGAZINES

The reason that *60 Minutes* is the best of the television news magazines lies in its fast pace. On the March 16, 1971, program, Mike Wallace, who has no rival at this sort of questioning, interviewed "William Crum, called the Money King of Vietnam," the man a senate committee investigating a PX scandal hadn't been able to find.

> *Wallace:* If all the things they say about you are untrue, why don't you go on back to Washington and testify before the Ribicoff Subcommittee. Why not cooperate with them?
> *Crum:* Because my doctors have requested that I do not travel that long a distance.
> *Wallace:* So it's purely for reasons of health. You're too ill to go to Washington to appear before the committee?
> *Crum:* Yes.
> *Wallace:* What if the committee were to send an investigator out here to talk to you?
> *Crum:* I'd have to consult my attorneys.
> *Wallace:* Well, you say you'd be happy to go to Washington to appear if you were — if you were well enough, so if they'll — if Mohammed won't come to the mountain, the United States will come to you?
> *Crum:* So I'll talk — I'll talk to them in the presence of my attorneys.
> *Wallace:* Your critics call you the unchallenged money king of Vietnam, sitting atop a consortium of corruption of forty million dollars.

Crum: As far as being a money king, I wish I knew where the money was hidden.

Wallace: The Senate Permanent Investigations Subcommittee would also like to know where the money's hidden and who else is involved, and why the PX and servicemen's clubs are evidently so vulnerable to charges of kick-backs, corruption, money manipulation.[11]

The Executive producer of *60 Minutes,* Don Hewitt, "a thin, tanned, cigar-smoking man in his early fifties," was interviewed on Tom Snyder's *Tomorrow* program, April 4, 1976. Speaking of *60 Minutes,* Hewitt said he had unabashedly patterned the program after *Life* magazine in that it stressed current manners, morals and mores.

We deal less with those who make news than with those who are victimized by the problems that events cause.[12]

When *60 Minutes* went on the air, September 24, 1968, Harry Reasoner explained "that it was an attempt to bring to television the flexibility and diversity of the printed page." The program did use blowups of printed pages to serve as prominent backdrops. But the stop-watch motif, ticking away as the program unfolded, linking various segments and cueing commercials, helped maintain the awareness that it was a broadcast news program, moving inexorably through time, spending only so much attention on a topic, then moving on.

"Being the executive producer of *60 Minutes,*" says Hewitt, "is like being the managing editor of a magazine. I have fourteen producers. [as of 1975] They're like contributing editors. I pick good guys, and once we determine a story, they go, and I don't see it again until what we call a rough cut. Then I go in and look at it. I figure what's got sex appeal. And that's how I put together the lineup."[13]

A prime reason for the rise in the segmented hour-long documentary or magazine show, featuring one or more presenters, plus the work of innumerable producers, correspondents and cameramen, is the polished use of the actuality. This skill came about as a result of the news work being done in Vietnam and at home, especially on political stories. Now the TV news magazines as well as the better-produced newscasts use actuality consistently and use it well.

60 Minutes shared only one thing with the traditional hour-long compilation documentaries, such as *Air Power, Eyewitness to History* and *Victory at Sea,* that used to proliferate on TV screens. It was a series. According to Hewitt, series documentaries tend to attract a somewhat larger audience than specials.

But *60 Minutes* differed radically from these programs in that it lacked a unifying theme. Often Hewitt didn't know what would be on the upcoming program.

We now have a new mandate which is, if we're on Sundays, if something big breaks on Friday or Saturday, we've got to get it on Sunday.[14]

Magazine-program producers like to feel they have some feedback from listeners, a sort of electronic "Letters to the Editor" department. CBS had a monthly daytime magazine called *Magazine,* which in 1975 carried a segment called "Face to Face," which was devoted to giving viewers a forum for their reactions to things on TV. A similar feature is at the end of *60 Minutes,* where the current presenters — Mike Wallace, Morley Safer, Dan Rather and Harry Reasoner — discuss letters from viewers complimenting or complaining about past stories.

Magazine programs alternate between reality and entertainment programming. On the first *60 Minutes* show, Mike Wallace interviewed Attorney General Ramsey Clark for a "cover" story about "Cops." Later, columnist Art Buchwald contributed a mini-essay on how journalists size up public opinion (they read each other's copy).[15]

60 Minutes has had its share of barbs as well as plaudits. *New Yorker* critic Michael Arlen deplored Dan Rather's handling of a two-part series in October, 1976, on corruption of officials in Wyoming. He said "those stories displayed a growing tendency to let prosecutorial indignation do the work of investigative reporting."[16]

Arlen found *60 Minutes'* zest for uncovering wrongdoing evidence of a "guard-dog mentality — they'll attack anything that moves. They are getting too drama conscious. One of the problems is that they need material, and once they commit themselves to a story it's tough to back down."[17]

On April 18, 1979, the United States Supreme Court ruled that public figures suing for libel may inquire into a journalist's "state of mind" and the editorial process that accompanied the allegedly libelous statement. The decision reversed the Second United States Court of Appeals ruling, saying it had misconstrued the First and Fourteenth Amendments. Producers and reporters, the high court stated, enjoy no constitutional protection from having to answer questions in a libel case.

The decision also was a victory for former Lieutenant Colonel Anthony Herbert, who was often touted as the Army's most decorated soldier; he had sued CBS and others for $44.7 million. In January, 1974, he sued CBS, correspondent Mike Wallace and producer Barry Lando in response to a *60 Minutes* segment, "The Selling of Colonel Herbert," the title of which ironically echoes CBS News's *The Selling of the Pentagon,* which also dealt with surrendering or not surrendering outtakes (film footage taken but not used on a newscast or documentary). In that situation, Dr. Frank Stanton, the CBS, Inc. president, had refused to turn over outtakes about the Pentagon documentary, even though he was subpoenaed to do so and was cited for contempt of Congress, a charge eventually overthrown by a full vote of the House of Representatives!

In the Herbert case, however, the Supreme Court was asking Lando, who had previously offered his full cooperation to the courts on everything but the answers to five questions put to him by Herbert's attorney, to answer those questions and, in effect, tell what he was thinking as he tried to develop the *60 Minutes* story on Herbert. Herbert claimed his interview with Wallace was a hatchet job because it was conducted under extremely aggravating circumstances for Herbert.[18]

Actual proof of whether Lando and Wallace acted with malice in producing, editing and interviewing Herbert on the air has not yet been decided at this writing. But, thanks to Herbert's stubborn efforts in the courts, the law regarding outtakes and even editorial attitudes toward those outtakes is — again at this writing — decidedly confusing.

Publishers, not broadcasters, have won the most clear-cut statements from the high court concerning whether or not an outsider has access to use the media that the publisher controls. Rosenbloom vs. Metromedia (1971), New York *Times* vs. Sullivan (1971) and Miami *Herald* vs. Tornillo (1974) support a publisher's right to determine access.

Only one recent Supreme Court case, CBS, Inc., vs. Democratic National Committee (1973), also grants broadcasters this same privilege, but numerous other important decisions — Red Lion Broadcasting Company vs. FCC (1969), *The Selling of the Pentagon* congressional inquiry (1971), NBC vs. FCC, the so-called *Pensions* case (1972), and now Herbert vs. Lando (1979) — at best — leave this whole area of federal law murky. As Justice Byron White wrote in the Herbert decision, "According an absolute privilege to the editorial process of a media defendant in a libel case is not required, authorized or presaged by our previous cases."[19]

In many ways, *60 Minutes'* popularity as one of the top ten most-watched TV programs has hurt the series. It enjoys enormous power over American public opinion. It must continually keep reaching for stories that will retain high audience interest, yet it can't make too many mistakes, either. Its success has also hurt other CBS documentaries, especially *CBS Reports,* which still clings to the traditional documentary format. Since its birth in 1969, *60 Minutes* has gotten tougher, zippier and more star conscious (Wallace, Safer, Rather and Reasoner). Despite competition from NBC and ABC with *Weekend* and *20-20, 60 Minutes* still rules the TV news-magazine field.

In January, 1969, the same year *60 Minutes* appeared, NBC News premiered *First Tuesday,* a casual two-hour monthly "magazine" which downplayed its presenters but gave correspondents ample time to display investigative as well as factual and feature pieces.

The clout that magazine programs have with their audiences is one of their unique features. As Reuven Frank has said (specifically in reference to "Chemical and Biological Warfare — the Search for Secrecy," *First Tuesday,* Feb. 1969): "In its earliest days, *First Tuesday* so aroused the public and official conscience about chemical and bacteriological warfare that it alone, *one* edition of *one* program, caused limiting legislation to happen."[20]

Still, *First Tuesday* had an identity problem. It became *Chronolog,* then *First Tuesday,* then *Special Edition,* then, after a hiatus, *Weekend.* Frank was put in charge, and he had his own ideas: "A magazine program includes more than one subject. It is expository in nature. That is all the definition you need, though critics like to speak of 'mini-documentaries'."[21]

Despite name changes, *Weekend* appeared most of its life at 11:30 p.m. on Saturdays. According to Reuven Frank:

> We took it as our primary obligation to be interesting. . . . Format: six commercial interruptions and two for station breaks. It seems like a lot but is, by special dispensation, less by a third than the normal for that period of broadcast time. Five pieces. Two must be, by anybody's criteria, serious journalism. Not solemn, serious. Not instructive, informative. But what most people write down or discuss, we took for granted: decency, concern, a capacity for anger, these exist inside or they do not; they are not proper subjects for meetings.[22]

Frank used Lloyd Dobyns, and later co-presenter Linda Ellerbee, to narrate. They used a low-key, dry-as-dust narrative style, which at 11:30 p.m. could put one to sleep. Frank liked them, however, as he did the verbals, which he admitted were "the least liked part of the program." These were trite two-or-three-liners placed before and after commercials: "Agnostic Chinese: Yee of Little Faith," "Johnny could read when his teacher could" or "A penny saved is a penny." Frank used them to keep the viewer watching. "People who are specific about those verbals they cannot abide seem to dislike most the ones in the middle of the commercial breaks. This, I submit, is absolute proof that they are watching. . . ."[23]

Looking back at what *Weekend* and its predecessors at NBC covered, it's difficult to see why the series didn't do better in the rating wars. Here are some of the stories covered; they give a good idea of Frank's approach: Twirling, Charles Atlas, British Weather, Rita Hayworth, Bathrooms ("The American Pipe Dream"), Beverly Sills, Smoking Clinic ("A Pack of Quitters"), Indian Sterilization, Maria Callas, Hemingway, Nuns ("Hide and Go Seek"), Machismo, Julie and David Look Alikes, Junked Cars, Yoga, Automated Radio, Gunbelts, Sinai, Herbicides and Gold.

News Specials

The investigative mode and the news-magazine format appear to cover all the possibilities open to the TV news documentarian.

Yet we have not considered two "News Special" approaches which differ greatly in aim and emphasis from the above and which have been consistently used throughout the decade with extreme effectiveness. The approaches are the hard-news actuality interview and the live, on-the-scene reporting sequence. Both are fraught with tension. Actuality interviews can tie knots in a viewer's stomach. On-going on-the-scene reporting can obtain equally spine-tingling results. Here are examples of each, one a carefully prepared commentary about capital punishment, the other, sensational instantaneous coverage nearly as accidental in its occurrence as the dreadful event itself.

First, the hard-news special based on actuality interviews:

The NBC News documentary, *Thou Shalt Not Kill,* was broadcast on July 28, 1972, at 9:30 p.m., with correspondent Carl Stern as narrator. Critic Val Adams called it "frightening. There were no charts or diagrams, yet it was all terribly graphic and horrifying. All it was were two men laughing and talking about the six people they had killed." [24]

These men, prisoners in Utah State Prison, were Myron Lance, 31, and Walter Kelbach, 34. In late December of 1966, they stabbed or shot to death six people in Salt Lake City.

At the program's start, Stern suggested "some parents may prefer that their children not watch" what was about to be told.

The program was mostly an interview with Lance and Kelbach, although near the end two psychiatrists said their investigations about the two killers showed them to be of average intelligence and without emotional disturbances that could be considered insanity in a court of law.

On parole for petty thievery, during their murderous tour of Salt Lake City, Lance and Kelbach had been gulping Nembutal and Methadrine pills, washed down with quantities of beer.

> Their first victim was an 18-year-old gas station attendant, who had taken the job ten days earlier to earn extra money for Christmas. After Lance and Kelbach robbed the gas station, they forced the young attendant into the back of their station wagon and headed for Tipp's Point outside of Salt Lake City. On the way they offered him beer and cigarettes. "We were human," Kelbach said with a smile. . . . Kelbach, who used a knife, and Lance, who preferred a gun, flipped a coin to determine who would murder the gas station attendant. "I lost, so I did it," Kelbach told the NBC audience, and he went on to describe how it's really easy to knife one to death. [25]

Over a five-day period, the two men, still eating pills and drinking beer, murdered another 18-year-old gas station attendant, a 30-year-old cab driver, and three others, including "a woman in a tavern."

"Both killers agree that they like to see their victims suffer." Filmed by KUTV, Salt Lake City, the film also revealed that after the killers were caught, police found numerous clippings about the murders in their rooms. "Stern suggested that Kelbach and Lance probably found glory in telling their bloody story on television."

Second, an example of the News Special documentary breaking as it unfolds:

At 4:10 p.m., Tuesday, June 24, 1975, an airliner crashed on its approach to JFK International Airport, killing 110 passengers. On television, WNBC's *NewsCenter 4,* a two-hour edition of local news that begins at 5 p.m., happened to have a 'minicam' crew taping a feature story at Shea Stadium and was able to provide live coverage from the nearby crash site beginning at 5:25, thus getting a jump of at least 90 minutes on its competitors. But those 90 minutes of coverage were unplanned, and the correspondents, either petrified by the thought of silence or hopelessly enamoured of their own voices, resorted to every cliché of disaster coverage several times. While trying to maintain dramatically hushed vocal projections, they described the mangled corpses, the shaken salvagers, the pervasive gloom. One veteran policeman, it was reported, solemnly announced he would never get in an airplane again. Later on, a former employee of Lockheed was interviewed on camera and asked if he would fly again. "Certainly (pronounced: soitenly)," he said, "I worked for them. I'd fly anywhere." So much for dramatics. (Perhaps it should be mentioned that Tom Snyder then added, "We are going to hear from all kinds of people who seem as though they don't know what to say. As a matter of fact, hardly anybody does know what to say after what happened here.")

Every so often, someone at *NewsCenter 4* would notice "several hundred people over the top of the hill." And it would be explained, with apparent disapproval, that "they've come to see the wreckage." But, then, so had the minicam crew, and the WNBC program scored its highest ratings ever.[26]

There's no question that TV has the ability to scare the hell out of audiences. That is why there is widespread belief both inside and outside the broadcasting business in an idea expressed in 1969 by former CBS president Frank Stanton. "TV's uniqueness," he said, "is in its power to let people have the intimate sense of meeting the great figures of the world and actually seeing many major events as they happen. . . . Great events of all kinds do not have to be filtered through the appraising accounts of reporters and editors. They can be witnessed by the people themselves, who can make their own judgments."[27]

When the 1966–67 television season opened, the late William R. McAndrew, then president of NBC News, announced that a "third format" — in contrast to "instant news specials" and planned specials — "will give NBC News increased flexibility in covering a story."[28]

"We are holding open time periods for timely or topical events that cannot be predicted," McAndrew explained. "It's an intermediate step between the instant special — designed for fast-breaking news — and our planned special, which can take from four to twelve months to produce.''[29]

Maybe the ''special'' was nothing more than the old-fashioned documentary dressed up to sound urgent and timely and newsy. Maybe it arose because there was so much hard news popping up everywhere, both at home and abroad. Certainly the news cauldron was bubbling just as fiercely at CBS and ABC as at McAndrew's domain. When he was in charge of documentaries at CBS, John Sharnik called the confusion about what exactly constituted a special ''one of those silly, imperceptible distinctions.'' To him a documentary was headed as ''A CBS News Special.'' He stressed the use of the upper case ''N'' and ''S.''

> Lower-case specials, which I think are actually called special reports, are the kinds of things that would be put on overnight; if, for example, there is a break in the Middle East peace situation. The distinctions are nonsense. Basically, there are a bunch of people around doing documentaries of lesser or longer form, taking more or less time to produce them.[30]

Alvin H. Perlmutter, former vice president, NBC News documentaries, said:

> A special here means a program that's not part of a series. It's on once and that's it. A documentary is called a special here. The regular documentary is a project that is in the works for perhaps four, five, six months or more, depending. An instant documentary is one that would be conceived because of a news break, a crisis of some sort in the morning and perhaps put on at night.[31]

Something clearly had happened in the network television news business. Documentarists had begun the decade worrying about making their documentaries dramatic and heroic so that the programs would earn respectable ratings. They built their shows around a hero or heroine. Later, however, as news story after news story — hard, stark, sometimes ghastly — rolled across the nation's TV screens, television documentary changed to meet and try to cope with this onrush. The special was invented. It came on like a freight train because there was a good market for news, because the traditional documentary could be tailored to fit the exigencies of the moment and because television journalism generally had become so much better.

For, along with the rise of quicks, instants and specials, another television-news trend had been underway during the decade: a trend toward better local TV news. Local stations were using more talent, a team that was usually made up of an anchorperson (sometimes two), a sports personality and a weather ''expert.'' Increased use of graphics, electronic projection systems and better photographic film footage helped, too. Networks and local stations learned there was money in news. Such programs started to deliver sizable audiences and, moreover, these audiences stayed on to watch programs that followed the news shows. As a result, broadcast journalism standards were increasingly bettered. Larger markets could afford longer as well as more sophisticated newscasts. In 1975, for example, WNBC-TV's *NewsCenter 4* was two hours in length, running weeknights from 5:00 to 7:00 p.m. in New York City.

All this meant news itself was sought after more aggressively. The tougher the disaster, the more eager local outlets were to cover it. Again in 1975, approaching within 500 feet of the blaze after a Liberian oil freighter and an American ship had collided in the Delaware river, KYW-TV Philadelphia newsmen risked the danger of further explosions. But their newsfilm was processed and ready for airing on NBC's *Today* show five hours after the accident.[32]

The incident was typical.

3 / Television Theme Documentary

THE ESSENTIAL characteristics of the theme documentary bear repeating: It is an attempt to control "life" by expressing a point of view by means of one or more of three basic approaches: *compilation,* wherein each contributor to the production lends his special talents to develop its theme; *biography,* wherein a person's will to surmount a series of confrontations is depicted; and *drama,* wherein facts are dressed up for the sake of a story line.

To put it another way, when you plan your documentary to consider history, society, nature or art, it is a theme documentary. As history, theme documentary celebrates anniversaries, recollects particular days or commemorates the deaths of the rich, the great or the powerful. As history united with drama, theme documentary can reconstitute the past and make it live again as legend.

In social terms, theme documentary can account for the culture of cities, countries and continents, appreciating, moreover, particular aspects of such places, such as their buildings, their peoples, their nations. And with adventure, geography or general travel, theme documentary is even more at home.

In this chapter we shall look at the theme documentary being applied to historical subjects, social problems, the literary essay, a continent and docudrama, which is one of the really significant changes to take place in television documentary in the years 1965 to 1975. These categories are meant to be helpful; they should be able to guide us as we seek out how a particular production either succeeds or fails. The question of effectiveness is important here. We must realize that with the theme documentary, whatever the documentarist does is done on his own. The resulting program rises or falls on the merits of what he has offered us. And in most cases, what is offered is an attempt to revivify history.

HISTORY AS THEME DOCUMENTARY

History as documentary originally used crude compilation methods in series such as *Twentieth Century* and *Crusade in Europe,* which were nearly always shaped from historical film, then backed up by strident musical fanfare and omniscient narration. Fortunately, shows within this genre of theme documentary have become better. The best examples of what I mean can be found in the work of George Vicas and Lou Hazam at NBC News and John H. Secondari, Jr., at ABC News. In George Vicas' *The Middle Ages* (1965) or in his *The Aviation Revolution* (1966), his method of dealing with history was to employ prominent actors for narration chores, using unusual camera angles to enhance fixed locations, such as galleries, palaces or museums, and sometimes using still photos or symbolical enactments to liven up the action.

Research, always a tedious necessity in preparing any documentary, is a monstrous requirement for the theme documentarist. For example, Vicas' *The Defeat of the Spanish Armada* (1965) enlisted the cooperation of the Van Stock collection, Rotterdam; Patrimonic Nacional, Madrid; National Trust, London; British Museum Library, London; National Maritime Museum, Greenwich; National Portrait Gallery, London; Lord Methuem; and Simon Singfield Digby, M.P.

Uncovering such sources and gaining their active help are only parts of the task; one must somehow project views of long, cold museum corridors, ill-lit and cavernous, and make them interesting. To do this, naturally, isn't easy. A suit of armor remains just that, and often camera work alone — that is, just showing the viewer something — won't do the trick. That's why the theme-documentary maker tries all sorts of stratagems to solve the problem of "interest."

To cite one example, Lou Hazam emphasized "landscapes and landmarks, artifacts and art works." His technique was "the subjective camera" — a high-sounding device that reached its fullest (and most absurd) expression in a 1946 MGM movie, *Lady in the Lake,* in which the detective hero appeared only once, reflected in a mirror; the entire movie consisted of what he *saw*.

Hazam used this method for *Michelangelo: The Last Giant* (1965–66), but an earlier effort, his *Greece: The Golden Age* (1963), gives us a better example: "Hazam's skill was such that he could suggest the Battle of Marathon by photographing a field of wheat (the Greeks) and poppies (the Persians) in a high wind — and get away with it."[1]

This method, however, hovers constantly between success and failure. Hazam, again, in the first half of *The Capitol: Chronicle of Freedom* (1965) "concentrated largely on the paintings, frescoes and statues to be found in the rotunda, the corridors and the senate and house wings. Visually, they were not shown to particularly good advantage and the accompanying narrative was not especially inspired."[2]

Theme documentary often lovingly dwells on what is left behind long after great personages from the past have left us. Magically, we see their works, their words, their intimate world. Sometimes we accompany the producer on a tour, allowing ourselves to be guided, informed, even provoked. Other times, the topic piques our curiosity without the presence of the subjective camera, heavy musical fanfare or the passionate wooing of our attention by one or more mellifluous narrators, who are usually professional actors, not network news correspondents.

People and places, then, are the real stuff of theme documentary. Vicas' *The Pope and the Vatican* (1965) was about such a combination since it was an examination of the Papal State of the Roman Catholic Church and its leader. During two months on location in Vatican City and northern Italy, Vicas talked with churchmen and laymen, filming their views on current changes in the church and on the personality and acts of the Pontiff. The only aspect of the program linked to current events was the knowledge in the minds of the audience that the late Pope Paul VI recently had appealed to world leaders to produce a peaceful settlement in Vietnam.

Another Vicas production, *The Middle Ages* (1965), covered the thousand years between the fall of the Roman Empire and Columbus' discovery of America. It studied the workings of the feudal system, the rise of courtly love and manners in the castles and the reappearance of cities. Segments touched on the 100 Years War, the great plagues, the role of religion and discoveries and inventions that soon would result in the Renaissance. It even examined the origins, motives and results of the eleventh-, twelfth-, and thirteenth-century crusades. If nothing persuades one that the theme documentary is distinctly different from its news counterpart, this rundown of the content covered in *The Middle Ages* should. And remember, it was all done in an hour!

If John H. Secondari, Jr., had done nothing else in his career except produce *Saga of Western Man,* he would be remembered. Even though this series was overly stylized, eccentric and grandiloquent, it was good theme documentary.

Secondari had been with ABC News since 1956, joining it as Washington bureau chief, after having been a CBS news correspondent in Europe, a producer of films and broadcasts in Italy for the Marshall Plan and a novelist (his novel, *Three Coins in the Fountain,* became a popular movie).

His second wife, Helen Jean Rogers, also an ABC News producer, was co-producer of most of his productions and director of many of them. Secondari wrote and usually narrated his works. His voice was good, but his delivery was so crisp it drew attention to itself, not a charitable quality when speaking into a microphone.

Before he produced *Saga of Western Man,* Secondari was in charge in 1960 of the first *Close-up* series, each program running an hour-and-a-half in length. They were sponsored and survived for three seasons. One program, "Meet Comrade Student," was filmed in Russia and was broadcast September 28, 1962. It later won the Overseas Press Award for its photography, but Fred M. Hechinger, then education critic for the New York *Times*, wrote: "The flaw in the approach was the mistaken belief that another country's education could be caught by television reporters, without apparent knowledge of the differences between American and European — let alone Russian — education. . . . Unfortunately, too, the commentary toward the end turned self-consciously propagandistic."[3]

Such criticisms of Secondari were inevitable. His talent for stating a case was always bounded by his inability to remain reportorial.

Saga of Western Man came in 1963, "a simplified, semi-dramatic history of Western civilization that would isolate certain years, people and incidents" to put across the ideas, as Secondari described it, that "man . . . develops haphazardly, but he develops — due to God, nature or whatever you choose to call the motivating force."[4]

Four programs in the series were part of the 1963–1964 season: *1492, 1776, 1898,* and *1964*. "I'm convinced," Secondari had said, "that (these years) . . . are the turning points of Western civilization — 1492, the renaissance and discovery of the New World; 1776, the initiation of a new concept of government; 1898, emergence of the United States as a dominant world power; and the present, logical conclusion of the current two-thousand-year cycle of Western civilization."[5] This remark discloses Secondari's dogmatism, a quality that nevertheless made him a marvelous theme documentarian. He knew exactly what he wanted to say and how to say it. His works were docudramas without overt actors or other fictional props. Instead, he used the voices of actors, speaking authoritative historical dialogue, and sound effects to resurrect the life that once had existed at some famous locale. He also used his camera as if it were a visitor capable of seeing things in any age: staircases, windows, doors, furniture, yards. "I introduce a new concept, the subjective camera technique," he said in 1963, even though Hazam's *Shakespeare: Soul of an Age* and *Van Gogh* and Vicas' *The Kremlin*, all productions of NBC News, pioneered this identical technique on network television; it is a film technique, by the way, extending back to Dziga Vertov's kino-pravda work in Russia (1919–22).

1776, for example, used actor Fredric March as the voice of George Washington, with other actors representing Sam Adams and other rebels; they spoke against camera shots of empty churches or colonial gubernatorial halls or with shadows cast by actors anonymously reliving the past. Paintings and statues of George III, as well as famous patriots, were scanned frequently. These shots were set up very carefully.

One difficulty resulting from this "subjective camera technique," at least for Secondari, was his willingness to extend our imaginations with sounds so that, on an audio level at least, he really was giving us reenactments. Yet, at the same time, he couldn't bring himself to practice visual reenactments because he knew, if he did, he would be completely over the line separating nonfiction from fiction, history from drama. *I, Leonardo Da Vinci*, for example, was described by Harriet Van Horne as "strikingly effective in its recreations."[6] Later, Jack Gould, reviewing *Custer to the Little Big Horn*, wrote: "The technique of (suggesting action without recourse to visible actors) has been wearing thin with repetition."[7]

Gould felt that "its application to General George Custer bordered on the ludicrous. . . . The ineptness of the staging of the battle was matched only by the incredible clumsiness of the offscreen dialogue. . . . Many of television's documentaries obviously are coming to the point where they will have to decide whether a given segment of history can best be represented as an illustrated reportorial narrative or as a play."[8]

Without meaning to, Gould was calling for the formation of the docudrama, a form Secondari probably would have been completely comfortable with — that is, if he had never been a broadcast correspondent and as such learned to appreciate the singular dramatic power of offscreen voices and sounds.

SIXTEEN IN WEBSTER GROVES: THEME DOCUMENTARY AS SOCIAL COMMENTATOR

A different theme is exemplified in *Sixteen in Webster Groves*, best of several excellent CBS News productions created by sociologist-turned-TV documentarian Arthur Barron. It is about teenagers and their education in a high school in an upper-middle-class suburb of St. Louis. Broadcast on Friday, February 25, 1966, at 10:00 p.m. EST, it was written and narrated by CBS Correspondent Charles Kuralt.

Sixteen is important for several reasons. The primary one is that Barron set out to do the program with a deliberate point of view in mind, a condition one never finds with a news documentary. Barron said, "It was my purpose to balance keenly the full range of the town. The program accurately and totally represented the major value structure of Webster Groves."[9]

To support this viewpoint, CBS had a $12,500 survey of 16-year-olds in Webster Groves undertaken for the network by a University of Chicago affiliate, National Opinion Research Center. "The survey's general findings coincided with what the cameras illustrated; but Richard Jaffee, assistant director of NORC added: 'There was an awful lot of Fellini in the show, which was artistic rather than sociological'."[10]

Running 52 minutes, after being edited from 27 hours of cameraman Walter Dombrow's fine filmwork, *Sixteen* opens with Kuralt telling us Webster Groves is "six square miles of the American dream," with "eight thousand, twenty-two pleasant homes, thirty-two churches, one public high school and no bars."[11]

   Talking heads of teenagers and teachers then support Kuralt's statements
about the questionnaire: that three-fourths of these teenagers listed as their main
goal in life a good paying job, money, success; that 90 percent liked Webster
Groves; that 50 percent wouldn't mind staying there the rest of their lives:

Jim Harwood: Well, I'm satisfied with the conditions I'm living in now and,
   well, we — it's really hard to say. I — I'm content. I live in a nice house
   and am doing all right.
Molly MacGreevy: I'm very, very happy. I — I don't have much that I can
   complain about.
Chip Covington: I'm perfectly happy the way I am and until I become unhappy with my present situation, I feel this is the way that I'll stay.
Mrs. McConachie: They're oriented toward big cars, toward big houses —
   well, now, that's what they're used to. I'm studying *Walden* right now.
   My kids think that Thoreau is one of the biggest weirdos they've ever run
   into. The guy goes out and lives in a cabin in the woods. He's nuts. He
   can live in a big house. He can make enough money to have a rug on the
   floor, to have silverware. My goodness, silverware makes you feel good.
   A girl told me this this morning, "If you've got silver to put on the table,
   it does so much for you." What? She couldn't say. The — just the accou-
   terments of the good life that they're used to and they feel are necessities.[12]

   Sixteen in Webster Groves was about the effects of strong parental inputs
into what their 16-year-old children did at home, in school, with their leisure.
Barron offers mounting evidence of this, with many sequences in counterpoint
to one another: Mrs. Condon's School of the Dance; the exclusive Monday
Club; the Queen of Friendship dance; a teenage nightclub, "where you think
you're free, you're not" — and numerous scenes in high school: socies, nor-
mies, intellects and weirdos; about working in Mr. Schraeder's shop class;
about being Black and being welcome on the football field as a player but not
on the sidelines as a cheerleader; about cooking class; about film shots of girls
and boys and their respective hair styles, accompanied by fast-moving music;
about the driver education program, also backed up by fast music at Mrs. Condon's or the Monday Club. Despite these scenes, however, it's the parents who
insist grades are all important.

Kuralt: Well, suppose to express their individuality, one of your children
   took part in a civil rights demonstration downtown in St. Louis, what
   would be your reaction to that?
Woman: I don't think I'd like it.
Woman: I wouldn't like it either.
Man: It'd be some time before they'd sit down, I'll tell you that.
Kuralt: Why?
Man: I can't see any excuse for it. What business is it of theirs? At sixteen
   years old, they don't have any firm convictions of anything.

Woman: They wouldn't do it, because we have a daughter in college and —
and we were talking about the problem at the college level. And somebody
had asked Bill about it, you know, what he thought about it. Would he do
that, demonstrate? "Aw," he said, "I don't have time for that. Doesn't
bother me at all."

Woman: Well, I think that if they did get into any of the demonstrations, it
would strictly be outside college, but I don't think they think enough about
these things enough. (sic)

Man: Well, you remember when I sent Clark down during those Jefferson
Bank demonstrations? And all any normal child has to do is look at the
demonstrators at Jefferson Bank. This was — oh, what — a year ago, I
suppose. And a bunch of beatniks, white, black, green, yellow, everything, and most of them felt this —

Woman: They do.

Man: — it looked like they pulled them out of some—out of some wine jug
or something and put them out there to demonstrate.

Kuralt: Mightn't a demonstration of some kind, though, sort of inject some
life into things around here? Shake the people — the kids up and make
them think about these things? Do you — do you think they need that
kind of shaking up?

Parents: No.

Man: No, I don't think any sixteen-year-old child should be burdened with
the problems of the world. But then to say—to say that they have to, at
sixteen or seventeen or eighteen, throw themselves into concepts of racial
prejudice or the haves and the have-nots, I think this is ridiculous.[13]

Barron may not consciously have been aware of it but the Emersonian
virtue of self-reliance was never touted openly as worthwhile in Webster
Groves. Thoreau, Emerson's disciple, was a weirdo, and the town's police
chief, Fred Zinn, says at one point that ". . . these youngsters are . . . not
learning self-reliance at all."

Parental control is too massive:

Mrs. Scrivener: I don't want her to be out past one o'clock even if it's a
very special dance that isn't over until twelve.

Kuralt: So you — you keep up with her. You know where she is.

Mrs. Scrivener: Yes, and this I insist upon, and this is one — one place
where we have felt a lot of parents perhaps are going wrong in that they
aren't — I'm snoopy — I guess that's it — downright nosey — so when
she was—now I'm not doing this anymore as much because I know pretty
much her friends, and I know the parents better than we did, say, two
years ago, but I do want to know where she is and what home she's
visiting, or what show she's going to and so forth, and I think this is
absolutely necessary. I think too many parents let this go by.

Patty Scrivener: Ma?

Mrs. Scrivener: Yes.

Patty Scrivener: I want to say something. You know the other night when I — when I told you — when one of my friends asked me if I could come over and spend the night because she was having about three other girls over.

Mrs. Scrivener: Um hum.

Patty Scrivener: And you wouldn't let me go, and I — I mean I was kind of mad at that because I figured that I'm old enough now that I know how to take care of myself, and if I want to go over there, and if they're going to do something bad, fine, I'll get up and come home, but it seems to me that you just don't trust me that far and that made me angry, and that's the first thing I've been angry with you about in a long time.

Mrs. Scrivener: Honey, you have to have — what night was it?

Patty Scrivener: Friday.

Mrs. Scrivener: It happened to be a girl who does not have any discipline at home, who's —

Patty Scrivener: Mother.[14]

Martin Mayer has said that the most important documentaries detail "situations that either were or should have been news."[15] This is not always the case; it may apply to news documentary, but many theme documentaries are done, I feel, for reasons that have little to do with news. Such documentaries are concerned with the same thematic materials that interest magazinists and publishers of hard-cover books. What is preeminently publishable is grist for the theme-documentary mill.

Theme documentaries have little to do with news but a lot to do with a producer's personal vision. I think, too, that whenever a particular theme works well, it is emulated over and over again, despite the fact that theme documentary offers one the freest form of opinion reporting imaginable. One's only limitations are 52 minutes of actual show time and the 5,000 words one must pack into those 52 minutes.

This power to state one's own case bothers critics. Kay Gardella of the New York *Daily News* felt Barron was suggesting that "materialistic comforts, the success treadmill and blind acceptance of parents' values had had a harmful effect on the development of a social conscience in the contented suburban youngsters. Their seeming indifference and lack of knowledge of problems that exist outside of their community was stressed — but not enough to support a point the program was determined to make . . . the architects of the hour started off with a premise they were determined to mold the teenagers to. . . ."[16]

Communications student David B. Baer has said, *"Sixteen in Webster Groves* is an interesting analysis of a population segment, but by no means a typical segment. . . . The piece is valuable as an insight into one type of community." However, Webster Groves was chosen to be studied by sociologists from the University of Chicago because it was statistically representative of middle-class suburbs, and its teenagers were considered typical. Still, Baer's criticism echoes in the review of Susan Szekely of the New York *Post:* "New York teenagers who watched the show did not see themselves in it. 'Maybe it's typical of the Midwest,' said Richard Welsh of Bronx Science, 'but it's not typical of my experience. A good deal of what was shown on the program was a bit disgusting to me personally'."[17]

Reactions to documentaries are one of their more interesting facets. Some merit hardly any response at all. Others agitate all kinds of people. CBS News must have realized this might happen with *Sixteen in Webster Groves* since, while it was being shown, three camera crews were busy in Webster Groves filming reactions, especially of those who were watching themselves on TV.[18]

Two months later, *Webster Groves Revisited,* produced by Baron and written and narrated by Kuralt, was broadcast on Friday, April 8, 1966, at 10:00 p.m. EST. The town's reaction came across first-hand with the teenagers liking — and the adults disliking — what they saw. John Horn said that the return also reinforced a conviction in the impartial viewer that *Sixteen in Webster Groves* had sounded the town's social and psychological depths correctly.[19]

A documentary about a documentary was something new. Parents who came on so negatively in *Sixteen* found that they had a second chance and tried to redeem themselves accordingly. One man repeated pretty much what he had said before but tried to qualify it with a touch of good humor. *Revisited* seemed to be both a justification and an apology by both CBS and the participants on the original program.

During the sequel, one of five teenagers who had been in the original said, "All these kids . . . they were really thinking something, and they were really feeling something. Their parents didn't even realize it. It was like two different worlds. They didn't understand them at all — the things that they believe in or the things that make them happy or sad. . . ."[20]

Sixteen in Webster Groves and *Webster Groves Revisited* are important theme documentaries because they anticipated and aired suburban familial conditions well before the video audience who saw the two programs realized such problems had arisen. Most documentaries aren't that prescient.

THE ESSAY AS THEME DOCUMENTARY: ANDREW ROONEY

Harold Clurman has described one of the mainsprings of most documentaries — the narrator — as "that loathsome presence in documentary films." Pitfalls await the theme documentary producer at every phase of his work. Narration is a major concern because so much of what is being "said" on a theme broadcast is relayed via narration. It's a potential bugaboo because no matter what else is being done on the screen and sound track, narration carries the brunt of the broadcast's exposition. A piece of film or videotape is dateless;

it can be about Arizona or the Sahara — you can't easily tell by just looking at it. Nothing on it tells you of what you're seeing or when or where it was taken. So some narration is always necessary, much in the manner of the caption written to explain a newspaper photo.

What Clurman objects to is the know-it-all narration extending way beyond the essentials of supplying the who, what, why, when and where. Narration *should* enable the theme producer to control his program, to release information in neat segments. Narration is all right when the program's objective is to be expository but all wrong if the aim is to divert your attention for an hour or so.

This leads us to Andrew Rooney, inventor of the television essay and supplier of scripts to innumerable CBS presenters. The success or failure of Rooney's scripts has depended on how well he managed to fill in information crevices around the blocks of film footage and music track. His usual narrator, Harry Reasoner, was never meant to be all-knowing in the manner of the old-time newsreel presenter. He was meant to be capable of bringing life to a Rooney essay by being wryly analytical and poetically appreciative, all the while retaining Rooney's completely personal point-of-view. Sometimes it worked; sometimes, it was plain "loathsome."

From February, 1965, through the end of 1966, Rooney was kept busy writing and producing one news documentary and four theme documentaries. The former was an hour-long News Special surveying the news events of 1966. The theme broadcasts were essay studies of the world from Rooney's angle: to see what we take for granted, to look again at the ordinary and find it startlingly refreshing; to see bridges (broadcast on February 2, 1965; rebroadcast on August 9, 1966), doors (broadcast on August 2, 1965), hotels (broadcast on June 28, 1966) and Scotland (broadcast on October 12, 1966).

John Horn said that *An Essay on Bridges* was "a lovely mass of film," and it truly does exploit the usual compilation features of the theme documentary: stunning film footage, original music by Glenn Paxton, adept editing by Jules Laventhol, highly skilled narration by Harry Reasoner and, of course, displays everywhere throughout the production of Rooney's extremely personal, almost eccentric viewpoints.

We see all kinds of bridges: the classic Roman arch, the railroad bridge, the covered bridge, the simple plank, the soaring suspension bridge. Examples were found in Rome, Italy and Bayonne, New Jersey, as well as above such bodies of water as Scotland's Firth of Forth and the New York Narrows.[21] "An eerie other-world sequence of happy workers bouncing on the Verrazano's first layer of wire mesh, high above the Narrows, was a good approximation of the way this film had a viewer's spirit leaping."[22]

Proving that you probably can do a theme documentary on just about any topic, Rooney decided to offer viewers *A Bird's-eye View of Scotland,* using an Alouette helicopter as a tour bus for himself, Reasoner and cameraman John Tiffin. Why on earth Scotland? Because, as Reasoner points out on the program, "it's beautiful country. . . . How can you hate a place that has highlands, lowlands, bonnie banks, tartans, bagpipes and Scotch whisky?"[23]

Reviewing the broadcast, Van Horne noted that Rooney "has a gift for the sudden, stabbing phrase, the quick summation. But he is also fond of sentences that produce, under analysis, absolutely no sense.

"We understand perfectly when Mr. Rooney writes, 'You can tell a great deal about people by observing what they have done to the land they live on.'

"But what are we to make of a sentence that reads, 'Sheep are not the only animals (in Scotland) though it is hard to show them to you'? Or: 'The view from the air is probably no more the way things really look than the view from anywhere else'."[24]

There's that omnipresent responsibility of narration. Narration cannot get too poetical as Rooney undoubtedly was trying to do in *Scotland,* which also featured an original score by Paxton and the lovely folk songs of singer Jean Redpath.

One condition Rooney demands his viewer go along with him on is sharing his unbounded fascination with his documentary subjects.

Take *An Essay on Doors.* You see all kinds of doors: bronze, wooden, plastic, French, Victorian, swinging, dentists', closet and screen. You see the door as a comic prop in a Charlie Chaplin comedy, as a fixture in a Douglas Fairbanks, Sr., epic and a Gloria Swanson drama.[25]

Take *An Essay on Hotels,* which delved into its subject in maddening detail, forcing Reasoner to narrate nearly 13 pages of script before the first talking head appeared on the screen.

Still, *An Essay on Hotels* had its moments:

No one has clearly defined a motel. Usually it's a motel if you carry your own bags and park near your room. It's a motel if there's a swimming pool . . . a coke machine down the hall . . . an ice dispenser nearby. It's a motel if you can hear the truck traffic from your bed in the middle of the night.[26]

With most hotels it is the beds that give it its ultimate purpose for existence. Maybe Las Vegas is the only city in the world with hotels where people stay but give final priority to something other than getting into bed. In Las Vegas, only the sore losers go to bed. The gambling rooms downstairs are 24 hours a day and hotel guests often come and go without unpacking anything but their money.[27]

The people who work in hotels say you can always see the manager coming because he walks on the edge of the carpet to save on wear and tear down the middle.[28]

Hotel and motel rooms are not like home and that's the way we like them. They are refreshingly clear of the miscellaneous paraphernalia that clutter our living rooms. You may have noticed that if you stay in a hotel room for a week you begin to not like it. That's because it's getting homelike.[29]

Kay Gardella pointed out about *Hotels* that "while it is true Conrad Hilton didn't sponsor the program, the fact is he didn't have to. His numerous cross-country havens for weary travelers and businessmen were well touched upon . . . ,"[30] which only proves that whenever a documentary gets off a bona fide news lead, it is apt to begin grinding out public relations — beneficial or adverse — for somebody.

When we reach the end of this study of documentary on TV from 1965 to 1975, we shall return to Andrew Rooney and allow him a last word.

AFRICA: SUMMING UP A CONTINENT

In May, 1966, Thomas W. Moore, ABC-TV network president, announced that ABC was about to pioneer "a new documentary form in TV journalism." It planned to screen a three-and-a-half hour study of the continent of Africa in prime time.

The resulting production was not a new form of documentary by any means; it was merely theme documentary applied to a monumental subject. But *Africa* turned out to be one of the best television documentaries ever made. It managed to make Africa understandable to millions to whom the "dark continent" was a jungle where natives ran around all day long waving spears. Seeing *Africa* repeatedly doesn't tarnish its impact. In fact, by creating this one program — although he had done dozens of others — producer James Fleming was catapulted into the front ranks of American television theme documentary. *Africa* illustrates again what a commercial network news organization can do when it has the will and means.

Hitherto, only NBC News had presented entire evenings given over to documentaries, such as its past looks at United States foreign policy and racial tensions. But Moore wanted his network to go beyond "a white paper or reportorial report. We want to turn loose the best talents in entertainment, sports, news and public affairs, all of which, for the first time will concentrate on one subject."[31] At the time, ABC officials, including Elmer Lower, then president of ABC News, envisioned the forthcoming project as encompassing "the broad areas of the continent (the geography and natural resources), then (moving) into a study of the people, their lives and degree of sophistication or deprivation and, later in the evening, examining the continent's culture and art, significance of its geographical position as well as the role of the emerging countries."

Depending on the success of the venture, ABC might, Moore suggested, do other studies. "We would do a different continent each year."[32]

To produce such a behemoth, a special production unit was formed, supervised overall by ABC News and actively assisted by ABC-TV programming and ABC sports. Fleming was named executive producer of the new unit. African correspondent Blaine Litell was picked to act as African coordinator, writer and producer for special projects. Eventually, anthropologist Robert Ardrey, photographer Eliot Elisofon, cameraman Skeets Kelly (who had filmed much of the movie *Lawrence of Arabia*), narrator Gregory Peck, ABC News commentator Howard K. Smith and composer Alex North contributed their respective talents.

Production took a year's combined efforts by six camera crews shooting 250 consecutive days, plus traveling over a million miles. They shot over 300 hours of color film, most of which had to be discarded. "One forty-minute sequence studied a Nigerian village through the eyes of a ten-year-old native girl. It was beautiful," laments Fleming, "but it simply couldn't be edited down and still remain effective."[33]

Ultimately the program did prove to be unique. It ran for four hours, for one thing, from 7:00 to 11:00 p.m., on Sunday, September 10, 1967. Moreoever, critic Jack Gould said of it: "By any conceivable standard, the effort was a landmark in commercial TV, fulfilling a notable educational and informational purpose."[34]

Covering the entire continent, *Africa* stressed the regions below the vast Sahara. It began sagely for that day and hour with emphases on jungle scenes, vistas and shots of wild beasts, but then moved on, hour by hour, into more serious considerations, such as the candid interview between reporter Richard Siemanowski and Sir Harry Oppenheimer of the South African mining and diamond dynasty, who "decried the automatic equation of the words 'white' and 'civilized'." At one point, Fleming's cameras showed a black boy at a South African colored New Year's carnival wearing white paint on his face. Other touches: a boy in Ghana learning the English word "shoe," though he is barefoot; and a Ghanan band playing "Auld Lang Syne."

The first hour also pictured Kalahari desert bushmen and the birth of Botswana, then a new country. The second covered tribalism, problems of disease, educational needs and excesses of African political leaders, such as the acts of Ghana's demented Kwame Nkrumah. The third hour disclosed African culture, sports and ethnic pride as well as Africa's people's bitterness against the rest of the world for enslaving their forebears. The fourth strongly indicted colonialism and its attendant horrors by citing Portugal's then African territories, as well as looking at imperial problems in Rhodesia and South Africa.

Other than Siemanowski, some who helped articulate these segments were: Tad Danielski, Edward Magruder-Jones and Pierre Streit.

Gould's enthusiastic review of *Africa* closed by congratulating Leonard H. Goldenson, then president of ABC-TV's parent corporation, Moore and Lower for having "outstepped their network rivals in documentaries. They encouraged four hours of independent reporting of genuine substance. . . ."[35]

Yet, despite ABC-TV's success with *Africa* and their high hopes for exploiting it ("We might use the audio track of the TV program for ABC radio. We possibly would want to edit portions for a series on radio, the radio network may be a contributor to the telecasts, or we may see fit to produce an entirely independent show . . . based on information provided by the TV study.''[36]), no new giant documentaries materialized. The next time ABC-TV talked about doing a three-hour telecast similar to *Africa* was in June, 1975, eight years later, when, with an eye on the upcoming Russian sponsorship of the 1980 Olympics, the network dallied with the idea of covering life in the Soviet Union.[37]

DOCUDRAMA: 1974

Until 1974, documentary was the only public affairs and opinion news format in commercial television to completely exclude commercial sales considerations.

Not that there wasn't always sponsorship for such programs, especially news documentaries. There had been — from the days when Alcoa sponsored *See It Now*. But such sponsorship always had a "compliments of a friend" tinge to it; the program was paid for, a gesture of good will was established and any resulting prestige was accepted as all to the good. Little else was expected. No need to raise one's hackles about the situation; documentaries just didn't earn an audience share that was commercially viable. All they bought was prestige and — if they weren't too realistic and hard-hitting — sometimes good will.

With everything else on the tube completely related to commercial sponsorship, it was an anomaly for documentary to be so excluded. Yet it was this freedom from worry about who was watching — and how many — that helped make the TV documentary so truthful and reliable. Not only the traditional hour-long news and theme documentaries managed to survive despite earning increasingly poor financial returns resulting from puny audience totals, but those other more current and popular expressions of documentary on TV, such as actualities (live coverage, mini-docs and Special Reports reconstructed from previous live-coverage tapes), thrived by bringing the news right into homes whenever the need arose and by amplifying that news through the appearance of well-produced, informative backgrounders featured on the regular morning and evening newscasts. Moreover, magazine formats, especially *60 Minutes,* always were sponsored and earned excellent ratings.

Sometimes, however, thirst for prestige *and profits* was too much. At such times, that form of theme documentary called docudrama emerged. Actuality was abandoned entirely, to be replaced by reenactment and fictional reconstructions superimposed on the truth. Yet, enough of the facts were retained to give an audience the sense of actuality — of real things happening again just as they had happened before — thus making docudrama an increasingly prevalent form, especially from 1974 on. By 1974, everything we had witnessed on TV was capable of being re-created and passed along to us again as an instantaneous experience. No matter what was happening on that piece of furniture called a television set, we saw its images in our homes, while sitting in comfortable chairs. To gain access to it, all we had to do was snap on the set and settle back. TV's inherent tendency to enhance the dramatic and minimize the routine worked to make even a documentary a cozy entertainment program. In a great many instances, that's what it was.

Thus, watching documentary on TV was home theater. It was recreation; it was diversion; it was not work. Thus also, with all the entertainment available on the tube, if we occasionally wanted "truth," better we got it comfortably couched in dramatic scenes than in bald, blatant actualities. True, forsaking actuality left us with a melon called docudrama, which contained only an outer shell of reality but a big inner shell of fictional pulp. That, however, was the price American television paid to win wide audiences, to deliver to a sponsor who would pay handsomely for such efforts.

Five 1974 productions on CBS-TV — *The Autobiography of Miss Jane Pittman, The Ambassador, The Migrants, 6Rms W Vu* and *The Whirlwind* — were all good theater. They had plots, stars, supporting actors and sets. They were meant to entertain large audiences, and they were produced to be sold.

Of them only two were bona fide docudrama — *The Ambassador* (November 21) and *The Whirlwind* (December 17). They were parts of four 90-minute specials CBS-TV had scheduled for Tuesday evenings from 9:30–11:00 p.m. in late March and April. Only the above were shown in 1974, probably because of the scheduling chaos caused by the lengthy live coverage of Watergate. In any event, CBS-TV geared up for the Bicentennial in 1976 by creating a series about "the man many students of American history regard as perhaps the greatest American of them all." The network promised *Benjamin Franklin* would be "afforded all the quality production and special effort that are dictated by so vital and vibrant a subject."[38] CBS-TV also noted that the series offered "an advertiser an extraordinary opportunity to be associated with a project as appealing as it is meritorious."

Lewis Freedman, long a network executive producer of dramatic programs, supervised the series, which followed four broad areas of Franklin's durable life: (1) his early years from birth (1706–57); (2) the London years (1757–75); (3) the Paris years (1776–85); and (4) the last years from 1785 until his death in 1790.

George Lefferts, whose writing and production efforts extended back to *Studio One, Armstrong Circle Theatre* and *Kraft Theatre*, produced *The Ambassador*, which starred Eddie Albert as Franklin; the script was by Howard Fast. As *Variety* noted, five actors were slated to play Franklin in the various productions. In addition to Albert as Franklin at 72 and as ambassador from the rebelling American colonies to France, Richard Widmark later portrayed Franklin in England, Melvin Douglas played him as an old man helping to get the young United States underway, and Lloyd and his son Beau Bridges respectively acted out Franklin the businessman and printer.

In *The Ambassador*, Franklin "was shown as wise, wheedling, brave, patriotic and shrewd."[39] In *The Whirlwind*, written by Loring Mandell, another veteran who wrote for *Studio One, Playhouse 90, CBS Playhouse,*

Franklin was transformed from a "self-educated journeyman-printer into America's elder statesman in the Revolutionary War years."[40] Franklin's wife and illegitimate son, William, helped show him in human perspective: as a youth who used his illiterate wife to rise in the world only to cast her aside when she failed to keep up with him intellectually and as a father unable to tolerate a son without talent. The script belied what Franklin later wrote of his marriage: "We throve together and ever mutually endeavored to make each other happy."[41]

Docudrama, it seemed, was everywhere in the fall of 1974. On November 29, Richard Burton played Sir Winston Churchill in NBC-TV's *The Gathering Storm,* which was based on Churchill's first volume of World War II memoirs. Although his physical appearance never reminded one directly of the essential Churchill, Burton's mastery of Churchillian mannerisms and props brought forth the British leader's courage and intelligence, qualities which led him out of the political wilderness and back to the seat of power, where he went on to inspire his countrymen and their allies to victory.

On December 18, ABC-TV presented *The Missiles of October,* starring William Devane as John F. Kennedy and Martin Sheen as Robert F. Kennedy as they confronted the Cuban missile crisis in 1962. *Variety* described exactly why the public found this form of fact-fiction so absorbing:

> Writer Stanley R. Greenberg used quick vignettes to convey the story . . . and the movement helped speed up the extremely long program. He also decided to juxtapose the hero JFK with a fairly sympathetic Nikita Khrushchev, who was portrayed as a man with decent instincts, but a powerful hawk constituency. Within the dramatic terms of the story, Kennedy and Khrushchev were in almost exact parallel situations politically. There's no way of knowing how accurate the Russian phase of the story was — but it made for absorbing television.[42]

Docudrama topics sometimes were too potent in political content and abrasive language to be carried over any American television network, commercial or public. A two-and-half hour program produced by the BBC, about the Chicago conspiracy trial, was turned down in 1971 by all American networks, but was shown eventually in New York on November 26, 1974, as part of a course in documentary at the New School for Social Research.

The production used such actors as Cliff Gorman and Morris Carnovsky in major roles, which were based on the Chicago Seven Trial transcript. Docudrama can occasionally stir up the past even though that past is essentially a reenactment.[43]

This proclivity for the re-creation of past history was not something TV producers invented. No less a writer than Shakespeare favored it, especially with his history plays, *Richard II, Henry IV,* Parts I and II, and *Henry V,* which are collectively entitled *The Henriad,* wherein the feudal past is shucked

away and a new age of order, science and power springs forth. Of course there
were novels — the historical novels of Scott, Thackeray and Dickens, of Fen-
imore Cooper, Kenneth Roberts and Walter D. Edmonds. There were the biographical novels of Robert Penn Warren (*All the King's Men*) and Edwin
O'Connor (*The Last Hurrah*), which, respectively, were based roughly on the
careers of Huey Long, governor of Louisiana and United States Senator, and
of Boston Mayor James M. Curley. TV's contribution to docudrama seems to
be this: it managed to make so much available in *actual terms* that it seemed
sensible to carry this ability along as far as it would go and ultimately *re-create*
the actual. Back in 1972, for instance, working with BBC-Time-Life films,
NBC presented the six-part series, *Search for the Nile*. It was produced by
Christopher Ralling, another BBC luminary, "who used African locations and
factual documents to stay 'as rigidly as humanly possible to the plain, unvar-
nished fact'."[44]

The series actually constitutes one massive whole, a six-hour epic dedicated to watching "nineteenth-century white man" work within and without
himself against the odds and hardships of locating the source of the Nile. Covering 35 years, the programs introduce six magnificent main characters: Richard Burton, John Speke, David Livingstone, Samuel Baker, James Brant and,
the best known of them all, Henry Morton Stanley — all diverse and different
yet bound together in a common passion for African exploration and adventure.

What is so unique about this excellent production is the acting. One never
is reminded of the countless white-man-in-darkest-Africa-safaris that riddle
most movies about this extraordinary continent. Here, we have true-to-life por-
trayals, wonderfully played by the actors. And so, the entire production comes
off despite the fact that it is all reenactment, something ordinarily horrendous
to documentary. But the touches are so deft, the characters of the various ex-
plorers so brilliantly evoked, that one cannot put down this series for being
make-believe, for it is not. Actors such as Kenneth High as Burton, Michael
Gough as Livingstone and Seth Adagala of the National Theater of Nairobi as
a guide are just right. As John J. O'Connor notes, Richard Burton, probably
the most prescient of the men depicted, sums up the quest for the Nile's source,
saying, "Men who go looking for the source of a river are merely looking for
the source of something missing in themselves — and never finding it."[45] The
series was narrated by James Mason, directed by Ralling and Fred Burley,
written by Derek Marlowe.

By 1974, the commercial networks had learned from the public television
channels that stories — well-mounted, well-scripted, well-acted — could earn
not only good will and prestige but also high ratings and consequent profits. It
was just another step to appropriate one's plot and characters from the day's
news, mix the facts (which always must be present) with appropriate fictional
props so that the story line is simple, dramatic and climactic, yet still identifiable with past real situations — and presto! You have docudrama!

The only difficulty with this formula is that it sullies theme documentary.

Too often, there is no theme in such productions. You can identify characters, recognize situations, anticipate the rise and fall of distinct heroes or villains, but all of it leads only to petty heroics or transparent gossip. In the end, *nothing has been said*. You've merely been on the inside for a short spell, spying on the rich, the well-born, the powerful or the infamous.

Part Two / PRODUCERS

Introduction

WHY ARE SOME PRODUCERS here and not others? Why, for example, is Fred Freed included but not Chet Hagen, an equally versatile documentarist?

With due regard for my fallibility as a critic and as a surveyor of the extensive amount of work done in the decade under study (which more times than not, may have caused me to overlook or even disregard some significant figure in TV documentary), I've tried to apply the following criteria to justify the choices that follow. A producer is included here if his work in TV documentary:

1. Is sufficient to reveal an understanding and skillful application of the documentary as a TV news form.
2. Is distinctive, that is, carries his own "brand."
3. Is concerned with journalistic subject matter important to understanding the decade under study.

If a producer or reporter meets all these standards, he has been included and his work singled out for critical appraisal. If he meets at least one of them overwhelmingly, he also is evaluated. (I realize this still leaves out a great many documentarists who deserve fuller attention than they may receive here.)

Many of the documentarists mentioned hereafter happened to be involved with News Specials teams. They were not part of the rank and file cadres producing traditional news and theme documentaries. Thus, viewers had frequent opportunities to see their work. Viewers were seeing more and more specials — those instant interpretative news programs that usually ran in the late evening hours. A new kind of news program, they weren't purely hard-news reporting, yet they weren't traditional documentary either. What they tried to do was explain some event that had been treated only cursorily on an earlier evening newscast because of deadline pressures and the need to cover other, equally important news. The men and women who worked on these shows gradually began to take over other, new areas of the documentary news field as the decade moved out of the sixties and into the seventies.

Another factor determined whether a producer fulfilled himself or not as a documentarist. Westin, of ABC News, has claimed that the impetus for making good news and theme documentaries is a cyclical situation. "Each network," he has said, "and I'll include Public Television, takes the lead and then loses it. *CBS Reports* held the lead for a long time. They were the first ones on the turf. They were because Frank Stanton and Bill Paley had to find out some way of defusing the payola quiz-show scandal, and it was at that time that they said that the best way to do it was to go on the air by saying we're going to do this once a month or once every two weeks."[1]

Westin was referring to the Tuesday evening CBS News hour, largely given over to *CBS Reports.* He believed NBC also had been tarred by the quiz-show scandals, so that network developed the NBC *White Paper* series of documentaries.

"For a while," Westin has said, "they were jockeying back and forth. Then CBS decided to go the *60 Minutes* route, and a considerable amount of their resources started to go into the shorter pieces on *60 Minutes.*"[2] Westin felt that the quality of *CBS Reports* began to decline as more and more investigative materials ended up on *60 Minutes.*

"The fin and feathers stuff," he has said, "CBS never really did, although they bought the *National Geographic* series for a couple of years. They never did much with it. Once in awhile Perry Wolff would do a kind of beauty show, like *The Mystery of Stonehenge.* So the lead, it seems to me, and I'm being very subjective and the guys at CBS would object, it seems to me passes to NBC. The NBC *White Papers,* the Fred Freed stuff took the lead."[3]

Westin believed that CBS never did get back to its former preeminence, that NBC held the lead up until around 1973, when ABC management decided to invest more heavily into investigative documentaries and ordered Westin to develop a stronger series of *Close-up* productions. With these, Westin claimed, ABC News took over the lead in news documentaries.

Many could argue with Westin's conclusions. I, for one, believe both CBS and NBC made spectacular strides in news and theme documentary in the mid-sixties. I think ABC News came on strongly with the *Close-up* series in the mid-seventies. But none of the networks, nor their respective producers, can accept many laurels for their work in traditional news and theme documentary from 1968 on. Other documentary news forms took over, but the level of quality achieved in the sixties was neither as good nor as prolonged as before. Vietnam had something to do with this. The office of the presidency had something to do with this. And the American people, no longer interested in hard news, contributed to the drop-off that occurred in traditional news and theme documentary at all three commercial networks in the years between 1968 and 1975.

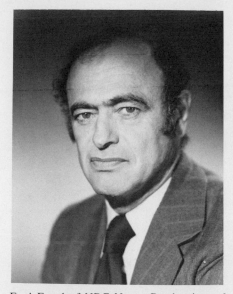

Fred Freed of NBC News. By the time of his death in 1974, he had produced nearly 40 documentaries and had won seven Emmys, three Peabodys, two Overseas Press Club awards and numerous other honors. Photo: *NBC News*

Reuven Frank, veteran NBC News executive and documentarist — guiding spirit behind *First Tuesday,* which also has been known successively as *Chronolog, Special Edition* and *Weekend.* Photo: *NBC News*

Robert "Shad" Northshield, now with CBS News as producer of *Sunday Morning,* a review of the week's news. He formerly was executive producer of *The Huntley-Brinkley Report.* As a documentarian, he handled just about any kind of project — from his 1963 three-hour news special on civil rights, *The American Revolution* of '63 to his poignant study of children in strife-torn Belfast, Northern Ireland, November, 1971, entitled, *Suffer the Little Children.* Photo: *NBC News*

Lucy Jarvis, NBC News. Her forte was the theme documentary: specifically, historical essays filmed on location. But she also produced several quality investigative programs, such as the 1970 *White Paper: Trip to Nowhere,* on drug abuse among the youth of Phoenix, Arizona. Photo: *NBC News*

71

Now with NBC News, Richard S. Salant was CBS News president throughout most of the Image Decade. Along with Dr. Frank Stanton, former CBS, Inc., president, and Peter Davis, writer of *The Selling of the Pentagon,* Salant deserves praise for taking intense critical heat from Congressional critics and others after that documentary first was broadcast in February, 1971. Photo: *NBC News*

Don Hewitt, perhaps the most brilliant documentarian in American television and executive producer of *60 Minutes,* first news magazine program ever to score consistently with big audiences so as to become one of the nation's top, most-seen shows. Photo: *CBS News*

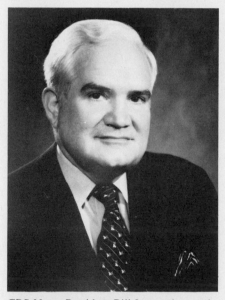

CBS News President Bill Leonard started at CBS News in 1945 as the creator and host of *This is New York* for WCBS, New York. His career neatly parallels the growth and application of television documentary. Photo: *CBS News*

Producer John Sharnik of CBS News. "I try to zero in on people telling their own experience." Photo: *CBS News*

Jay McMullen of CBS News. His *The Tenement,* broadcast in 1967, although obviously cast in the investigative mode, also was complete with marvelous poetical touches rarely seen in a TV news documentary. Photo: *CBS News*

Peter Davis, formerly with CBS News, produced and wrote *Hearts and Minds,* a made-for-theater documentary which was widely shown throughout the country in 1974. It probably summarized the Vietnam conflict more succinctly than any of the war documentaries which the three commercial networks ran April 29, 1975, the day South Vietnam collapsed and surrendered. Photo: *Irv Broughton*

Irv Drasnin. His *CBS Reports* documentary on Rhodesia, broadcast in March, 1977, had to fight for an audience against the NCAA finals on NBC, the Academy Awards on ABC, and *The Pallisers* and *Soundstage* on PBS. Documentaries commonly encountered competitive program conditions such as occurred in this particular instance. Photo: *CBS News*

Perry Wolff of CBS News. "One of his most ambitious programs, the 105-minute *A Day in the United States,* marshalled 43 cameras at 33 locations across America in 1970 to shoot 200,000 feet of film." Photo: *CBS News*

73

Eric Sevareid. Always the cerebral presenter, utterly devoted to the well-written statement, he never tried to influence his audience by manipulating his vocal delivery or altering his facial expressions. With him, ideas always came first. Photo: *CBS News*

Andrew A. Rooney, inventor of the television news essay, in his New York office, the walls of which are covered with blow-ups of government agency pronouncements, some of the materials he gathered while writing and producing *Mr. Rooney Goes to Washington*. Rooney looks "again at the ordinary and finds it startlingly refreshing." Example: Rooney on motels: ". . . no one has clearly defined a motel. Usually it's a motel if you carry your own bags and park near your room." Photo: *CBS News*

Charles Kuralt, CBS News, is one of the best narrator-reporters in TV news documentary. He has the common touch of personable humanity. Nowhere does this deft quality exhibit itself more luminously than on his *On the Road* series, which clings to some aspect of individuality as its recurrent theme. Photo: *CBS News*

Morley Safer's reporting in Vietnam in 1966 first made the American public aware of the new, unusual tactics being employed by both sides. He predicted that after the battle of Ia Drang Valley, American casualties would sharply increase, and they did. Photo: *CBS News*

Elmer Lower became head of ABC News in 1964. In his eleven years in that job, Lower saw his news budget jump from $4-million yearly to $50-million; his news staff rise from 250 to 750. Photo: *ABC News*

Martin Carr, who has produced award-winning documentaries for all three network news staffs. Photo: *Franc David Maratarella*

ABC News' Stephen Fleischman: "The documentary has got to be more than the sum of its parts. If you're coming out with four segments of a documentary, a documentary interrupted by commercials, you're seeing four mini-docs. If that happens, I feel I've failed." Photo: *ABC News*

Harry Reasoner, now back at CBS News after a stint at ABC News where he anchored *The Reasoner Report*, a half-hour weekly series from 1973 to 1975. A well-crafted program, it deserved a better prime time slot than the Saturday night supper hour. Photo: *ABC News*

Av Westin, ABC News. In 1973, he said, "Heretofore, a documentary unit was a little conclave set apart in the news division that researched its own projects. But we plan to open up the doors and to make use of the 400 plus employees around the world. All will make their contribution . . ." Photo: *ABC News*

4 / Producers at NBC News

FRED FREED

NBC WHITE PAPERS already existed in 1965, being the handiwork of Irving Gitlin, who had come to NBC in 1960. As NBC's executive producer in charge of creative projects, he supervised the series, especially the work of producers Al Wasserman and Fred Freed. Wasserman was responsible for "Sit-in" (1960), a study of the civil rights movement in Nashville, and the first news documentary on TV to tell the story solely in the words of its protagonists. Wasserman's "The Battle of Newburgh" (1962) was NBC News' first investigative documentary. A probe into welfare problems and official corruption in the Hudson River-area city of Newburgh, it also was the first to show the teeth a good documentary could bare by generating a wide public outcry.[1]

Freed, the most prominent talent to arise at NBC News, had been a news writer working for Bill Leonard at WCBS in 1949. After a long stint there, he went to NBC where, since 1961, he had been producer and executive producer of the *White Paper* productions. He died in 1974, having made almost 40 television documentaries and having won seven Emmys, three Peabodys and two Overseas Press Club awards as well as other major honors.[2]

He once wrote:

> People get the news from us. We shape the way they look at the world, sometimes not the way we mean to, but we shape it. I believe people should know *more,* not less. I believe people are entitled to know more. I believe they are better able to decide how they want to live if they know more.[3]

Freed had done slice-of-life documentaries for NBC, including *Comedian Backstage* (1963), in which Shelley Berman threw a tantrum backstage after completing his nightclub act out front. Freed was one of the first documentary producers to write and direct his own shows and interview his sources. He is rivaled only by Murrow and Friendly in his skill to get people to talk and to talk well. For instance, in his first major news special for Gitlin, *The White Paper,* "The Decision to Drop the Bomb" (1965), he filmed members of the wartime Japanese government, eliciting their first public comments on Hiroshima. It was a considerable advance in production techniques over past compilation documentaries, which relied on voice-over narration, musical fanfares or mood statements and interrelated film footage derived from old newsreels or other outside sources. Moreover, the program "employed what seems to be a prevailing technique these days in documentaries. From still photographs of the principals in 1945, there were instant dissolves to moving pictures of the individuals as they now look 20 years later."[4]

Freed produced a major documentary in September, 1965: *American White Paper:* "United. States Foreign Policy." It was another in a series of occasional super news specials offered by NBC News that consumed an evening of prime-time programming.

Freed's 20-year survey of our foreign policy was divided into three parts. The first, confrontation with the Soviet Union, spun through atom bombs, Churchill's Iron Curtain speech, civil war in Greece, the Marshall plan, the Berlin blockade, formation of NATO, the Korean war, European prosperity, Stalin's death, the Hungarian revolution, Sputnik, the U-2 incident, the Cuban missile crisis and De Gaulle's intransigence.

Part two, confrontation in the emerging world, was the best, taking in United States actions in Guatemala, Lebanon and Santo Domingo to show "the role of the United States in confronting the emerging world with humanitarian aid and military might."[5]

The program remained, despite its unique length, a pastiche of film footage, using battle scenes wherever possible. Without analysis, a program of such length cannot help but flounder, leaving the viewer numb as the words and images of 16 successive NBC correspondents tickety-tick past him like broken-down freight cars.

Still, "Policy" won Fred Freed an Emmy and an Overseas Press Club award.

With the single exception of ABC News' *Africa* (1967), NBC News was the first and only network to preempt entire evenings in this way. It began the practice in 1963 with *The American Revolution of '63,* a study of the civil rights movement. It ran for three hours on Labor Day, and was the brainchild of Robert E. Kintner and Robert Sarnoff, then respectively NBC president and chairman. These long shows were a new kind of TV movie: they were prime-time reality programs.

In addition to *Revolution* and "Policy," NBC News has produced three other *White Paper* news documentary blockbusters in prime time: *Organized Crime in the U.S.* (1966); *The Energy Crisis* (1973); and *Of Men and Women* (1975). Freed also produced the programs on crime and energy, a distinction no other television documentarist possesses.

Another Freed White Paper documentary appeared in mid-April, 1966: *Count Down to Zero*. It attempted, not too successfully, to survey the burgeoning missile arms race throughout the world. Using color for the first time, Freed spent six months on the program and employed his usual battery of NBC correspondents, plus experts and authorities on missile warfare. Like *Bomb* and *Policy, Count Down to Zero* stressed factual understatement of an intensely dramatic theme saying pointedly that the whole world, and specifically America, now lay open to missile attack. The program, however, never developed the tense pace its topic deserved.[6]

Another Freed effort in 1966, *The Hill Country: Lyndon Johnson's Texas,* was telecast the following Monday, but instead of showcasing Freed's hallmarks — tight interviewing, understated theme and copious presentation of facts — this particular program focused on LBJ's roots and biography in terms of the "country life along the sloping banks of the Pedernales river." Sequences revealed "the more lovely side of southcentral Texas — the wildlife, the cattle, the flowers, the endless sky, the green fields and the restful shaded trees."[7]

A more definitive treatment of Johnson and his presidency would come later when Walter Cronkite would interview the President — again at home in Texas — but well after he had left the office.

NBC telecast Freed's *American White Paper: Organized Crime in the U.S.,* a three-and-a-half-hour prime-time news special on Aug. 25, 1966. It was his second blockbuster to take over an NBC evening in prime time.

Freed's statement on organized crime warned his viewers that crime did pay — was, in fact, our biggest business. To embellish this claim, he paraded a long list of underworld types before his cameras, thereby giving viewers an understated but visually fascinating look at crime.

Freed had a frantic 1967. Three instant specials — on the State of the Union address and a two-part treatment of the China crisis — hit him in January alone. In March, he presented another instant news special, *Assassination Conspiracy,* based on the opening of New Orleans District Attorney Jim Garrison's investigation into an alleged conspiracy to assassinate JFK. Later, in June, he did an investigative turn in New Orleans, trying to walk the centerline between objectivity and sensationalism, trying also to state, at bottom, that Garrison had no case against New Orleans businessman Clay Shaw, who, two years later, was acquitted.

Also in March, Freed produced *Whose Right to Bear Arms? An NBC News Inquiry,* the first of a long line of treatments on TV about gun control. In this case, Freed was strongly against the free use of guns. It was a perfect theme documentary, well-written and edited.

But his third Emmy resulted from *Summer 1967: What We Learned,* an hour-long probe into what happened in Detroit just after the riots there had ended. Freed again was on location: first, it had been New Orleans; now, Detroit's still-tense ghetto.

Yellin, in his study of Freed and his work, says to Freed during an interview, "Since *Summer 1967: What We Learned,* there's been a shift in priority, in emphasis. In filmic language, the image creates the word; in print and radio, the word creates the image." To which Freed replied in his eccentric lower-case style:

> i want to be able to say in my script, "this is cleveland," and then show a picture of a slum. i don't have to say, "this is a slum in cleveland," and i certainly don't have to say, "this is a dirty, mixed-up, unhappy, miserable slum in cleveland." the simple declarative sentence is the guts of any documentary script.[8]

The program on Detroit had this quality — in the writing, in the video. It was a superb documentary.

Two of Freed's *White Paper* urban documentaries (1) *Cities Have No Limits,* and (2) *The People Are the City,* a two-hour program, were telecast in 1968. A third show, still part of the same theme, *Confrontation,* aired in 1969, featured the "why" of a lengthy faculty-student strike at San Francisco State College. It was a successful program, as was the first, which toured San Francisco, New York, Tokyo, Rome, Detroit, Chicago and Cleveland, and concluded with a lively discussion between Daniel P. Moynihan, then presidential adviser on urban affairs, and Charles V. Hamilton, a black political scientist. In it, Freed did what NBC Correspondent Sander Vanocur said earlier in the year about TV while he was covering the RFK assassination: "If TV is worth anything, it is the transmission of experience. You see it as we saw it."[9] Freed used every technique possible to keep the program moving: split screens, long lenses, montages, folk-rock music groups, juxtaposed slices of life contrasting black and white urbanites: black children in a city hydrant spray, white children in a backyard pool.

The second part, *The People Are the City,* directed on location in Boston, was beset with problems, concerning both what the program revealed and what its producers underwent before it was completed. First of all, the documentary was a study of blacks trying to obtain better housing, careers, education and civic participation. To achieve all these complex aspects, Freed had to overcome a $200,000 shakedown attempt by some Boston black militants, a boycott against him and his crew that prevented them from interviewing anybody and the murder of two people appearing in the documentary. Officials of a black anti-poverty program, the two victims were shot shortly after they had been interviewed by Freed's people. "For the next few days, the NBC team, led by investigative reporter Walter Sheridan, tapped their many contacts in Roxbury for leads. Finally, an informer was persuaded to talk and the NBC film crew filmed his resolution."[10]

Sponsored by A.T. & T., the urban series was worth the candle because both the sponsor and NBC News felt Freed knew what he was talking about when he said, while working in Boston, "There are three kinds of programs you can do. One makes you feel better. The second makes 'them' feel better. The third, the hardest of all, makes somebody who isn't committed involved in a problem. But with them you have to say it so they don't tune out."[11]

Besieged Majority was an hour look at crime from the victim's point of view — "how robberies and senseless violence were spreading fear in many urban neighborhoods and altering the life style of individual citizens."[12] Looking at what a high crime rate was doing to a white, middle-class Philadelphia neighborhood, Freed allowed his talking heads — plain people in the area, local businessmen and law enforcement agency bureaucrats — plausible answers. For instance, "one woman whose husband was murdered at work wanted to know why the ordinary person should be deprived of safety on the job or at home."[13] Freed's program conveyed the anger, fear and frustration that people felt over the rising crime rate, but it also, according to critic Jack Gould, "left a viewer with a feeling of complete helplessness."[14]

In 1971, Fred Freed's major effort resulted in the two-part *White Paper: Vietnam Hindsight*, which tried to answer the question: Why did we blunder into Vietnam?

Part I is about the Kennedy Administration and Vietnam; Part II, the assassination of President Ngo Dinh Diem. Both fail to answer the key question. For one thing, Freed was attracted to a complex subject. His documentarian modus operandi was built on the urge to simplify recent happenings for viewers. That was what the documentary was for, he felt. For another thing, Vietnam was far more complicated causally than emphases solely on the JFK and Diem stories would have us believe. Freed could have as easily taken a look at French involvement in Vietnam and it would have been just as helpful but not necessarily *the* answer as to why we were there. Or he could have tackled a detailed analysis of World War II in the Southeast Asia theater and obtain the same vacuous results.

Freed wanted to reveal flashes of insight about American policy. He wanted to do with video what Walter Lippmann did so well in print. Lippmann was unparalleled at using print to tell us what was happening. He could discuss complexities and supply answers. With him, it was a matter of cogent writing.

But Fred Freed couldn't get television to help him supply answers, not consistently at least. He could only describe problems — the inherent emotionalism of TV got in his way. True, maybe he saw an unspoken parallel in what his two programs tried to express. True, JFK and Diem both were cut down by acts of political murder. Maybe interruptions in regimes caused by such murders alter policy, and policy, once altered, tolerates disorder — it may, in fact, become a disorderly policy.

Freed also produced *Opinion and Comment,* featuring Edwin Newman, a new weekly series to give NBC News a video op-ed page. The programs did just that, but stirred little reaction and soon fell into the customary public affairs programming rut despite presenting a sterling means for letting public men speak out editorially.[15]

Freed oversaw three *White Papers* in 1973. There was the two-part study: *And Now The War Is Over . . . The American Military in the 70s,* which appeared in January and February, each program being two hours long. Later, in the early fall, Freed and his staff presented another of his super specials, a three-hour study, *The Energy Crisis.*

Part I of the program on the military, "If You Want Us to Stand Down, Tell Us," surveyed the past and present of America's armed forces and posed questions about their future. It discussed what Churchill called "the balance of terror" — the enormous stores of arms with which we and the Soviet Union face off one another. It cited the fact that we have 1,054 intercontinental ballistic missiles and 2,000 nuclear warheads, of which the smallest is ten times bigger than the bomb that destroyed Hiroshima.

It mentioned three paradoxes: that we have become used to the "balance of terror," that we always must convince the Soviet Union that we will retaliate no matter what they do and that "each year we have more weapons and each year we are less safe."[16]

Freed's script reads:

> The weapons are still there. Russian and American cities are still targeted. We have not found a way to end the balance of terror. And we cannot be sure that our weapons will always deter, that the other side always will be rational. We know that no weapon has been invented that has not been used. We will only be allowed one mistake. This is the nightmare we will continue to live with in the seventies.[17]

The second hour of Part II was entitled "One Billion Dollar Weapon," and was about the CVN 70, an aircraft carrier which cost billions to build as well as defend. This particular segment won another Emmy for Freed, both as executive producer and writer. He was actively assisted in creating these productions by Alvin Davis and Craig Leake, producers, and by Freed's longtime film editor, Darold Murray, as director.

Murder in America was shown in June, 1973, and John J. O'Connor of the New York *Times* called it "extremely effective in both conception and realization."[18] Freed's documentary deserves close comparison with Peter Jeffries' *Thou Shalt Not Kill* (1972). Both deal with murder, murderers and Western locales, but approach their subject matter from widely different points of view. Jim Hartz narrated Freed's script, which was made up of broad statistics, a characteristic of Freed's. "More Americans were murdered in the United States in the last three years than were killed in Vietnam in ten years." In 1972, 18,000 murders occurred. "Murder has become epidemic in America and no one knows why," although the documentary lists drugs, racial tension, permissiveness, more young people, lenient courts and even TV as possible causes.[19]

Moving from national statistics to a local example, the program focuses on Denver where, in 1965, 35 murders took place; in 1972, 100.

Freed used the talk and work routines of several Denver homicide detectives to reveal that 60 percent of Denver's murders occur on weekends, liquor is involved in two-thirds of the cases, drugs in more than half and guns in three-quarters.

His script continues: "On Sunday they stop killing in the bars and in the streets and begin to kill at home in neighborhoods . . . where the poor, the jobless, the troubled, the violent live."

Again Darold Murray was Freed's director; camera work was by Dexter Alley and film editors were William Lockhart and May Ann Martin.[20]

Freed's third 1973 documentary was an *NBC Reports: But Is This Progress?* shown July 31 in the usual Tuesday 10–11 p.m. EST spot. It explored changes in society.

"You wouldn't think this was a prune orchard only a few years ago," observed the late Frank McGee, opening the program. "Because it was, they call this shopping center 'the prune yard.' Around us is the city of San Jose. When the Spanish first came here this land was untouched. It was just as it had been for centuries, and here we are now. Is this progress? A lot of people aren't as sure as they once were."[21]

Freed chose San Jose because it was the first civil settlement in the state, the state's fastest growing city, and because "we regard California as the cutting edge of change in America."[22]

Freed used three generations to reveal our changing world: a couple aged 79 and 73 respectively; another couple in their forties; and 26-year-old Linda Lappin, "who ran away from home, lived in the Haight-Ashbury section of San Francisco, got into drugs and religion, married and separated."[23] Now she lives near the beach, talks of the free life and the terrible society and would like to escape from everything — except her car, hi-fi and dishwasher.

Craig Leake was producer of *But Is This Progress?* Adrienne Cowles was associate producer and Darold Murray, director.

Freed's blockbuster, the three-hour-long *White Paper, The Energy Crisis,* took temerity to run in prime time. Though timely, the subject certainly had its limits of interest. Just before it was shown on Tuesday, September 4, from 8–11 p.m. EST, to kick off the new NBC season, Freed said, "You're going to meet a lot of interesting people and hear them say a lot of interesting things." He sounded tentative and hopeful. But his know-how paid off. After all, he was one of the most experienced and talented producers of television documentaries, and he ended up giving "a solid and valuable survey of a staggeringly complicated subject."[24]

Freed built the show around the question, "How do you balance the needs of the environment against the needs of energy?" To expand on that, he used enough talking heads to fill two single-spaced pages of an NBC News press release.[25]

"Nothing we can possibly do in three hours will satisfy everyone," Freed said. "We can't even hope to cover it all. . . . Yet it needs to be done, and I think it is right that we are doing it. And I think that it is right that it is being done on TV, because that is how most Americans find out what is going on in the world."[26]

In any event, *The Energy Crisis* did what a *White Paper* is supposed to do: alert the public to a situation, define as clearly as possible what that situation is and how it came about and never — repeat never — offer conclusive answers. As Freed said, "We're going to tell you what we know about something you should know. . . ."[27]

Freed died on March 31, 1974, at age 53. A maid discovered his body in bed at 11 a.m. He was described as "the very model of the modern major newsman — tweedy, serious, cautiously skeptical—a tireless stalker of the specters of social unrest that haunt the television-watching average American."[28]

LUCY JARVIS

NBC News producer Lucy Jarvis' forte was the theme documentary — specifically historical essays filmed on location. She had been an associate of George Vicas in 1963 when NBC film crews were allowed to photograph the inside of the Kremlin. She had persuaded the Russians to grant NBC this privilege at a time when it was being denied even to Soviet cameramen. Four years later, when she was again in Russia, secretly gathering home movies, stills and voice tapes of Khrushchev, Jarvis again asked to enter and photograph the Kremlin. The Russians told her they might be interested in selling her film about the Kremlin, footage which, of course, turned out to be her own earlier documentary, *The Kremlin*.[29]

Because she could speak Russian and through her friendship with Khrushchev's son-in-law, Aleksei I. Adzhubei, she did manage to use Russian sources to obtain camera and tape recordings of the Khrushchev household, a dacha near Moscow where the former Soviet premier played with his dog, gardened and indulged a passion for photography.

Jarvis' 1967 documentary has grandfather Nikita romping with his grandchildren as well as expressing himself pungently on the American leaders he had confronted: Vice President Nixon, "a son of a bitch;" Ambassador Henry Cabot Lodge, "no fool;" President Kennedy: "I think if Kennedy had been alive today, we would have had an excellent relationship with the United States, because he would never have let his country get into such a sticky situation as it is in now in Vietnam."[30]

The Jarvis documentary was well-paced, giving the viewer a tantalizing glimpse of one of the sixties' most colorful political leaders.

Another example of the hour-long news documentary wending its investigatory way through a thicket of competing news material was Jarvis' 1970 *Trip to Nowhere,* a *White Paper* about a broad effort in Phoenix, Arizona, to fight a severe drug problem among the city's youth. Narrator Edwin Newman observed at the program's close that "somehow, we have failed them . . . we have turned our sons into cannon fodder for an incomprehensible war that seems without end."[31]

Lucy Jarvis broke new ground again in 1971 when her NBC News crew was the first to make a detailed video tour of Scotland Yard. She chose David Niven, the movie star, to narrate the Sidney Carroll script about the inner workings of the Yard. "He is bilingual," she explained. "There are very few personalities in the entertainment field who are equally at home in the English language and the American language."[32] A pleasure to watch, *Scotland Yard* featured detectives, their police methods and areas inside the British police unit never before shown to the public.

Jarvis' *The Pursuit of Youth* was a 1974 study of this country's "frenetic clutch" to keep young. Written by the eminent science-fictioneer, Isaac Asimov, the program asked:

> Why begin the hint of your retirement by your looks alone? Why point yourself toward an ending anywhere from ten to thirty years before the actual end — if, by altering your appearance and hanging on to the pretense of youth by every fingernail . . . you can deceive the world into accepting you as a human being — at least a little longer.[33]

The Pursuit of Youth employed a hodgepodge of sight and sound gimmicks to liven up its story, using clips from movies and pop records.

The Russian Connection — Armand Hammer was hinged to a news hook its producer couldn't control — the détente then existing in 1974 between America and the Soviet Union. It described the business machinations of Dr. Hammer, 76 years old and a bizarre figure who had come out of retirement to resurrect successfully the fortunes of Occidental Petroleum. He had had an adventurous life and at one time had done business with Lenin. But the Jarvis documentary took a year to put together and in the interim, Hammer's fortunes took a series of adverse turns. The program was scheduled, postponed, finally rescheduled. It was a biographical essay roosting on a risky news lead that did nothing ultimately to help it along.

Mrs. Jarvis produced another strong investigative news documentary in 1975: *A Shooting Gallery Called America.* It was narrated by Correspondent Carl Stern, written by Rafael Abramovits and Stern, directed by Tom Priestley and used Ira Silverman as an investigative reporter. Broadcast on April 27, it is another example of the 1975 model of news documentary: carefully, almost compulsively documented yet not without sequences designed to sensationalize the topic or aspects of it. The rise in the sale of handguns was just the kind of subject to produce such contrasts, for the program could be both fact-filled and death-drenched.

Gallery also had its share of early storm warnings from irate viewers. It had been originally scheduled for broadcast on March 2, until postponed until April by Mrs. Jarvis. Between the two dates, mail poured in to NBC — both pro and con, but mostly con — about a program not yet telecast. Mrs. Jarvis delayed it because she felt the need for additional reporting and because of what she called "the incredible concern" about the program while it was being researched.

"People knew we were doing it, and we began to get lots of mail," she said. "Probably they were alerted by a national organization. Because there was such an emotional reaction, I didn't want the program to go until I was doubly sure that everything we had checked out."[34]

Carl Stern wrote:

> This program is about handguns. Not rifles, not shotguns, but handguns. What we do with them and what they do to us.
>
> Ten years ago, Americans owned an estimated ten million handguns. Today: forty million. In the next hour, we'll find out why some people have handguns, how they got them and how the explosion in handgun ownership has affected our lives.[35]

Illustrative of the statistical-sensational polarities in the program is this sequence:

Gun Store Clerk: But, a gun, of course, is like an insurance policy. You don't want a sorry insurance policy . . . a bad one, you want one that's gonna pay off if you need it. Now, er, we do have a, a charge system . . . we use all the local charge cards — the Bank Americard and the Master Charge and such.

NBC Reporter: How long did it take you to get your first gun?

Blinky: . . . about fifteen minutes.

NBC Reporter: About fifteen minutes, yeah . . . you got it in the street?

Blinky: Yeah.

NBC Reporter: What did you want that gun for?

Blinky: I wanted to kill somebody.[36]

Blinky's amoral remarks are intercut throughout the documentary with less sensational material. He provides some of the best actualities in the program.

ROBERT "SHAD" NORTHSHIELD

1971's real significance for NBC News was the emergence of "Shad" Northshield. The network already had Freed, Lucy Jarvis, Lou Hazam and Craig Fisher, among others, and had recently acquired Martin Carr. Northshield, beginning in 1971, was to create several stunning documentaries, winning over a dozen awards in the process. A former reporter, picture editor and columnist for the Chicago *Sun-Times,* he joined NBC in 1960, where he produced the *Today* program, along with other assignments, until 1962. Previously, he had been doing public affairs programming at both CBS and ABC. At this writing, he is back at CBS News as a news producer.

A major production in 1963 for NBC was his three-hour news special on the civil rights movement in the United States, *The American Revolution of '63.* The program received ten major awards.

Other documentaries produced by Northshield in his first three years with NBC included: *The Trial of Adolf Eichmann;* five specials on the integration of the University of Mississippi; *The Chosen Child,* a program on child adoption; *An Experiment in Excellence,* a report on new techniques in education; *The Making of a Pro,* a look at the role of the quarterback in professional football; and *The Art of Collecting.*

As general manager of NBC News in 1964, Northshield supervised primary, convention and election coverage. As executive producer of *The Huntley-Brinkley Report* and *The Scherer-MacNeil Report* in 1965, he oversaw the changeover to color film coverage of news stories. He handled the former show for nearly four years.[37]

His *Man's Thumb on Nature* (1971) would appear to have been a simple "Oh, gee! Isn't nature wonderful!" theme documentary, since it defended the argument of most conservationists at the time that Man must control the populations of certain wild species if those creatures are to survive. In this case, Northshield's cameras were looking at seals inhabiting Alaska's Pribilof Islands, but his direct concern was the specific issue of controlling their population. Jack Perkins was narrator. As a news documentary, *Man's Thumb* had a point to make and made it well. *Variety,* however, disagreed. Commenting on the Pribilof Islands sequence, where baby seals were shown being clubbed to death in order to assure the survival of their species, *Variety* said:

It is difficult if not impossible to reconcile such coldly pragmatic considerations with the act of a man clubbing a helpless seal to death; and it is all the more difficult because of the manner in which that clubbing was shown on this program. Repeatedly, at the key moment, as the weapon struck the animal, the camera withdrew to spare the viewer's sensibilities. What about the seal's sensibilities? . . . Perkins' script had a disturbing bias — it has fulsome praise for what Americans have done to save wildlife, the sort of thing that leads to smugness when so much remains to be done . . . a curious, though consistently interesting hour.[38]

Northshield's second 1971 production, *Cancer Is the Next Frontier,* described the fight against this disease, showing four leading doctors talking about advances in surgery and chemotherapy, devices used to combat cancer and patients undergoing treatment. At the same time, Northshield gave the viewer a primer on what exactly cancer is while stressing the point that cancer research needed much more money than it currently was getting. Northshield made no effort to enhance the television presence, which often was quite awkward, of his medical experts.[39]

Executive producer for his third 1971 documentary (John Lord was producer), *Xerox Presents the Quarterly Report,* Northshield gave viewers an overview of the recent past, similar but far more modest than his lengthy *Revolution '63* and *From Here to the Seventies.* The documentary scanned a number of subjects: moon rocks, Harvard-Radcliffe youth voter registration and capital punishment. Its production values, especially the graphics, were of high quality. But the program lacked Northshield's usual firm, clear statements.[40]

Two NBC News documentaries in 1972 were supervised actively by Northshield: *Guilty by Reason of Race* and *Suffer the Little Children.* The first described the tragedy of 110,000 Japanese-Americans being uprooted and moved to inland detention camps during World War II, suffering in the process incalculable losses in pride and property.

The second, *Suffer the Little Children,* was the result of an NBC film unit at work for a month in Belfast, Ireland. As an hour-long, network news documentary, it is nearly perfect. Cameras follow the Catholic child, Joe McCann, throughout Belfast. Serving as his own narrator, Northshield says, "Everything you will see and hear in the next hour was seen and heard in that one month, November, 1971. It is very little of what happened to that troubled city that month."[41]

A psychiatrist, a doctor, British soldiers, Catholic and Protestant women were interviewed by Northshield. They discuss what terrible violence is doing to them all, especially to Belfast's children. A penny whistle's tune is the documentary's main musical motif. One sequence also uses a musical group, "The Flying Column," to contrast the lyrical Irish mind and heart with the camera's probing views of the Lower Falls ghetto:[42]

Sequence making complete portrait of Lower Falls Ghetto. Most shots backlit with long shadows. Again emphasize children running, standing and crouching on street, playing in wrecked cars and torn-up roads and vacant lots. Natural SOF (sound on film) very low; entire sequence edited to rhythm of narration and song.

Northshield: Violence and pathos are ever more common in Belfast now. But they are only a part of the long tradition of poverty, unemployment, bitter hatred and family love that form a boundary around a Catholic ghetto. Within it, there are a subjugated minority, few hopes, many fears and dozens of myths about an Ireland that once included four kingdoms but now has but three. Ulster, this place, is the one that's lost.

Picture sequence continues silent, with "Four Green Fields" sung full over.

THE FLYING COLUMN (VOICE OVER)

"What did I have?" said the fine old woman,
"What did I have?" this proud old woman did say.
"I had four green fields, each one was a jewel,
But strangers came and tried to take them from me.
I had fine, strong sons, they fought to save my jewels,
They fought and they died and that was my grief," said she.
"Long time ago," said the fine old woman,
"Long time ago," this proud old woman did say,
"There was war and death, plundering and pillage,
My people starved, by mountain, valley and stream,
And their wailing cries, they reached the very heavens,
And my four green fields ran red with their blood," said she.
"What have I now?" said the fine old woman,
"What have I now?" this proud old woman did say.
"I have four green fields, one of them's in bondage,
In stranger's hands that tried to take it from me.
But my sons they have sons, as brave as were their fathers,
And my fourth green field will bloom once again," said she.

Last two lines of song are over boys walking with priest on Falls Road. Cut to vigorous playground action, then to street scene, Lower Falls and action of two British armored cars roaring through children's rubble.

As cars race through street again, pan to child hiding behind curtain in window, zoom in and freeze. Super moving title: "Suffer the little children." Fade out.

Later, Northshield questions two pre-teen boys in school uniforms. "What do you think of the troubles? What do you think is happening?"

1st Boy: It's all the Catholics. It's the IRA doing it.
Northshield: Do you know what a Catholic is?
1st Boy: Yes.
Northshield: What is a Catholic?
1st Boy: Aye, he's a man who believes a different religion.
Northshield: Do you know?
2nd Boy: Aye, a man that causes trouble. He can join the IRA, and the IRA burns up, bombs up all the pubs, and the Catholics are — the Catholics make the trouble.

CU (CLOSE-UP) JOE MCCANN

Northshield: How do you know what a Protestant is?

Joe McCann See, I always knew, because Mommy always told us don't be going up there, maybe getting beat up by some of them . . . because there are some bad ones up there, and she told me they are Protestants.

Northshield: Well, what is a Protestant, do you know?

Joe: No, I don't know.

This news documentary is deceptively simple because it is based completely on the producer-narrator handling plain interviews, complemented by footage indicative of the setting and atmosphere of Belfast and of the difficulties between Catholic and Protestant in Ulster, rather than depending upon films of the actual troubles themselves. Ordinarily, this would be a dodge, a stratagem to avoid doing true investigatory reporting. Yet, by means of a penny whistle and other musical instruments, through discerning questions and corresponding literate answers from adults, through poignant close-ups of Joe McCann and the other Belfast youngsters, we are captivated. Its children, although lovely and innocent, are nonetheless trapped in a hell they sense but cannot understand. Moreover, Northshield makes no judgments, preaches no sermons. He doesn't have to. The documentary delivers what it promised — the results of a month's work in Belfast, recording some things that happened there to its children.

Northshield was executive producer-writer-narrator for *The Sins of the Fathers,* broadcast on June 19, 1973, which described the plight of thousands of racially mixed children in Vietnam, abandoned by their soldier fathers. *Variety* said:

> While the sheer numbers of the indigenous orphans is grim enough, the life of the racially mixed children is wretched beyond seeming endurance. Living in a country that is racist in its own ways, the half-breed orphans are pariahs and virtually non-people . . . Northshield's treatment of the subject wisely let the brute horror of the situation speak for itself . . . he was aware that the showing was more important than the telling in this case . . . Vietnamese kids born to lose in "our" war. The United States has given money for the 133 licensed orphanages handling these cases, but draws the line there so far.[43]

Northshield's other 1973 hour documentary, *The Long Winter of Henry Aaron,* was an excellent example of biographical theme documentary. Aaron had just hit 713 home runs, one shy of toppling the hallowed Babe Ruth's record. Using Tom Brokaw as narrator, Northshield on the October 21 broadcast adumbrated Aaron's career from his childhood in Mobile, Alabama, up to the early days when a black man still had to avoid certain hotels and restaurants.[44] He outlined Aaron's personality through interviews with his family and fellow ball players. He "effectively caught a portrait of the superstar as 'dig-

nified loner'.''[45] He concluded with a sequence, showing some of the hate
mail Aaron was getting because a black dared challenge the immortal Babe.
      Brokaw concluded, saying:

> Most Americans are probably delighted to be alive when a lone
> athlete makes as many marks with grace and strength and true dig-
> nity. The fact that not everyone is delighted says more about this
> country than it does about this man, Henry Aaron.[46]

A sampling of Northshield's 1974 work gives us some idea of his continuing versatility. In his *White Paper,* for example, *And Who Shall Feed the
World?,* narrator John Chancellor says:

> There is no answer. . . . But if the world is not fed, it will be a
> difficult, dangerous world, and soon. Let's conclude with one fact:
> In the hour of this program, more than thirteen thousand more people
> have been born; half of them are dying now, because they don't have
> enough to eat.[47]

For *The Navajo Way,* Northshield was his own producer, director, writer
and narrator. It was an obvious labor of love, since he was returning for a six-
week stay with people living on the Arizona-Utah border whom he had filmed
20 years earlier while doing a CBS documentary.

"That first program," he recalls, "was seen in black and white on forty-
one stations on a Sunday afternoon. The second one was seen in color on two
hundred stations in prime time."[48]

When he first went out to see the Navajos, Northshield filmed Mary Gray
Mountain bringing her sick baby boy to Long Salt, a 65-year-old medicine
man. When Northshield returned, he sought out the man who had been that
infant and found him, his mother and the now-ailing medicine man, Long Salt,
since crippled by a stroke. "Like Mary, he (the son) needed to be put in touch
with 'the way,' to be told that his strength was permanent and grand enough to
let him take from both the cultures."[49]

This documentary again exhibits Northshield's compassion for those who
must confront a more dominant way of life than their own but who still respect,
despite terrific pressures not to, where they came from and who, doing so, gain
strength from the past.

Probably being not so much news as spectacle, the Bicentennial was
building up impetus slowly and began receiving its share of attention at NBC
News in 1975. Northshield, working with David Brinkley as narrator-writer,
was to prepare the first three 90-minute Bicentennial programs based on the
meaning of Thomas Jefferson's words, "life, liberty and the pursuit of happi-
ness."

The first documentary in the series was shown on October 28, 1975.
Called simply *Life,* it was a hybrid affair, replete with history, personages,
momentous moments. Yet it still was able to chronicle the plain, common,
daily events that made up the bulk of the nation's past.

Brinkley's cynical but apposite style made *Life* perhaps seem more dramatic than it really was. It "begins with the concept of '*e pluribus unum*' and the fact that this nation has attracted 42 million immigrants in its first two centuries. Traveling about the American land and to key places in other parts of the world, Mr. Brinkley explains that 'these are the *pluribus* who want to be part of the *unum*.'"[50]

Northshield, whom NBC News executive Al Perlmutter has described as having "a certain poetic feeling about what he does," counterbalanced Brinkley's levities by focusing much of the program on his beloved outsiders: New Mexico Indians, New York Puerto Ricans, Louisiana Cajuns, and America's Blacks, who came here from Africa, "shackled, chained, bewildered, terrified."[51]

One of the best sequences, using a technique usually reserved for the theme documentary (which *Life,* of course is) is made up of photos of immigrants commingled with shots of Ellis Island then and now.

An almost impossible assignment, *Life* has a *con brio* quality that keeps it upbeat and zestful, completely in the heraldic mood it wanted to convey. Curiously, however, it failed to ignite very much enthusiasm, for either itself or the Bicentennial. But, then, no documentary program or series was destined to do that.*

---

*NBC News from 1966 to 1975 is covered further in Chapter 14.

5 / Producers at CBS News

THE BIRTH OF CBS REPORTS

To OFFSET THE malodorous aftermath of the network quiz-show scandals, CBS News, already sensing an upswing in hard news, in May, 1959, created "a single informational series."

Sig Michelson, then vice president of CBS, Inc., and general manager of CBS news, told a Toronto broadcasters meeting that time had been preempted and such CBS News producers as Fred Friendly, Les Midgley, Av Westin, Burton Benjamin, Don Hewitt, Paul Levitan, Al Wasserman and Stephen Fleischman were scheduled to work on the new series.

"These nighttime specials will take up the momentous political, social and economic developments of the day," Michelson said. "The contents, in the main, will be dictated by affairs of urgent national interest at the time of the broadcast, so it is not possible, at this time, to provide a full rundown of topics."[1]

Dr. Frank Stanton, president of CBS, Inc., who was credited with creating the new series, said the forthcoming programs would be in addition to the flow of news specials scheduled irregularly as events warranted.

Although as yet lacking a name, but destined to become the most comprehensive and accomplished news documentary series ever produced, *CBS Reports* was launched.

*   *   *

Faces change, positions alter, programs rise and fall. Nowhere were these truisms more in evidence than at CBS News in 1965. So constant is change in American journalism, and in broadcast journalism in particular, that one can only account for people and programs by finding out how they relate directly to a particular period or production being surveyed. Quality news work has an inbred side to it. Its practitioners move around a lot from job to job or location to location, but still remain a select, inbred community. Maybe all this happens because quality news work is so hard to do well. That's why, perhaps, you'll find that this producer or that writer, safely ensconced at one network this season but off to the Fiji Islands next year for another network, resurfaces so often. Even those who are fired come back many times to former jobs. Thus, shifting patterns in news administration and program destinies require that we revisit the fifties and early sixties.

At CBS News, for instance, Fred W. Friendly had taken over that news operation in 1964, serving as president, a post he would resign from two years later. Previously, he and Murrow had produced a remarkable series of *See It Now* and *Small World* programs. As executive producer of *CBS Reports* from its birth on October 27, 1959, with the program *Biography of a Missile,* until he named Arthur D. Morse to succeed him, Friendly gave that series its distinctive verve and remarkable informational insights.

According to Bill Leonard in *Television Quarterly:*

> He was an extraordinary editor, temperamental, driven by a sense of personal discovery and mission. One day Fred discovered *water!* and the fact, which some of us had known and accepted along with the moon and the stars, that there wasn't enough water to go around. Overnight the *CBS Reports* shop was whipped into a water-reform machine. Research! Film crews to the ends of the earth! Fred had all of us in water up to our eyes. But out of it came a broadcast, and a good one, on the water famine.[2]

By August, 1963, *CBS Reports* had completed a total of 97 broadcasts. Ten future shows, at any one time, at various stages of preparation, were always listed on the status board. It was a major contributor to the News Hour that Stanton and Michelson initially had envisioned — an hour of prime time regularly given over to interpretive news coverage. Ray Oviatt of the Toledo *Blade* said, "This series continues to prove that television can be exciting, even terrifying, as well as enlightening when it looks at real life."[3]

Friendly sincerely believed that television was meant to be a news medium. "There's a limit," he said in February of 1965, "to just how much entertainment can be created. You can be overentertained, but never overinformed. Years ago, I used to *think* that reality was far more exciting than fiction. Now I *know* it. The fact remains that shooting a man up in a rocket is more exciting than shooting a cowboy on *Bonanza* and seeing catsup seep out of his shirt."[4]

Friendly found himself contending with many pressures that year. Commercial interference was one; the poor ratings of *CBS Reports,* another.

Sometimes the commercial interference problem couldn't be avoided. This happened when the quiet-spoken, almost subdued Arthur D. Morse, Friendly's successor as executive producer, came to *CBS Reports* in 1960 as a producer-writer. He developed *Who Speaks for the South?*, *The Other Face of Dixie* and *The Catholics and the Schools.*

In 1964, he was put in charge of the series "but soon ran into trouble in completing *Cigarettes: A Collision of Interests.*" [5] According to the New York *Times:*

> The reference was to the collision of health hazards and the economic security of the tobacco industry, then a major television advertiser. But Mr. Morse sensed a lack of support from his superiors and that December, when he read that the program was being shifted to a less desirable hour, he made an issue of it and resigned. [6]

After Morse left, Palmer Williams, veteran broadcast operations director at CBS News, was put in charge of the series.

Meanwhile, the ratings picture revealed that *CBS Reports* was picking up around ten million or so viewers (a fifth of *Bonanza*'s audience). Friendly was beginning to hear complaints about people not watching public affairs shows. Despite its numerous prizes, the series was in trouble: it had been moved from 7:30 p.m. on Wednesdays to 10:00 p.m. on Mondays because it no longer was sponsored and, therefore, no longer would be rated by Nielsen, which only ranked commercially sponsored programs.

Commenting on this open speculation about the "value" of *CBS Reports,* Friendly said, "The day they take away this hour of public affairs programming, I'm leaving. That hour is inviolate." [7]

Fortunately nothing came of these rumors and Friendly was able to re-orient CBS News in 1965 to meet what he called a new, exciting era in broadcast journalism. He stated:

> Television news is just now reaching a point of a realization of its potentials of bringing not only the news to the viewer but the viewer to the news . . . the growing complexity of world and domestic affairs and the increasing appetite of the public for more comprehensive, more sophisticated and more encompassing television news and cultural broadcasts pose an editorial challenge of the most stimulating kind. [8]

Then he made several moves. Gordon Manning, formerly executive editor at *Newsweek,* was appointed a vice president and director of television news, and Bill Leonard also was named a vice president and handed direction of news programming. Manning was responsible for hard news — CBS-TV then was scheduling 70 minutes of regularly scheduled news, exclusive of weekends. He also handled news extras and supervised all CBS News bureaus and correspondents. By this time, exclusive of operational and per diem people, CBS News was employing nearly 600 persons.

Leonard, who had managed the election unit, was in charge of *CBS Reports, 20th Century,* cultural programs and the election unit, as well as "special broadcasts on the contemporary and historic world of Man, which has become increasingly proper 'copy' for the non-fiction program."[9] He joined CBS in 1945 as the creator and host of *This is New York* for WCBS, New York. He eventually became closely associated with *CBS Reports.* One of his programs, *Trujillo: Portrait of a Dictator,* won the Overseas Press Club Ed Stout award.

Another Friendly move was the appointment of Herbert Mitgang, at that time an 18-year-veteran as an editor, writer and critic with the New York *Times.* Friendly made Mitgang his assistant and an executive editor of CBS News. According to a CBS News press release:

> Because CBS News will become more concerned with ideas and words, with the "why" of the news, its management must direct as much of its time and attention as possible to the creative aspects of broadcast news. Herbert Mitgang's long experience as a newsman and historian, his versatility and experience in the visual crafts, his judgment as a critic, make him an ideal choice to help us implement this goal.[10]

Just the preceding summer, Mitgang had accompanied former President Dwight D. Eisenhower, Walter Cronkite and Friendly to the Normandy beaches. He had been serving as historian for the forthcoming *CBS Reports: D-Day Plus Twenty Years: Eisenhower Returns to Normandy,* to be broadcast on June 5.

Mitgang would ride out the months ahead under Friendly, remain with Richard S. Salant, Friendly's successor as president of CBS News until July, 1967, then resign. At that time, he said, "There was no friction involved. I decided to leave the tube for the typewriter. It's where I prefer to be. That's all." While at CBS News, Mitgang was associated with the series *Vietnam Perspectives.* He also was executive producer of the news special *Ben Gurion on the Bible,* and he wrote the script of the program *Henry Moore: Man of Form,* which won the Ohio State Award in 1965 as best cultural program of the year.[11]

He returned to the New York *Times,* joining its editorial board.

NEWS BECOMES DOCUMENTARY

CBS Reports finally went to Tuesdays at 10:00 p.m. in October, 1965, sharing the CBS News Hour with News Specials, Special Reports, *Town Meeting of the World,* and *National Tests.*

Palmer Williams, then executive producer for the series, was to be followed in future years by Burton Benjamin and Perry Wolff. Williams had come to CBS News in 1951 as production manager of *See It Now*. During World War II, he had worked with Frank Capra on the *Why We Fight* series, and with Garson Kanin and Carol Reed on *The True Glory*. He also had been a producer for the War Department of several newsreels and documentaries for use in Japan and Germany. He later became senior producer on *60 Minutes*.

Others working in 1965 on *CBS Reports* were: Jack Beck, David Buksbaum, Gene DePortis, David Lowe, Bill McClure, Bill Peters, Bob Richter, Phillips Scheffler, and Joe Wershba. Lowe produced *Harvest of Shame,* and McClure and Wershba had been on the *See It Now* team.

Additional specially organized units, headed by executive producers Les Midgley, Don Hewitt and Av Westin, were set up for the Special Reports — hard news requiring more interpretive treatment than was available in regular news coverage. These treatments, ranging over the decade and covering every major story of that period, constitute a valuable history. Many times, they are more informative and pertinent than the traditional news and cultural documentaries.

Before I conclude this initial look at CBS News in 1965, that news department's National Tests program deserves a word. On May 24 of that year, CBS News presented a new kind of news-feature broadcast that gave, in the words of the Washington *Post* "true meaning to that much abused broadcasting term 'audience participation'." Titled *National Drivers' Test,* it offered the nation's millions of motorists a graphic test of their driving perceptions, skill and knowledge. It earned the number-one rating in the Nielsen report for June; governors of eight states proclaimed the day of broadcast as National Drivers' Test Day; and the show was cited on the floor of the United States Senate.

Pleased with its success, CBS News planned more "tests" — shows designed to test citizenship, current events and a new version of the driving test.

It should be obvious by now that CBS News in 1965 was quite different from its sister news departments at NBC and ABC. Public television and radio had not yet appeared. CBS, Inc., not only dominated the entertainment-program ratings season after season but also usually led in the news field as well. NBC News, operating under the aggressive eye of its president, ex-newsman Robert Kintner, did what it could to confront the CBS News juggernaut.

Knowing it was the leader in broadcast network news helped CBS News overcome that old bromide about news being good public service programming but a poor revenue producer. CBS News in 1965 was a viable commercial operation for CBS, Inc. Most of its regularly scheduled broadcasts were sold. Moreover, those news events that, for various reasons, could not be adequately handled in a regular newscast were set aside as News Extras — shows scheduled at any time, day or night — and preempting, of course, regularly scheduled programs.

Some 13 CBS News Extras already had been sponsored in 1962–1963 by Metropolitan Life Insurance Company — representing over 100 commercial minutes at a total cost of $1,320,000.

One lucrative source for Extras was the United States space flights. CBS News worked up a pattern with which to cover them. The pattern's scenario ran something like this: first, the evening of launch (a half-hour preview of the personalities and the preparations); next, launch (from a half-hour prior to lift-off through the first orbit, for coverage of about two hours); then, in-flight reports (at least one five-minute period daily, plus so-called "crawl" bulletins); then recovery (running from 90 minutes prior to retrofire through recovery, again for a minimum of two hours); and finally, wrap-up (a half-hour on the evening of the day of recovery to summarize the entire mission).

Nothing like this had ever been attempted before. Still the frenetic tempo continued. At the time CBS News was scheduling these Extras, Gemini had a launch set roughly for every 70 days; by early 1966, a 14-day flight was in the works; by 1966–1967, the Apollo three-man operation and the Air Force's Manned Operating Laboratory were set to go.

Such exciting fare would certainly produce audiences, but CBS News, wanting to make sure potential advertisers knew exactly what the makeup of the audiences would be, could only claim that "weekday daytime space-shoot coverage attracts the 'housewife' viewer normally present in those hours." These "off-hour" portions of space-shoot coverage also would produce a sub-stantial "bonus" of adult men. But in 1965, CBS News salesmen couldn't prove the efficacy of these claims directly. That data was still to come. Instead, it said that ARB (American Research Bureau) figures revealed a similar audi-ence composition for the 1965 presidential inaugural ceremonies, for All-Star and World Series baseball in 1964 and the John Glenn flight in 1962.

Salesmen at CBS News concluded, therefore, that "it seems quite clear that 'extraordinary' news events develop extraordinary viewer response in the sense of creating audience mixtures not normally present in certain time pe-riods."[12]

A potent combination had appeared: eager sponsors for news, articulate news people and an interested audience. All the moves had been completed and the stage was set. Yet no one realized how extensive and penetrating the news drama to come would be. Ultimately, events — sometimes awful, but always dramatically decisive — dictated what Friendly and his successors, col-leagues and competitors would report and what American audiences would view between 1965 and 1975. That's why all the rules that seemed to work so well in 1965 were, by 1975, sundered, thereafter causing numerous news series to be tossed aside and untold broadcast news personalities to be abandoned in order to cope with a brand new kind of news audience in America.

POWER ALWAYS THINKS IT HAS A GREAT SOUL

On February 10, 1966, CBS News President Fred W. Friendly watched an NBC monitor showing George F. Kennan, architect of several major policies in United States foreign affairs, criticize American actions in Vietnam before the Senate Foreign Relations Committee. CBS was carrying a fifth rerun of *I Love Lucy*. Friendly wanted his network to carry Kennan's testimony. He called his superior, Jack Schneider.

"Jack, this is extremely good stuff. Have you been watching?"

"Watching what?"

"George Kennan's testimony . . ."

"No, Fred," said Schneider, "things are too hectic over here . . . I'll call you back."

Schneider never did and Friendly, fed up, resigned.[13]

Thus ended Friendly's stint as president of CBS News. Replacing him was Richard S. Salant, who had held the job from 1961 to 1964. A lawyer, he had joined the networks as a vice president in 1952. Resented at first for his lack of a journalism background, he went on to become an able news-staff administrator and an excellent judge of broadcast news. He was to become especially aware of the premier position CBS News shared in most broadcast markets. "Broadcasting," he said, "is not solely in the uplift business; it needs its mass audiences to survive."[14]

If anything substantiated Salant's new responsibilities and Friendly's past achievements, it was the announcement in May of 1969 that CBS had won 10 of the 14 Emmys awarded in 1968 by the National Academy of Television Arts and Sciences. Three of the prize-winning documentaries — *Don't Count the Candles*, a visual essay on aging; *The Great American Novel;* and *Justice Black and the Bill of Rights* — will be discussed shortly.

The key move in the fall of 1968 at CBS News was the introduction of *60 Minutes*, which premiered on September 24, with Mike Wallace and Harry Reasoner as host correspondents. By 1975, Dan Rather had joined Wallace and Morley Safer, who had replaced Reasoner. Don Hewitt, who remained throughout those years as the successful series' executive producer, admitted patterning the new interpretative magazine newscast after *Life* magazine. "We always have been interested in manners, mores and morals," he has said.[15] *60 Minutes* moved from the Tuesday night News Hour to early Sunday evenings, first at 6:00 p.m., then at 7:00 p.m. — because 7:00 p.m. on Sunday nights, by 1975, had become a new kind of hour. The FCC earlier had decided to return that hour to affiliates but excepted Sundays if the networks would use the 7:00–8:00 p.m. hour for children's or public affairs programming. With *60 Minutes* competing against NBC's *Disney World* and ABC's *Swiss Family Robinson* that year, the durable magazine series on CBS had nowhere to go but up, since it now was the only adult show on at that hour on commercial television. Result: *60 Minutes* soon was one of the top ten programs on TV, the first documentary series ever to achieve that status.[16]

Of course, placement in a propitious time slot was only one factor in the long-term success of *60 Minutes*. Besides crediting Hewitt's editorial genius with a story and citing the respective on-air talents of the three "stars," we also should credit the durable Palmer Williams, the series' senior producer, "who handles the complex logistics of where producers (now up to 18 in 1977, with 6 assigned to each correspondent) are or should be at any given time," and who funnels all story ideas for quality, then assigns the survivors, then oversees their completion.[17]

Lord Snowdon's *Don't Count the Candles* was shown on March 26. If such a subject — aging and old age — seems out of line compared to the extraordinary coverage the news division was giving to other 1968 stories, it was not. Two-thirds of the older people in America were living in cities. The 1966 population was 199,118,000. The life expectancy of men was 66.7 years; of women, 73.8. True, there were more young people — the median age was down to 28.6 years — but there were also more oldsters.

"Lord Snowdon has a photographer's eye for compassion, in his close-ups of people of advanced years experiencing the loneliness that attends limited mobility," wrote Jack Gould, ". . . in Noel Coward, 68 years old; Baroness Asquith of Yarnbury, 80; Sir Compton MacKenzie, 86; and Leopold Stowkowski, 81. Here he illustrated the few who live remarkably active lives with full control of their mental capabilities."[18]

Gould liked the Earl's compassionate eye but said he failed to get into the real problems of the aged. Still, the documentary was a winner largely because of moments such as the time "those splendid octogenarians, Lord and Lady Ramsey, having a peevish argument, suddenly halted when her Ladyship — who happens to be Queen Victoria's granddaughter — snapped, 'If one of us was not deaf, it would be a help, you know'."[19]

The Great American Novel was Arthur Barron's attempt at "a demonstration, in a new way, that great literature lives because it is as relevant today as when it was written." To do this, Barron used John Steinbeck's 1939 portrait of rural poverty, *The Grapes of Wrath*. To evoke the contemporary relevance of that novel, Barron sent Walter Dombrow and his cameras to trace the flight of an Appalachia farm family to industrial Chicago. Eric Sevareid was the reporter.

"Arthur's idea," says Dombrow, "was to maintain as much naturalness as possible. As a result, we worked under very adverse conditions. Many of the sequences were shot with only a three-hundred-watt bulb in the ceiling providing light; some were shot with just the existing natural light.

"But as demanding as the project was, it had great rewards. In filming the story of the farmer and his family, I became so concerned with their problem that it seemed as though I was experiencing it with them."[20]

Barron's coverage of *The Grapes of Wrath*, narrated by Richard Boone, was accompanied on *The Great American Novel* by a contemporary version of *Babbitt*. For the latter segment, narrated by Pat Hingle, Barron and his crew went to Duluth, Minnesota, which is generally considered to be the model for

Sinclair Lewis' Zenith City of the novel. There Dombrow and others filmed activities of members of a local club, as representatives of a mid-sixties version of Zenith's Booster Club. One sequence features Hingle delivering the same speech to the club that George F. Babbitt gave to Zenith's Boosters in the novel.[21]

Perry Wolff was executive producer of *The Great American Novel;* Barbara Connell was associate producer.

Salant heralded *The Great American Novel* as the means for "a new form of television documentary . . . to emerge from this special to demonstrate that great literature endures because it is as relevant today as when it was written."[22]

Most critics, however, were uneasy with a format that required the viewer to have read the two novels surveyed before it was possible to evaluate their present-day relevancy. Bob Williams of the New York *Post* noted:

> The CBS cameras pursued an impoverished Tennessee farm family in a broken-down car to a Chicago slum future. But the father got a job amid the squalor, and social assistance was available for the pregnant daughter, whose husband quit the horrible scene fast. From the CBS hour, one would have to gather the impression that the George Babbitts of society, however unhappily, are doing as well as ever while the Joads of Steinbeck's *The Grapes of Wrath* are doing just a little better.[23]

Barbara Delatiner was disturbed and terrified by the fact that maybe Barron's thesis was correct, that he had found "the same hard-drinking, success-worshipping social-unconscious Babbitt, . . . the same, hungry, defeated, desperate hillbillies who inhabited the worlds created by Lewis and Steinbeck two and three decades ago."[24]

Lawrence Laurent, TV critic of the Washington *Post,* felt that although Barron could "find many contemporary parallels with books published 46 and 29 years ago," his "new form of documentary" committed "the documentarian's small sin of intensification and manipulation of reality," but if it made "a documentary more entertaining, then it was a success."[25]

"It was a heavy burden to place on a TV program, and the documentary suffered some from the selective editing required to support the thesis," said George Gent of the New York *Times,* "but while the ambitious goals of *The Great American Novel* were not entirely realized, the experiment itself is definitely worth pursuing."[26]

Justice Black and the Bill of Rights was broadcast on December 3. Produced by Burton Benjamin, it used Sevareid and Martin Agronsky as reporter-interviewers, and set a precedent for a television interview with a sitting Supreme Court justice, who discussed the law, the Constitution and the Court itself. The Court, of course, refers to the so-called Warren Court, named after Chief Justice Earl Warren, who was appointed in 1953 by President Eisen-

hower; the Court made several noteworthy decisions concerning racial prejudice, reapportionment and civil liberties. Probably *Brown v. Board of Education* (1954), holding that racial segregation in public schools was
unconstitutional, was its major decision, although it also ruled permissively
concerning obscenity and rigidly concerning constitutional restraints affecting
law officers.

Justice Black, then 82 years old, "with charm, eloquent simplicity of
language and a proud expression of faith in constitutional processes," spoke
up during the broadcast on such issues as pornography, racial segregation, the
Chicago riots and the Fifth Amendment.[27]

On absolute interpretation of the Bill of Rights:

"Congress shall make no law respecting an establishment of
religion" — that's the First Amendment. I would think: Amen, Congress should pass no law. Unless they just didn't know the meaning
of words. That's what they mean to me. Certainly they mean that
literally. And I see no reason to attribute any less meaning than they
would have had then, or would have now.[28]

On what justice best fits the times:

What best fits the times. Now that's a very prevalent philosophy. I'm
not sure but what it's the controlling philosophy in this government,
as far as lawyers are concerned, or government is concerned.

Agronsky: You don't feel that the judges should judge according to
what fits the times?

Black: No. How would they know?[29]

On coping with crime and widespread public disorder:

Black: This country has always been called a country of violence.

Sevareid: That's true.

Black: Right after it was organized, they had a "Whiskey Rebellion"
up in Pennsylvania. George Washington had to send the Army up
there to stop it. Nothing new about crime. Now it's true different
types of crime increase from time to time. Or decrease. That's not
saying we should have it. For I think the purpose of an organized
government with a Constitution is hoping that the people would do
just what they said they would, what this Constitution was written
for.

Sevareid: Mr. Justice, if one could assume that there may be a really
serious threat to American society, from within, would it be in the
direction of greater oppression by authority, or a kind of spread of
anarchy and disbelief? What is the progression of dissolution of
society, if that sort of thing happens?

Black: Well, that's a case that no two people probably could agree on. I do know that a study of history convinces me that nations have risen, their stars have gone up, and then they begin to grow dimmer. Particularly, if they get too big, and try to run the world. And that's what happened. I don't know what will happen here. I hope this nation will have a longer life than all of them. Nobody knows. Nobody could say with any degree of certainty.

Sevareid: I think John Adams said once that "power always thinks it has a great soul."

Black: That's right.[30]

Finally, on why the American constitution has survived:

I think that if this government lives permanently, it will be because the people stick to a government like the one we created. Government of the people. It's intended to be a government of the people, by the people and for the people. It's failed at various times and in various localities. But it's done mighty well, compared with the other nations of the world. It's certainly better than the empire Augustus had. I think this country has lived because of its Constitution and its laws and its ideals of liberty and equality and freedom. I think every time we take a move in that regard, to make it what they said, to improve the public tranquility under law, that it moves another step toward lasting a longer time.

Agronsky: Thank you, Mr. Justice.

Sevareid: Thank you, Mr. Justice.[31]

The CBS policy that the Tuesday evening News Hour at 10:00 p.m. EST would be presented regularly as a public service regardless of audience ratings (the percentage of TV sets tuned to each station), was severely tested by the Justice Black broadcast in the New York City area. A. C. Nielsen Company ratings, obtained by statistical samplings from 300 homes located in 17 counties in metro New York, showed Justice Black had a 9 percent audience share; *That's Life,* a musical on ABC-TV starring Robert Morse, had a 20 percent share; and NBC-TV, with a show starring French actress Brigitte Bardot, earned a 44 percent share.

But that was not the least of it. The interview with Justice Black started with a 5.7 rating; it eventually dropped to 4.7.*

Throughout the fall of 1968, CBS News covered the flight of Apollo 8 to the Moon with several instant specials, devoting parts of six days in October, one day in November, and eight in December, including, on December 23, pictures transmitted live from the space capsule back to Earth, 202,000 miles

---

* A rating is the percentage of TV households in a market a TV station reaches with a program. A share is the percentage of sets in use tuned to a particular program.

away, plus the reentry and splashdown after a report at the Moon on December 27. News, truly, had become documentary.

1969

Special events coverage in 1969 at CBS News was heavy: several stories demanded attention consistently throughout the year — the presidency, the Apollo missions, the deaths of President Eisenhower and Senate Majority Leader Everett Dirksen. Each consumed innumerable hours of live air time.

The Nixon inaugural was followed, for example, by extensive coverage of the President's European trip in the early spring. Again in August, TV cameras were busy recording Nixon's trips to India, Pakistan, Romania and Great Britain.

Successive flights of Apollo 9, 10, 11 and 12 — with Mission 11 showing Man actually walking on the surface of the Moon — were given 46 hours and 7 minutes of live air time. The climax of Mission 11 came at 10:56:10 p.m. EDT, on July 29, 1969, when Astronaut Neil Armstrong stepped onto the Moon and said to a TV audience watching and listening back on Earth, "That's one small step for Man, one giant leap for Mankind." Just to show that moment meant leaving $1¼ million in electronic and camera equipment on the Moon.

Other vital stories broke that year: the accidental death of Mary Jo Kopechne, the first reduction of American troops in Vietnam, the defection of Russian diplomat Anatoly Kuznetzov, the death of Ho Chi Minh, the Vietnam moratorium. All were covered.

CBS News was increasingly giving more air time to live coverage of these events or covering them as News Specials.

As for traditional news and theme documentaries, CBS News clung pretty much to tried-and-true formulas in 1969. Two exceptions can be found in the work of Don Hewitt and Arthur Barron.

Hewitt was given permission to develop *60 Minutes* because he had long felt the traditional, hour-long, one-topic documentary always reached the same audience. He wanted to test his theory that there was a more general audience out there for a multi-topic public affairs program. As we all know, he has since overwhelmingly made his point.

When Arthur Barron's *The Great American Novel* was broadcast in 1968, Salant had heralded it as a new form of documentary. So Barron was allowed to try again in 1969, this time with a production called *The Great American Novel: Moby Dick*. A News Special, it was the study of life aboard a schooner in the North Pacific with appropriate commentary from Herman Melville's great novel itself, which had been written over a century earlier.*

*Other 1969 CBS News productions will be reviewed later in Chapter 18, which covers social issues and confrontations.

6 / Two-Ton Pencil: CBS News, 1970

1970 WAS THE YEAR television news became America's prime news source. Nowhere was this fact more evident than at CBS News, where the technical competence, reportorial talent and news information imparted to viewers were of a complexity and magnitude never before experienced.

By 1970, there was an amplitude to TV news coverage on the commercial TV networks that was unique because so often big news subjects that year were covered live and for lengthy periods; in effect, they dominated everything else that was shown that day or, sometimes, that week.

This is not to say television hadn't before undergone long, penetrative coverage of major news stories. We know it had. But 1970 was distinctive for the volume and variety of its TV news broadcasts. If events occurred, television had to cover them. What was happening, of course, was that TV news was becoming more acceptable, believable and profitable. Such budding circumstances would make any network TV news producer a bit dizzy with the power over public opinion now available to him, and those at CBS News were no exceptions. One could say that the craft and attention which the making of a documentary required were especially worth hanging onto during the successive deadline pressures placed on the news divisions by daily newscasts and instant specials. Stories were as hard as diamonds: the Chicago Seven trial had ended in February, when the defendants were found not guilty of conspiracy; in April, Apollo 13 climaxed; that same month, four students at Kent State were shot dead by National Guardsmen; finally, in early May, students demonstrated in Washington and on numerous campuses.

At CBS, the news division preempted the Sunday evening prime time Ed

Sullivan Show to broadcast a special report on Cambodia. The air was glutted with news, especially about President Nixon's decision to toughen up American strategy in Southeast Asia by sending troops into Cambodia. These days of crisis occurred after November 13, 1969, the day Vice President Spiro Agnew attacked TV news before a Republican party conference in Des Moines, Iowa. He had asked his audience, ''Is it not fair and relevant to question (the) concentration (of power) in the hands of a tiny, enclosed fraternity of privileged men elected by no one and enjoying a monopoly sanctioned and licensed by the government?''[1]

After Agnew's attack on the press, a state of war existed between the Nixon Administration and the press. The Administration made no bones about dispersing a thesis which Nixon successively had used with voters since his first try for elective office after World War II when he unseated incumbent Congressmen Jerry Voorhees: namely, that the press filters the truth, that its reports are suspect, that a voter therefore should expect bias from every source except one — Nixon himself, because he was the one manifest source unallied with the press.

These attitudes permeated the Justice Department, which used subpoenas to require reporters to submit notes, news films, tape recordings and unedited files containing any information, confidential or not, that might be useful in controversial court cases. Major news agencies — among them CBS, the New York *Times* and *Time,* Inc. — protested such acts by going to court. In November, 1970, a United States Circuit Court of Appeals decided that the government could demand of a reporter that he or she testify before a secret grand jury, but only if the government could show an overriding necessity for such testimony.[2]

Meanwhile, in the relatively calm waters of documentary production, CBS viewers saw, only a few days after news about Kent State, a magnificent panorama by famed French photographer Henry Cartier-Bresson, *California Impressions,* a program televised without narration, a cinematic essay in the genre marked out by another photographer, Lord Snowdon.

Kay Gardella wrote in the *Daily News:*

> As Bresson's quiet but critical camera swept across the state, which apparently is also a state of mind for some, we listened to an impassioned plea to curb the use of DDT on grapes, we went surfing in Malibu, were caught up in an anti-war demonstration, to say nothing of bumper-to-bumper traffic on the Los Angeles freeways, and visited a commune.[3]

But reviewer Kay Gardella didn't pretend to know — without narration —what producer Bill McClure may have had in mind.

An underlying theme to this program as well as to many of the programs considered in this study is that, in our time (America in 1970) we have seen an ongoing push asserting itself in just about everybody to enjoy pleasure for its own sake but, while so doing, to not fall under anyone else's control. In fact, true pleasure and contentment was not having anyone bother you. Yet, to gain such freedom, you must somehow possess some degree of power over others to ward off poachers on your territory. It was a Catch-22 paradox: to be free, you need to control that same freedom in others. Rich people, I suppose, always have had this sort of thing down pat. Now it was becoming available to everybody, thanks to the egalitarian effects of taxes, government beneficence, a workable legal system; thanks to a general affluence predicated on advertising sustaining a broad mass distribution, consumption and media system; thanks to the loss of regionalism and a growing awareness of other nations and other peoples; thanks, finally, to the leisure given us by a technology and energy apparatus doing most of our hard work for us, leaving us no longer brutalized and stunted by excessive physical work but "free" to realize our needs. In short, life was becoming increasingly fair and equitable for most of us. Only bad luck could hurt us. Diseases, disasters and disorders were the enemies — irrational, naturalistic forces unharnessed and unchecked either by our marvelous technological modes or by the new lifestyle of self-satisfaction. Perhaps an awareness of this new way of coping in America in 1970 was what Father Theodore Hesburgh, president of Notre Dame University, had in mind when his campus was shutdown for two days in May. Those two days, he said, "were two of the most educated days in the lives of our students."[4]

Another example of TV's mastery of newsgathering was the Xerox Corporation's claim that its sponsorship of *Opening Day: Japan's Expo '70,* broadcast on March 13 via satellite from Osaka, Japan, was the first time an American advertiser had sponsored a program simultaneously in the United States and abroad. The production used 61 cameras. Anchored by Charles Kuralt, the broadcast also used other commentators to translate his narration into Portuguese for Brazil and into Spanish for ten other Latin American countries.

Kuralt had "difficulty trying to report on the limitless pavilions spread over 815 acres in a country with which he was obviously not too familiar. . . . He was most impressed with Switzerland's aluminum tree of 35,000 lamps but on TV it appeared somewhat confusing."[5]

Among other shows Xerox had sponsored were: *The Making of the President* programs for 1960, 1964 and 1968, as well as the *Of Black America* documentaries on CBS. David J. Curtin, vice president of communications for Xerox, speaking of his firm's sponsorship programming guidelines, said:

> Each program will have an overall purpose. It will not only entertain,
> it will tend to stretch the mind, to inspire, to stir the conscience and
> require thought. Our programs should try to advance TV over what
> it has been. Where possible, we should use our money to lead, not
> to follow. We should take roads least traveled on.[6]

Satellite transmission required space communication stations be placed exactly 22,330 miles above the equator, orbiting the earth at the same rotation speed as the earth. Meeting these requirements made the satellites "synchronous" — that is, acting as if they were stationary, hovering above the earth in the same "fixed" position.[7]

Earth Day, on April 22, dominated much of television: NBC jumped around the country covering rallies in Philadelphia, Miami, Madison (Wisconsin), Chicago and Washington. National Educational Television gave six-and-a-half hours to Earth Day. On ABC, Howard K. Smith said "that any of us who owns a flush toilet, or drives a car to work . . . shares some blame for fouling our air and water." Walter Cronkite took almost everybody to task, especially the politicians, warning them that fighting for a cleaner America means "treading on more special interests than ever before in history."[8]

Concern, or the lack of it, toward the environment was a big issue in 1970. CBS News, following its usual inclination to scatter information far and wide whenever possible, ran another "test" on May 19 called *The National Environment Test*.

These "tests" received a mixed reception from critics (and presumably, viewers). In this instance, Kay Gardella of the New York *Daily News* lauded the show:

> For some reason, we always approach these tests with tremendous negativity and, by the time the hour is ended, come away singing the praises of CBS News for the clever way they make us swallow our informational medicine. And that's really about what it amounts to. Currents begin to build on a certain subject and in jumps CBS News to pull us up by our bootstraps and test whether we've been paying attention or not.[9]

Harriet Van Horne, headlining her review 'A Miserable Mess," said:

> For several years now CBS has been making parlor games out of such public issues as auto safety, the nation's health and political attitudes. The quiz idea has its merits, but one finds the repetition of each question terribly tedious. . . . Still, a great deal of basic information is imparted.[10]

In response to these critics, it's only fair to hear from the program's Executive Producer, Robert Chandler, who had written a book with Patricia Lynch based on the broadcast script. Agreeing with the critics, Chandler said the purpose of *The National Environmental Test* was "to impart *significant* information in a manner that would involve viewers to a greater degree than the normal television documentary does." Chandler believed that deeper involvement in the broadcast would help viewers become more aware of issues of ecology and remember them better. He might also have had in mind the problem TV — as a medium — always gives the purveyor of outright information: the inability to handle factual data as easily as it does emotional situations.

How, then, did Chandler and his staff cope with such a "heavy" subject on a prime-time documentary? They would "cut as wide a swath on the subject of environment as possible in the limited time available," thus sacrificing detailed explanations for quick considerations of a wide variety of ecological aspects. Part I included subjects with a "news peg." Part II catered to the individual and showed how pollution, particularly as a potential health hazard, affected him. Part III dealt with both water pollution and conservation. Part IV "essentially looked at what technology has done to the environment." The final segment related population and consumption to the ecology.

To write the script, Chandler and Lynch obtained materials from the United States Department of Agriculture, the United States Department of the Interior, the National Forest Service and the National Park Service. They also got valuable assistance from Dr. Glen Paulsen of Rockefeller University. In addition, a CBS News poll tested a national sample of 450 people, so their scores were available for comparison with those of the home audience and a studio audience. Among others who helped create the program, the always reliable Walter Dombrow was responsible for photography; Rudi Bass and the Graphic Arts Department produced some of the animation, with the John Hubley Studio doing the animation for the final segment.[11] Correspondents who helped were Mike Wallace, Harry Reasoner, Bill Plant, Terry Drinkwater, Ike Pappas and Phil Jones.[12]

DISSENT

Among the Russian people one will always find a dozen persons who are so dedicated in their ideals, and who take their country's plight so much to heart, that they readily sacrifice their lives for their cause. Men like that cannot be intimidated by anything.[13]

These words were spoken by Alexander Ulyanov, Lenin's older brother, in his last statement in 1887 just before being sentenced to hang for plotting against the life of Tsar Alexander III. They would fit just as well the situations of four Russian dissidents interviewed by CBS News Moscow Bureau Chief William Cole for *Voices from the Russian Underground,* which was broadcast on July 28, 1970. Cole was expelled for filming interviews with historian Pyotr Yakir, 43; Andre Amalrik, 31 and an historian and writer; and Vladimir Bukovsky, a 26-year-old poet who had spent six chilling years in an insane asylum. These talks were followed by a taped statement from the poet Alexander Ginzburg from his prison camp.[14] All had been or were in labor camps. All four quite consciously ran the risk of being shut away again.

Yakir said the underground press, or *Samizdat,* consisted of typewritten books and pamphlets circulated privately. He had been thrown into a concentration camp in 1936 at the age of 13 and had stayed there until Stalin's death in 1953. During those years, his family perished. He said, "I'm dissatisfied with the political system but do not want to leave. If I would have had a choice before my birth, I would have chosen another country."[15]

The interviews took place in the woods to avoid the police. There, amid the ferns and trees, secluded and remote, Cole talked to the dissenters, who answered his queries gently and dispassionately. The documentary's executive producer, Perry Wolff, nicely integrated the narrative between Cole and Harry Reasoner with the interviews with the Russians. CBS later made the films available to Holland, Sweden, Switzerland, Denmark, France, Austria, West Germany, Japan and Great Britain to use as each wished.[16]

On May 21, Amalrik was arrested and charged with violating article 190–1 of the Russian Republic Criminal Code, which deals with "falsehoods derogatory to the Soviet state and social system." Maximum sentence: three years in prison. His trial began November 11 in Sverdlovsk. Five documents formed the basis for his trial: a letter to Anatoly Kuznetzov; his second book, *Involuntary Journey to Siberia;* and his interviews on two TV films made by Cole. One film was confiscated by Soviet customs. The other ended up as part of *Voices from the Russian Underground.*[17]

Showing Off: Perry Wolff

Nothing exemplifies better the heady intoxication that TV news producers brought to their profession in 1970 than the glorious attempt by Perry Wolff to commemorate July 20, 1969, with a film portrait of America and Americans on that historic day when Man first landed on the moon. Until the arrival of the Bicentennial blockbusters at NBC News produced by Shad Northshield, nothing else like it had been tried; not even Fred Freed had tried anything like it.

TV news, as Fred Friendly had once described it, truly was a two-ton pencil. On the above date marking the moon landing, for example, Wolff marshaled 43 cameras at 33 locations across the country and shot 200,000 feet of film. His purpose was to expand the "day in the life of" format to fantastical proportions. Wolff literally created a 105-minute broadcast titled *A Day in the Life of the United States* that he hoped would reveal "America captured, frozen in a day of time."[18]

But Wolff, writing in his script, called it all "a letter to history . . . human evidence about the place the first moon voyagers came from."[19] It was an interesting concept because it was not a record of reactions to the moon landing. Emphasis was placed on what was important to us on that day.[20]

Broadcast as a News Special on September 8 at 9:15 p.m. EDT, the program opened with Narrator Charles Kuralt standing on the Maine coast at 5:25 a.m. with the sun rising over his shoulders, and closed with the sun passing beyond Hawaii. Wolff interconnected symbolic sequences such as these with "mini-documentaries" that broke away from the poetical master camera to scan, for example, the life of a child hospitalized for fever, who subse-

quently went into convulsions; mine-stripping operations in Kentucky ("an act
. . . of supreme greed"); and Chicago's Black slums.[21]

It was clear, however, that Wolff was not so much interested in exposés
as in showing "our great grandchildren the sounds of our accents, the look of
our faces, how we were to one another on the day Man first landed on the
moon."[22]

Of course, the documentary's scope was immense. It took in a Newport,
Rhode Island, folk festival; a hippie commune in Taos, New Mexico; a horse
ranch in Birney, Montana; and Travis Air Force Base in San Francisco, where
wounded Vietnam veterans were returning.[23]

The narrative sometimes bogged down into statistical trivia. It was estimated, for example, that Americans consumed 635.3 billion calories that day;
that a Las Vegas slot machine may have 8,000 possible combinations.[24]

Of the mammoth telecast, Jack Gould said, "The program could have
been done any time. The moon landing was clearly a gimmick for an occasion
that took an easy way out of merely concentrating on the obvious."[25]

This may be true, but Wolff operates very creditably at combining different vignettes, contrasting locales and patterning the talk of vivid people into
a clear story line. I know of no one else who could have produced A Day in
the United States as well as Wolff.

7/ Retrospective at Lincoln Center

A VALUABLE RETROSPECTIVE of CBS News broadcasts, 1952–1971, was held from November 29 to December 4 at Lincoln Center, New York, and was sponsored by the Center's Film Society. Sixty-one productions were listed in the program as being "of high artistic merit" or "of great impact and influence at the time of their broadcast." The list began with *Biography of a Missile* (1959) and concluded with *But What If the Dream Comes True?* (1971). Others included: *Henry Moore: Man of Form* and *The Battle for Ia Drang Valley* (1965); *The Volga* and *Sixteen in Webster Groves* (1966); *The Italians* and *Morely Safer's Vietnam* (1967); *The Viet Cong* (1968); *The Japanese* and *The Battle of East St. Louis* (1969); *A Day in the Life of the United States* (1970); and *The American Revolution: A Conversation With Lord North* (1971).The program also generously referred aficionados of the documentary to the work of documentarians at NBC, ABC, NET and the independents, such as Group W. It was dedicated to seven deceased artisans of documentary: David Lowe, Harry Morgan, Edward R. Murrow, Jules Laventhol, Arthur Morse, J. C. Sheers and Ted Yates — "documentary journalists of the very highest order." Harry Morgan had died at the age of 41 on May 26. He had received Emmys for *The Wyeth Phenomenon* (1968) and *Fathers and Sons* (1970). His credits included: *The Farthest Frontier; LSD: The Spring Grove Experiment; The Mystery of Stonehenge; The Homosexuals; The Anti-Americans;* and *JFK: The Childhood Years.* Morgan had joined CBS News in 1953, becoming a producer a decade later. Bill Leonard said of him: "He was serious about his work, humble about himself and we loved him around here."[1]

Leonard, then vice president and director of news programming at CBS

113

News, was moderator at the several panel discussions. On November 29, he was joined by Fred W. Friendly, Palmer Williams and Joe Wershba. Together they recollected the work of Murrow and Friendly after the audience had seen two *See It Now* shows, *McCarthy* and *Annie Lee Moss*.

On the 30th, "Covering the War," featuring panelists Les Midgeley, Ernest Leiser and Morley Safer, was discussed. Screened were: *This Is Korea . . . Christmas '52* from *See It Now; Vietnam: How We Got In — Can We Get Out?* (1965); *Morley Safer's Vietnam* (1967); and the *CBS Reports: A Timetable for Vietnam* (1969).

On December 1, the documentary as investigative reporting was dealt with and featured Jay McMullen, Peter Davis and Mike Wallace with the *CBS Reports: Biography of a Bookie Joint* (1961) and *Hunger in America* (1968) shown on screen.

The next day's session looked at documentary as history and featured Burton Benjamin, Perry Wolff and Pamela Ilott, director of the network's religious broadcasts. Shown to the audience were 1945: *Year of Decision* (1965); and *Of Black America: Black History, Lost, Stolen or Strayed* (1968).

Burton "Bud" Benjamin, a pillar in documentary has credits extending well back into years preceding this study (see Bluem's *Documentary in American Television*). Considering only the years 1967 to 1975, the year Benjamin assumed control of the CBS *Evening News,* he produced or supervised production of five programs in 1967, 13 in 1968, 11 in 1969, 20 in 1970, 17 in 1971, nine in 1972 and 1973, and 8 in 1974 and 1975 — a total of 92 Instant Specials, News Specials, series or *CBS Reports*. Hardly anyone at CBS, unless it is Perry Wolff, can boast such quantity and quality.

On December 3, *The Mystery of Stonehenge* (1965); *The 21st Century:* "The Mystery of Life" (1967) and *Incredible Voyage* (1968) were shown, with panelists being Dr. Frank Stanton, Salant and Martin Mayer, author and television critic.

The retrospective concluded on December 4 with the topic "The Documentary as a Series." Showcased that day were: *The 20th Century:* "Paris in the Twenties" (1960); *World War I:* "Summer at Sarajevo" (1964); and two *60 Minutes:* "What Really Happened in the Tonkin Gulf" and "How to Succeed in the PX Business" (1971). Panelists were Don Hewitt, Isaac Kleinerman and John Sharnik.

These discussions frequently turned up precise insights. Speaking about the documentary as history, for instance, Perry Woff said:

> Newsmen get exasperated by finding cultural documentaries or historical documentaries on the air; and we often get exasperated by seeing just the machine of news working day after day. And the fact is that there is a mix. And I don't figure we can come to any percentage as to what the mix should be. But it is necessary.[2]

Wolff's panel then discussed whether or not television was turning everybody into a nation of listeners and watchers. Wolff had some interesting ideas about that:

Bill Leonard: At least a third, or in some cases, two-thirds, of the modern library complex today is records, films, tapes and all . . . the appurtenances — and movies. Is education fundamentally changed? Are we becoming a nation or a world in which we're getting very little material from the pages of a book, and most of it through our eyes and ears? That after awhile nobody's going to read, really. It isn't necessary to read. All you have to do is be able to sign a Diner's Club card. From then on, it's all coming in ears and eyes. And we're a part of that. Revolution, good or bad."[3]

Ilott: . . . I sometimes wish someone would invent a machine that wuld enable me to see, you know, ninety minutes of film in five minutes, in a brain injection. You can't keep up with the amount of material that's flowing in that deserves seeing and listening to, and evaluating . . .[4]

Wolff: Well, there's a kind of law here, that I've been trying to work out for some time. It starts with a baseball game. If you're going to do a baseball game on television, you have to do it live. Except for a few crazy people who watch baseball and football all the time. San Francisco clubs particularly. You want — you have it live because you don't know what the answer is: you watch those football games on Saturday. You really want to go away from it; if you just knew what the end of the game was, you could get away from it. But you've got to stay to the end. That's the rule of live broadcasting.

If you don't know what the answer is, put it on live. If you don't know who the Convention is going to nominate, put it on live. The next thing that happens is, that you know the answer, but you want to show the event that led to the answer, and that, usually, you put on tape.

And then the thing that happens after that is you want to tell a story. Then you use film. People always get these things (live coverage, tape and film) mixed up. They want to make a film that looks like it's really, really real. That's a contradiction in form and in term. The next thing that happens is that you want to tell a story for other purposes. You want to tell it well and precisely. You usually verbalize it. This is in defense of the writer here.

Then, the more abstract you become, the more you want to manipulate the symbol . . . until finally you have Korzybsky and you have the statisticians, and you have sigmas and rhos, and they stand for whole cultures.

Now, the rule is, the further away you are from the reality, the easier the symbol is to manipulate. That may be called Wolff's law for anybody who's taking notes out there. The easier it is to manipulate the symbol. But the more you have left out — the more tactile reality you have left out. . . . So these people who say that it's all going to end up visual are wrong. Because the human brain, human communication and human culture are verbal, mathematical, oral. It's not going to end up in one place. A writer has to say that. I'm stuck very often with people who want to put two pieces of film together, instead of putting one good sentence together.[5]

On December 3, the panel, consisting of Stanton, Salant and Mayer, discussed the future of TV documentary. Mayer forecast that "we're going to lose public affairs programming within this decade in prime time unless there is some requirement put in that this thing continue, because I think the economic pressures will get too severe."[6]*

---

*The year 1971 at CBS News will be further covered in Chapters 16 and 17; 1972 and 1973 will be discussed in detail in Chapter 18.

8 / CBS News, 1974

TWELVE PRODUCTIONS in the *CBS Reports* series, one of which was a summer retrospective (*Murder and the Right to Bear Arms,* 1964), and another (*The Rockefellers,* 1974), a rehash tailored to fit a current news lead about the new Vice President, Nelson A. Rockefeller, were aired in August, 1974. Other *Reports* were: *Shanghai* and *The Colleges* (March); *Food Crisis — Feast or Famine?, The Palestinians* and *Inflation —How Much, How Long?* (June); *Peace and the Pentagon* (September); *The Case of the Plastic Peril* and *Castro, Cuba and the U.S.A.* (October); and *Caution: Drinking Water May Be Dangerous to Your Health* (December).

Most of these were run for 60 minutes at 10:00 p.m. in the customary Tuesday News Hour slot. The "Castro" show contained the first interview with the Cuban leader since 1968. It also was unique because Dan Rather appeared for the first time on *Reports* as an anchorman.

Actually, this interview was a hodgepodge of footage derived from two sources: Rather's interviews with Castro, which explored changes in foreign affairs and trade relations between Cuba and the United States since President Nixon's resignation, and an earlier exclusive talk in July, which had been arranged and recorded by Frank Mankiewicz, the former John F. Kennedy advisor and newspaperman. CBS News bought the Mankiewicz footage for use in its documentary, then arranged for Rather to see Castro to procure additional film.[1]

According to *Variety:*

The core of the Castro piece was produced outside CBS News by Frank Mankiewicz and Kirby Jones with Saul Landau as director (Landau via public station KQED-TV San Francisco produced a full documentary on Cuba at the revolution's tenth anniversary). But Rather went to Cuba with the independent producers, who get a special correspondents credit here, and his interview of the Premier, with an interpreter, was interwoven with the previous long interview by the special correspondents.[2]

Most of the time, commercial networks didn't allow for such arrangements and CBS News found it had its problems absorbing a previous piece of work and putting out the final effort as its own. There was the matter of credit, of sequences between one interview and the other, of the entire matter of who had access to a network news documentary production: only the network staff — or also others, working independently but just as skillfully and professionally? At this writing, the issue still isn't resolved.

The roll call of *CBS Reports* was especially impressive in light of the consistent pressures placed on the news division to monitor Watergate live, to produce the instant specials required to recapitulate that live coverage and still be willing to introduce additional news series such as the daytime *Magazine.* Premiering May 2 at 2:00 p.m., it was described as "a series of occasional CBS News Specials of particular interest to women." Another new series was *The American Parade,* composed of theme documentaries highlighting our historical roots, which first was broadcast on May 2 in an afternoon time period, featuring the topic *We the Women.* Two other shows followed that year: *The 34th State,* in late August and *The General* on December 5, the latter of which was telecast at 9:00 p.m. in prime time. *Variety* found that Kansans who saw *The 34th State,* which depicted the early days in that state, were unhappy with it because "it dwelled on the dismal and hard aspects of life in early Kansas."[3]

With these programs, CBS tried to break away from the usual daytime game shows and soap operas. *Magazine* especially brought the real world to daytime TV by presenting, as it did in mid-October, stories about "Sex After 60," "Ten Ways to Kill Your Husband" and "Coffee, Tea or Radiation." Produced directly by Vern Diamond, Irina Posner and Mary Drayne, and supervised by Perry Wolff, the program lived up to its title: the first two pieces on "understanding geriatric emotional needs" and heeding "dietary injunctions" were, *Variety* said, already "heavily gone over in print." But the final segment about passenger planes carrying radioactive materials as cargo "was a chilling report."[4] Hughes Rudd and Sylvia Chase anchored the program.

CBS News also found time to produce four fine tributes to mark the deaths in 1974 of Duke Ellington, Mahalia Jackson, Earl Warren and Jack Benny. The obituary tribute now had become a standard format at the network, which also offered a half-hour special report to commemorate Walter

Lippmann's death. It was only fitting that the nation's premier journalist, probably the most cogent commentator on the day's news flow since Daniel Defoe, should be recognized by broadcasting's most competent news organization. Similar to the Truman obituary, the broadcast depended heavily on past interviews made in the 1960s between Lippmann and CBS Correspondents Howard K. Smith, Charles Collingwood and Eric Sevareid. The latter, after the program provided "glimpses of Lippmann, the man, and the working of his mind," summed him up, saying:

> He was a fastidious, sensitive soul. He would not bear violence in this century's politics of hysteria. Vietnam literally sickened him.[5]

In addition to magazine and theme series, CBS ran a few other theme productions. The first of three scheduled "Smithsonian Specials," called *Monsters! Mysteries or Myths?* was broadcast on November 25 at 8:00 p.m. It was produced by David L. Wolper's organization working with the Smithsonian Institution of Washington, D.C., and was later heralded by Wolper as delivering the season's top audience ratings for a TV documentary. Its subject matter would appear to have guaranteed such results. The hour program was about the Loch Ness Monster in Scotland, the Abominable Snowman in the Nepalese Himalayas and "Big Foot" in the United States' Northwest. *Variety* said, "It contained a couple of dramatized reenactments for more graphic illustrations of certain eyewitness accounts."[6]

More important, though certainly less popular, were the transatlantic efforts of CBS News Vice President Gordon Manning and Producer Burton Benjamin to nail down an interview with the then far less well-known Soviet dissident and writer, Alexander Solzhenitsyn. Solzhenitsyn was a twice-decorated Soviet Army captain in 1945 when he was tried and sentenced to eight years of hard labor. In 1956, his name was finally cleared. Six years later, his flawless account of Soviet prison life in Siberia, *One Day in the Life of Ivan Denisovich*, was published but only at the personal behest of Soviet Premier Nikita Khrushchev. Since then, Solzhenitsyn dedicated his writings to exposing Stalinist Russia.

In 1974, Burton Benjamin found him in forced exile at Zurich, Switzerland, where Walter Cronkite had just cut short his coverage of a presidential Mideast trip to join Benjamin. "I was tremendously impressed with him," Benjamin said of the 56-year-old writer. "For a man who spent years in a prison camp and who has had cancer, he's amazingly virile and young looking . . . scarcely a white hair on his head, very upright, very vigorous and very warm and outgoing when you get to know him."[7]

The broadcast consisted of 24 questions put to Solzhenitsyn about the personal safety of his family — who were then with him in Zurich — about his writing and work habits and about his attitudes toward the West both before and after his forced exile from a Russia that, despite its dreadful dealings with him, he obviously still loved deeply.

Earlier in February, Andrew Rooney and Harry Reasoner pooled their respective talents as essayist and presenter with a CBS producer who hated New York — to balance off Rooney's love of the place. *New York, New York,* broadcast on February 1, at 9:00 p.m. EST, echoed the Dan Rather analysis of England and Texas but is saved from that program's tendentiousness by Rooney's light touch.

Producer Warren Wallace, in his segment, "To Hell with New York," hit every negative stop he could. Crime in Central Park, crowded subways, expensive apartments — the plain fact that just too much was happening: all these substantiated his "creeping suspicion that somehow in this city we are losing hold of things."[8]

Rooney's portion found it "hard to say anything about New York that isn't true . . . very often in New York, ugliness is only skin deep. . . . Whether New York is a pleasure or a pain depends upon what it is you wish to fill your life with. . . . No one keeps statistics on life. The feeling is that like everything else, there's more of it in New York. . . . New York is the cultural center of the world."[9] The Wallace-Rooney production, filled with images espousing two distinctive attitudes, was an excellent example of what a theme documentary can accomplish.

THE TROUBLE WITH ROCK AT BLACK ROCK*

A spokesman for Arthur Taylor, then president of CBS, Inc., pointed up a unique dilemma in August when CBS News aired the investigative documentary *The Trouble with Rock* on Sunday, August 11, at 6:00 p.m. EDT, the time slot that year for retrospective documentaries. The program would confirm "that officials and employees of a sister company, CBS Records, bought protection and drugs from organized crime figures."[10] Newspapers and periodicals had disclosed such allegations a year earlier. Now CBS News was flatly confirming them. Taylor's spokesman said Mr. Taylor would have no comment on the documentary since it involved a dispute "between two of his children," meaning, of course, CBS News and CBS Records.[11] This was a rather Olympian view of the matter; CBS Records did nothing to help CBS News produce the documentary; CBS, Inc. — on May 29 — already had fired Clive J. Davis, president of CBS Records, and was suing him for misappropriation of the record company's funds; it also dismissed two of his assistants, David Wynshaw and Anthony Rubino. These actions, in turn, prompted a Federal Grand Jury investigation by the United States Attorney's office in Newark into alleged payoffs to disc jockeys by recording firms anxious to obtain broadcast time for their hit records. Some of these payoffs, it was alleged, took the form of drugs.[12]

---

*Black Rock, nickname for CBS, Inc., corporate headquarters in New York City. It was derived from the movie title *Bad Day at Black Rock*.

Aside from these developments, CBS News was interested in rock music for other reasons. Bill Leonard, then a senior vice president and director of public affairs, told critic Kay Gardella what was important from a news point of view was that culturally the rock revolution was "one of the most important things happening in this country." He noted also that CBS News during the previous year had presented the News Special: *The Rock Revolution*.

"Rock Music has a powerful influence on our young people today," Leonard said. "Young people who are at an impressionable age. They're interested in the musicians and their lifestyle. It's a big cultural explosion."[13]

The investigative hour featured David Culhane as on-camera reporter. It was produced by Stanhope Gould, Linda Mason, Bernard Birnbaum and Lee Townsend, with Les Midgley overseeing their work. Salant had assigned Gould the task of heading up a three-person investigative team a year earlier, following Davis' dismissal, saying the team's assignment would be "a no-holds-barred news investigation of the record company's practices." He said Gould's team would follow through "even if it leads to the top."[14]

The Trouble with Rock deserves a close look if for no other reason than that it is probing the activities of part of its own producers' corporate body. After going through several examples of just what rock music was ("the music that infuriated so many people in the fifties and sixties; the music that so many thought too loud, vulgar and somehow dangerous to our morals"[15]), Reporter Culhane got into what rock really meant: a $2-billion industry in pop records and tapes or "about three times the amount of money taken in by all spectator sports, college and professional, including football, baseball, basketball, hockey and tennis."[16]

Then he reprised rock's history, from 1955's "Rock Around the Clock" through Chuck Berry to the Beatles and on to the Rolling Stones. He cited critic Albert Goldman:

> The Rolling Stones have made a career out of being professional bad boys. They're the flip side of the Beatles. The Beatles were the sweet, adorable, innocent, oh, if I could just — ice cream cones, you know. And the Rolling Stones are the nasty little ugly freaky punks, you know. They represent a tremendous adolescent desire to sort of up-end mature values: be bad, be naughty, say it, do it, screw them all up, be outrageous, drive them crazy.[17]

Culhane saw Bob Dylan's arrival on the rock music scene as the coming of the music of politics and protest. "His songs were hymns for hundreds who marched. . . ."[18]

Then came massive festivals — first at Monterey, California in June, 1967. They were showpieces for flower children as well as ports of entry for rock eccentrics such as Janis Joplin. Later, Woodstock drew 300,000 fans — further evidence of "the industrialization of rock." Four months later, during the Rolling Stones' concert at Altamont, California, four concert-goers died, one of a stabbing.[19] The dark forebodings predicted earlier for rock music appeared to be coming true.

Culhane noted that in 1955 the record industry earned $275-million. Nine years later, the Beatles alone rang up a stunning $758-million. Then the bonanza: by 1973, pop tapes and records were bringing in a legendary $2-billion!

"Rock music," Culhane reported, "had become the biggest money tree in the history of entertainment."[20]

Five percent of the record artists delivered 75 to 80 percent of that revenue. The major vehicle for profits was the record album. Costs for making one of these included recording the music in a studio, paying fees to artists, writers and producers, then meeting promotion costs. If 50,000 copies of an album could be sold, a firm broke even. Thereafter, profits could run better than a dollar per album.[21]

The key to the big money, according to Culhane, was winning radio air time for the firm's big stars' records. Disc jockey Larry Lujack told the audience:

> I am convinced that you can take any half-decent record, and if
> you ram it down the public's throats enough, I'm convinced that you
> can make any half-decent record a hit, if you play it enough.[22]

The trouble with rock came, Culhane said, when the pressure of competition and money got out of hand. Result: payola. Recording-firm promotion people even began using the expression "standard practice" when they talked casually about bribing radio station personnel.

At this point, the documentary began using the silhouette technique whenever various informants talked to the camera about payola, whether it be about supplying drugs or indulging in other covert shenanigans concerning recording companies, their stars, disc jockeys or the underworld.[23]

The program finally got to CBS Records when Culhane began basing his conclusions on the Gould team's probings. "CBS News . . . talked with dozens of radio and record industry figures across the country," he reported. "Most insisted that their identity remain secret. Only two would appear on camera."[24]

Back in May of 1973, CBS, Inc., had fired Clive Davis, the head of CBS Records, whom Culhane now described as earning $350,000 a year and as being "the most powerful man in the music business." Davis was charged with misusing large amounts of company money. By using phoney receipts, Davis allegedly appropriated $80,000 for his own use. Davis denied the charge.

CBS, Inc., also fired David Wynshaw and Anthony Rubino, Davis' "right-hand man" and a CBS Records marketing and budget executive respectively. In a separate civil action, CBS, Inc., charged them with stealing money "believed to exceed $300,000." Wynshaw and Rubino also denied the charges.

Culhane said the CBS News investigation unit also uncovered the use of

CBS Records' funds by some personnel for illegal purposes. Pat Falcone, a convicted heroine smuggler, was a frequent visitor to Wynshaw's office "at CBS headquarters in New York." Moreover, in Falcone's apartment, federal agents found phoney bills, which were traced back to Wynshaw, that had been submitted to CBS Records for "goods never delivered and services never performed."

"Names of non-existent companies were at times fed into CBS computers by employees who were cheating the company, and . . . checks were issued to the phoney companies."[25] Culhane said one of these dummy firms — a so-called trucking outfit — was paid almost $15,000 by CBS Records. "The money reportedly went to David Wynshaw . . . to organized crime figures and possibly others."[26] Best-selling albums also were made available to organized crime figures, since they could easily be converted into cash.

"Protecting" CBS Records' artists was another part of the action for Anthony "Fat Tony" Salerno, an alleged Mafioso chief who controlled big gambling and loan-sharking empires in New York and Florida. Singer O. C. Smith had recorded for CBS until August of 1973. When his life was threatened earlier by West Coast gamblers in a dispute over gambling debts, Smith reportedly asked Wynshaw for help. Wynshaw turned to Falcone who turned to Salerno, who supposedly used his "vast influence to end the death threat against Smith."[27]

Falcone, armed with a gun, and two other men also acted as 'round-the-clock guards for another CBS Records star, Jeff Beck, who said, "He was . . . protecting me against this threat on the telephone, you know, the — the chaps that — that threatened to shoot me on stage. . . ."[28]

Culhane said sources close to the federal investigation in Newark knew of several other occasions when Falcone and others "protected" CBS Records recording artists.

An independent record producer, silhouetted to prevent making known his identity, told Culhane's audience that both black and white Mafia intimidated "a lot of the super rock stars."

> If he were a musician, they'd threaten to break his playing hand; if he were a vocalist, they'd threaten to slit his throat, unless they got twenty-five percent of the artist's fee in kickbacks.[29]

Drugs and rock music were inseparable. Jimi Hendrix, a heroin user, died of an overdose of barbiturates at age 27; Janis Joplin also was dead at age 27 of an overdose of heroin. Culhane mentioned "a man associated in the management of a famous rock group who told CBS News: 'If you needed an ounce of cocaine that minute, there was a place at CBS Records you could get it'."[30]

Despite denials from the network's sister operation, "We don't permit drugs or drug trafficking of any kind. . . . ," *The Trouble with Rock* quoted a former CBS employee who claimed:

I mean, there was no — there was no budget for drugs, you know. When I bought — when I would buy dope, you know, what I thought was a legitimate expense — marijuana, or some cocaine or something — (I don't know if I want to say it or not) — I would just write it up on my expense account, you know, as expenses. I didn't say what it was. And the same — the same thing goes down through the whole — through all the promotion people. No one said that there's got to be a budget for drugs. And if anyone was ever asked, I'm — I'm convinced that no one at CBS would ever approve that, you know what I mean? There was a double standard, of course, which is — which is — you know, it's a Watergate, you know. In a sense, it was a Watergate morality, you know. What we don't know, you know, doesn't hurt us, you know. And, we don't want to know.[31]

This documentary had two goals in mind: (1) to explain the rock music phenomena of the fifties and sixties and what they had done to the recording industry; and (2) to make clear exactly what CBS Records, and the other recording companies, had been doing to deserve federal investigation of charges of dummied accounts, payola, drug and extortion payoffs and illegal promotional methods. It achieved both goals and did so graphically, accurately, and interestingly.

Still, a hot issue tends to burn those most affected by it. The Recording Industry Association, for example, said on August 11:

CBS failed to distinguish between hearsay and reported allegations regarding a few, and the honest, moral, law-abiding practices of the overwhelming majority of those in the music and radio industries.[32]

Many television critics also said the program reworked year-old materials that had been extensively publicized. Yet, it took nerve for CBS News to face the wrath of another corporate group and attack it. This wasn't the first time CBS newsmen had pointed their cameras at "themselves" and it wouldn't be the last.

The talented Tom Zito, of the Washington *Post,* thought the hour "provocative, well-produced." He also caught a statement made on the program that signalized how weird the world of rock music then was. Zito quoted Joe Smith, president of Warner Brothers Records, who said, "I would like to see someone from the Genovese family dealing with the Rolling Stones, trying to understand that whole mentality."[33]

That proved to be the same problem for the TV audience viewing *The Trouble with Rock.*

9 / CBS News, 1975

NEWSGATHERING BY CHECKBOOK

NEWSGATHERING, at best, is an aggressive occupation, marked by excesses concerning both the sensitivities of sources and those of the audience. Not only is what a source offers often cruelly manipulated to produce a lead but it's often necessary to pay a source to say something newsworthy. Often, too, the result is hardly worth the time, trouble and money put into it.

Such was the case when CBS News decided to pay H. R. Haldeman, the Nixon White House's Chief of Staff, about $50,000 for two interviews with Correspondent Mike Wallace. Executive producer was Perry Wolff; producers were Gordon Manning and Marion Goldin. The first interview was broadcast on Sunday, March 23, 1975, from 6:00–7:00 p.m. EDT. The second appeared the following week at the same time.

Many program reviewers believed Part II produced more hard news than the first, which largely concentrated on the Watergate tapes and Haldeman's relations with Nixon.

Wallace: About three months ago, Mr. Haldeman, you and I were sitting in the Hay-Adams one night, and the White House was illuminated behind you; and you said something to me that night that I didn't follow through on because I was fascinated that you had said it, and I'm very curious to — to hear you elaborate on it. You said to me, "Mike, Richard Nixon was the weirdest man ever to sit in the White House." What in the world did you mean?

Haldeman: What I meant was that he is — is one of — as a man, as a

125

human being — probably one of the least understood, most complex, most confusing men who has ever sat in the White House.[1]

Throughout the broadcast Haldeman insisted that what he had done was mismanage, not conspire or obstruct justice. He dealt "with Watergate within its own parameters. . . ." He was concerned about *his* image just as, in the past, he had worked so diligently to enhance the President's public postures.

The second interview featured Haldeman's home movies. One excerpt, recorded just about the time Watergate got underway, showed John Ehrlichman's wife grinning and holding up a newspaper to Haldeman's camera as she and her husband sunned themselves on a Florida beach. The newspaper said, "Probers Eye Haldeman."[2]

Haldeman also mentioned a frustrated Agnew, who thought of resigning during his first term, and the chances of his being succeeded by John B. Connally. He said Henry Kissinger threatened to resign several times; that the late J. Edgar Hoover, to bolster presidential support for FBI programs, fed Nixon "tidbit-type information" about "major figures."

Were the two programs worth the money? Cyclops, writing in the Sunday New York *Times,* said:

> If I held stock in CBS, I'd be grumpy about that much money going into a watered-down-for-TV remake of "The Apprenticeship of Duddy Kravitz." When the president of CBS News, Richard S. Salant, concedes that "I cannot preclude the possibility that my decision drew the line between permissible and impermissible payments at the wrong place," what he is really saying is that Haldeman's leftovers turned out not to be worth as much as Salant paid for them.[3]

Most viewers at that time would have agreed.

But seeing the national networks' journalistic efforts as similar to those of national magazines, Cyclops admitted that they will buy stories, even though he considered doing so as always a gamble. He concluded, "I don't see why paying for your mistakes is immoral."[4]

The CBS News rationale for making such payments wasn't based only on network resources to exploit newsmakers for exclusive rights to their stories but also on the value of those stories as "memoirs." Sometimes in the past, some news sources had stories that did smack of history. What these sources had to say — I stress this — may linger on importantly and continue to illuminate past affairs for future generations. In August, 1969, for example, CBS News documentarian Burton Benjamin paid an undisclosed amount to Anatoly Kuznetsov, a Russian writer who had defected to seek asylum in England. His interview, broadcast in early September of that year, was handled by Morley Safer and a Russian-speaking journalist of the London *Daily Telegraph,* David Floyd. The program mostly was on Kuznetsov's escape. The network also paid for interviews with another exiled Soviet writer, Alexander I. Solzhenitsyn, as well as with the convicted Watergate conspirator, G. Gordon Liddy. Moreoever, CBS News had paid for interviews with Presidents Eisenhower and Johnson. Again, however, these interviews were seen by CBS as more of the memoir variety than as talks based on hard news.

Once when a hard-news situation occurred, CBS News was criticized for not frankly acknowledging its interview sources. The network had bought interview footage of Fidel Castro from Frank Mankiewicz and his associates, then presented parts of it in a news documentary produced and edited completely under its own control: *Castro, Cuba and the U.S.A.* (1974), which was reviewed in Chapter 8. Al Pearlmutter, then head of documentaries at NBC, told the author:

> No one knew at the time that that was aired by CBS that one of the people involved in the production had business dealings with Castro, was making money from the Cuban government for exposing — or let us say giving exposure to — Cuban business activities to American businessmen who might be interested in investment there or (in) doing business with Cuba.[5]

Reactions such as Perlmutter's made all three commercial network news staffs leery about sharing production responsibilities with outside sources. But the gist of the criticism leveled at CBS News by its rivals was that it was paying for an exclusive story.

"We would not pay Haldeman or anyone else for a news interview," William Sheehan, then president of ABC News, insisted. His counterpart at NBC News, Richard C. Wald, while not admitting he never would pay for an interview, said, "I dislike the idea of buying a news story."[6]

CBS News still stressed it was paying for "a magazine article or book 'for which fees normally are paid . . .'" Robert Chandler, vice president of public affairs broadcasting, said it was against CBS News policy to buy interviews "for hard news purposes"[7]

Reuven Frank, of NBC documentaries, raised a good point:

> You will notice that most men in public life nearly always fail to answer a question. They all learn how to skirt it. If you let them run, they will use you to say what they want. If, like Mike Wallace, you try to get them back on the track, you seem rude and win sympathy for the interviewee.[8]

Even more interesting was the payment in May of $2,500 to radical activist Abby Hoffman for a public television interview entitled "In Hiding," which was apt because he was a fugitive from a narcotics charge. It was broadcast on May 24 at 11:00 p.m. over WNET, New York.

"We wanted the Hoffman interview because we have always chosen to cover what does not normally get on the air," said Michael Shamberg, who produced the interview for his company, TVTV.

Calling the Hoffman program "a total rip-off," Fred Friendly, speaking as a journalism professor and not as a Ford Foundation television consultant, said, "I don't think any news organization should pay a fugitive. It's neither good journalism nor good broadcasting, and it is not any way defensible."[9]

What was most alarming about "checkbook journalism" in the spring of 1975 was the sudden rash of paid TV interviews. Despite cash payments and the consequent appearance of their recipients before the public on TV, these particular interview programs just didn't add up to much.

But that didn't mean CBS News wouldn't go on paying for an occasional story. It would.

SUMMING UP 1975 AT CBS NEWS

1975 followed Hammond's law of broadcast media circulation: namely, whenever viewers are not watching general TV programming in large numbers, documentaries appear or are rebroadcast frequently. July and August were favorite months at CBS for running opinion programs. When the potential for large audiences again reappears — as in the fall — then documentaries fade away or, if they do run, they must be investigative blockbusters on the order of *The Guns of Autumn,* with which CBS led off the 1975 fall schedule.

Ordinarily, the frequent appearance of documentaries signifies not only small audiences but also the passing of "black weeks" when Nielsen takes no national program ratings. Or their appearance can mean last-ditch counter-programming strategies, when nothing else will serve to fill the time.

CBS Reports offered nine quality productions in 1975. It again nicely catered to the news staff's need to stir up excitement by knocking about a sizable number of viewers. This year, it zapped devotees of hunting. Besides exciting the national gun lobby, imploding the macho instincts of thousands of gun-toting Americans, *The Guns of Autumn* and its reaction sequence, *Echoes of the Guns of Autumn,* caused one curious upshot: the Michigan United Conservation Clubs filed a $300 million slander and libel suit against CBS, charging that the two documentaries had held about one million Michigan hunters up to ridicule.[10]

Vietnam got a two-and-a-half hour retrospective, *A War That Is Finished . . . ,* and a Special Report, *Indo China 1975 — End of The Road?* Women continued to receive *Magazine,* a series featuring six shows, each with three excellent mini-docs, mostly conceived and produced by women. The serious-minded could tune in on *Conversations with Eric Sevareid* during the dog days of July and August, when Sevareid successfully presented banker-diplomat-administrator John J. McCloy, German politician Willy Brandt, ex-Ambassador George Kennan and the Peabody family of Massachusetts. History was highlighted with three productions of *The American Parade.* Young people saw three shows in another series called *What's (the CIA/U.S. Senate/Apollo-Soyuz) All About?* which played Saturdays at noon.

For almanac buffs, CBS News closed out the year with *1975: A Television Album*. It covered President Ford's year (in which two assassination attempts occurred against him); economics and unemployment generally, plus an accounting of New York City's financial woes; Vietnam and the South's fall; Cambodia's defeats; and America's jingoistic attempt at martial face-saving, the Mayaguez incident.

A Television Album also covered Portugal, détente, Franco's death, terrorism, the slow heating up of Campaign '76, trials of the CIA, the International Women's Year, crime and the upcoming Bicentennial.

10 / Producers at ABC News

BEGINNINGS

CREDIT FOR CREATING ABC must be shared by its various founders with the federal government which, from time to time, stepped in to keep ABC independent and viable.

Although ABC was formed in 1943 when Lifesaver candy magnate Edward J. Noble bought and operated NBC's Blue network, which the government had ordered sold, the broadcasting organization we think of as ABC really was born on February 9, 1953, the day the Federal Communications Commission approved the merger of ABC into United Paramount Theatres, Inc. UPT, in turn, had come into being in 1950, when the government forced Paramount Pictures to separate its movie theatre chain from its film studios. AB-PT (American Broadcasting-Paramount Theatres, Inc.) began with 708 theatres, a radio network of 355 affiliates, a 14-station television network, and TV, AM, and FM station properties in five big cities — New York, Chicago, Detroit, Los Angeles and San Francisco.

Former political columnist Robert E. Kintner, then president of ABC, retained that position and reported to Leonard Goldenson, president of UPT and chief of the new corporation.

In 1965, with broadcasting revenues far outreaching income from its other sources, the corporation recognized this dominance and renamed itself American Broadcasting Companies, Inc. In the years 1953–1965, ABC inaugurated its first regular TV news report, the quarter-hour *John Daly and the News,* expanded the TV network to 100 affiliates and strengthened its news operations by picking President Eisenhower's press secretary, James C. Hagerty, to head the news division, which by now was a distinct entity. By 1960, Hagerty had acquired correspondents Howard K. Smith, William Lawrence and John Scali; ABC News also had produced the third and fourth Kennedy-Nixon debates and had introduced two public affairs series, *Issues and Answers* and *Directions*. Slow-motion instant replay was shown during a 1961 Thanksgiving Day Texas-Texas A & M. football game — the first of many ABC-conceived technical innovations used to buttress sports telecasts. In November, 1963, ABC devoted 60 hours of TV time to cover the John F. Kennedy assassination. A year later, Elmer W. Lower became head of ABC News.

Lower's appearance at ABC was fortuitous. In his eleven years at the helm of ABC News, its budget went from $4-million yearly to $50-million, its staff from 250 to 750. This growth came despite ABC's financial problems, despite ABC being forced to go to color and set up new production centers, despite involvement with merger overtures (such as those by ITT and Howard Hughes) and despite ABC News' lack of an identity. In the mid-sixties, for instance, the ABC *Evening News* was carried by only 95 stations. As a result, evening-news-show ratings usually allotted CBS News a 38 to 40 share, NBC News a 35 to 40, and ABC News an 18 to 26.[1]

ABC News had to put up with this kind of ratings horse race for well over two decades. Yet neither network brass nor the news division ever quit. There were years when they ran the course and that was about all that could be said about it. They lacked program clearances with many affiliates; they lacked news stars and correspondents to fill assignments; they lacked prime-time periods and, most of all, audiences. But there always was a news schedule.

Perhaps this sort of tenacity enabled ABC to finally set a managerial pattern which its rivals eventually would have to follow and which would help bring it from its lowly third position in popular-program ratings to a surpassing Number One by the mid-seventies. That pattern was its reorganization into four operations: as a television network; as a television entrepreneur (owned and operated stations, spot sales, films and international); as a radio production group; and as a manager of various non-broadcasting activities, such as Florida properties, a part interest in Disney enterprises, recordings and publishing.[2]

When surveying ten years of news work at the three commercial networks, one discovers they are not "notable for their similarity," although, when their common product is viewed on the home screen, one might think so.

Having the bulk of the audience watching most of its programs most of the time makes a network very different from its rivals, who must settle for smaller audiences. ABC News, a distinct unit of ABC, the then chronic ratings loser, was quite different from CBS News, a distinct part of CBS, Inc., which was always the number one network. Therefore, imagine the enormity of the problems facing ABC News, nestled so deeply into an outfit lacking high-rated programs. Strong, highly rated programs usually get stronger. Popular evening lineups can even deliver a high rating to the occasional documentary thrown into such a golden galaxy. However, the one fact of life at ABC News was that documentary had its distinct place, but, most of the time, that place wasn't prominent in the network's overall programming mix.

Documentaries at ABC News received various amounts of air time throughout 1965–1975, ranging in 1965 from 16 hours out of 147 : 10 hours totally given over to regular news, public affairs and — what ABC News termed — miscellaneous (which covered documentaries, news bulletins and special reports, pre-announced news specials and live coverage news) to 39 : 10 hours of documentaries out of a general-news mix of 332 : 58 hours in 1975. The exact relationships were:

YEAR	DOCUMENTARY HOURS	TOTAL NEWS AND OPINION HOURS
1965	16	147 : 10
1966	29	448 : 25
1967	46 : 30	546 : 26
1968	47	549 : 53
1969	34 : 30	548 : 34
1970	23 : 30	483 : 57
1971	24	489 : 26
1972	30 : 30	533 : 42
1973	63 : 14	659 : 59
1974	23 : 44	255 : 12
1975	39 : 10	322 : 58

(Source: ABC News statistical summary, 1965–1975)

ABC News committed itself most heavily to both documentaries and general news programming 1973. Both categories had peaked earlier in 1968 only to drop precipitously in 1970, to reach a new high in 1973, then to fade again back to mid-sixties levels in 1974 and 1975. 1968 was noteworthy for its catastrophes, including Tet and the deaths of Martin Luther King, Jr., and Robert F. Kennedy. 1973, of course, brought us Watergate, a prolonged news drama. ABC News gave more coverage to it than to the Vietnam war in any given year of the decade under study.

When considering the above figures, we should keep in mind that ABC News was the network news organization with the fewest stations, the lowest ratings and the least acceptable (to audiences) news personnel. Often, as a result, ABC News was damned if it did nothing (limited coverage of the national political conventions) and damned if it tried to outshine its network rivals (i.e., with *ABC Scope*).

ABC News also found that its rivals had preemptive news formats and documentary approaches that it had to ape if it wanted to compete — either that or come up with something completely different. At CBS News, for example, correspondents had considerable clout. Their authoritative opinions were respected. Most CBS News documentaries, therefore, were interpretative.

Those that were not primarily news-oriented still reflected the presence of a savvy news organization at the top of its form.

NBC News favored a 90-minute format, giving over an entire evening on occasion to a documentary. It strove for the blockbuster effect, an approach which also harmonized nicely with the emphasis NBC programming moguls gave to the so-called "big event" — multi-hour movies, entertainment specials and other popular series.

Wherever ABC News looked, it found the territory overrun and developed. CBS and NBC entertainment shows dominated the ratings; their news staffs infrequently spiced lucrative schedules with well-crafted news and theme documentaries costing hundred of thousands of dollars. Some were even sponsored and all were given, most of the time, choice prime time.

What could ABC News do?

It looked around and discovered that documentary news staffs still could anticipate trends and problems no matter which network they worked for. They still could help point out a situation to the public before the public fully realized it had occurred.

And that's what ABC News did. It didn't always win the attention its efforts deserved, either from its own managers or the public, but it tried. For that alone, ABC News documentaries deserve an accounting.

DOCUMENTARY MAKERS

In 1965, four producers developed the 17 hour-long documentaries (including two repeats) aired over ABC: David L. Wolper Productions, Robert Drew Associates, Stephen Fleischman and John H. Secondari. The Wolper organization was responsible for six programs, all narrated by actor Van Heflin: *The Way-Out Men, The Bold Men, The General, The Teenage Revolution, Mayhem on Sunday Afternoon* and *In Search of Man*. They were, successively, about scientists working to shape mankind's future, about men who regularly defy death on their jobs, a study of Douglas MacArthur, teenagers' problems, professional football and a look at mankind as one family.

Robert Drew's group accounted for *The Daring American,* about Peace Corps volunteers, and *Phil Hill: Assault on LeMans,* which showed Hill prepping "himself and his car for the treacherous grind of the 1964 LeMans Grand Prix." Both were narrated by ABC Correspondent Bob Young.

Wolper specialized in strongly commercial themes and worked in association with ABC News. Drew, a devotee of vérité and creator of some of the best news documentaries screened in the early sixties, was billed as chief of one of ABC News' documentary units.

Fleischman, an early stalwart in network TV documentary, was responsible for *Man Invades the Sea,* narrated by actor Robert Montgomery, which probed the ocean's "inner space," and *Everybody's Got a System,* narrated by that gadfly comic, Terry Thomas, which was a funny treatment about American and British attitudes toward gambling. Cut out of entirely different cloth was *The Agony of Vietnam,* narrated by commentator Edward P. Morgan. It was a backgrounder on the Asian conflict, trying to explain the enemy, the roots of the war and why the United States was there.

Secondari did some of his best work in 1965. Using the theme documentary consistently in his award-winning series, *Saga of Western Man,* he produced *I, Leonardo Da Vinci, Custer to the Little Big Horn, The Pilgrims' Adventure* and *A Visit to Washington with Mrs. Lyndon B. Johnson* — all co-produced with his wife, Helen Jean Rogers.

The above titles pretty well spell out the range of the documentary at ABC News in 1965. It was experimental with tinges of vérité (Drew); it was demographic, seeking out mass audiences whenever possible (Wolper); it was heavily thematic and instructive (Secondari); and it was versatile, treating both light and somber subjects (Fleischman). But, above all, it was the traditional hour-long, off-camera-narrated compilation. ABC News still saw the television documentary as a big-D production, as a direct carry-over of what Grierson and Flaherty and Van Dyke had accomplished with past nonfiction theater films. In 1965, ABC News was still treating documentary as a genre completely set apart from its other newsgathering activities. It either was unaware of or unconcerned with the fact that, by this time, all television news was documentary, either big-D or small-d. Compensating for this "ignorance," perhaps, was its satisfaction with past triumphs at ABC, which had showcased not only the talents of Fleischman, Drew, Wolper and Secondari, but those of Richard Leacock and Al and David Maysles.

STEPHEN FLEISCHMAN

The Agony of Vietnam appeared on August 25, 1965, at 8:30 p.m. An hour long and narrated by Commentator Edward P. Morgan, it was produced, written and directed by Stephen Fleischman, who, together with Secondari, Thomas H. Wolfe, Lester Cooper, Robert Siegenthaler, Gordon Thomas and Arthur Holch, presided over most documentary programs produced at ABC News that year. But even then, he and Secondari appeared to possess more leeway to work out whatever they wished. The others, possibly with the exception of another important ABC News producer, James Fleming, devoted most of their energies to the series, *ABC Scope.*

Fleischman was especially good at conceiving and producing the traditional hour-long television news documentary. Jack Gould described *The Agony of Vietnam* as possessing vivid close-ups, sensitive narration and "at its best in probing the reaction of the South Vietnamese to the United States presence."[3]

Fleischman used one sequence to describe "the culture of the rice field, where survival of a family's water buffalo can have a greater economic importance than a man's life. . . ."[4]

Documentaries such as *The Agony of Vietnam* were derived from position papers or outlines of what the producer planned to do, running in length anywhere from a couple of pages to twenty. Sometimes subjects were assigned at ABC News; sometimes, just dreamed up. The fact that another network documentary unit might have been working on the same topic never troubled Fleischman. "I learned that from Fred Friendly, because we were always coming up to him and saying, 'Hey!' because NBC was doing the same subject. His answer: 'We can do it better'."[5]

Film and news elements of actuality often were complicated by the producer's use of correspondents and vice versa, depending, of course, on each party's respective clout. Sometimes, according to Fleischman, a correspondent merely did the narration the producer handed him or her to read. Maybe a minor word change would be made by the correspondent, but little else. Other correspondents, however, would fight the producer right down the line, wanting to take over production as well as the writing of the program. Usually it was a constant struggle, especially if the correspondent happened to be knowledgeable about documentaries.

"I had an interesting experience with David Schumacher on the CIA show," Fleischman once recalled. "I think the program benefitted from this struggle between us. We didn't have a conflict on what we were going to say; we had a strong one on how to say it."[6]

Before going to Vietnam with Morgan to do *The Agony of Vietnam,* Fleischman had seven weeks to prepare. Along with associate producer Susan Garfield, he worked out in advance what the thrust of the show would be: no prior assumptions as to whether the United States was right or wrong to be in Vietnam. Then Fleischman and Morgan went off to Vietnam, Garfield staying stateside to handle a series of interviews about what was happening at home. Once he arrived, Fleischman talked to United States Ambassador Maxwell Taylor, General Westmoreland, peasants in the field, marketplace women, newspaper editors, journalists, educators. Meanwhile, Morgan lined up other key interviews. Then Fleischman wrote the script and Morgan narrated it.

Earlier, Fleischman had used the same technique with Eric Sevareid for CBS News in 1960 when they did *The Freedom Explosion,* a documentary about Nigeria's independence. From 1959 to 1963, Fleischman produced about ten shows for *CBS Reports.* Since then he has done programs on music, health, the environment and foreign affairs. He likes subjects offering strong contrasts that can be played off each other. Film, he has said, doesn't move in a gentle flow but is most effective when contrasts are present.

Never tell a story chronologically. Talking heads, usually the bane of TV documentary, can be exciting. That's our whole story, nothing but people talking. If the talking heads are dull, then you've got a dull show. If you've got some interesting personalities, and they're saying exciting things, and they're juxtaposed correctly, talking heads are fine. A lot of people run them too long. Let him make his point; don't let him run on to make other points.[7]

Even though he admits a documentary always must tell a story and he believes ardently that it takes a good writer to produce a good story, Fleischman has said:

The thing to remember is that you can say it with a great deal more impact visually. When you write a script, you sometimes belabor a point, saying the same thing over and over again in three or four different ways. This is a process I've seen through many times. No matter how many times I'm working on a script and I say, 'My God! I'm up to page one hundred already and I haven't finished developing my idea.' I find I can whittle it down to about fifteen pages when you're in the cutting room, and say as much, if not more.[8]

He also has stressed the need to tell a cohesive story.

I don't believe in segmented documentary; one of the problems I'm having to face is the tendency to do four ten-minute segments instead of doing a one-hour documentary. Each segment is telling its own little story and may lack any relationship to the others. I like to build a story so, even though you're interrupted by commercials, if you cut them out and put it all together, it's got a beginning, a middle and an end — a dramatic climax. You come out the other end feeling you've witnessed a total experience. The documentary has got to be more than the sum of its parts. If you're coming out with four segments of a documentary, a documentary interrupted by commercials, you're seeing four mini-docs. If that happens, I feel I've failed.[9]

Born in 1918, Fleischman majored in English at Haverford College, graduating in 1940. He worked for an advertising agency but discovered his real interests were journalism and film. He tried to join the Navy but was turned down because of a heart murmur. While everyone else was being drafted, he decided to stay in New York, taking a job with a Gotham film company, which was producing training films.

His first exciting moment in the business came when he began work on a manual of arms film.

It was just a very elementary training film. I went out with the film director and we shot film of soldiers marching up and down, doing present arms and so forth. I snuck into the cutting room that night and took film we had shot a couple of days prior to that. I was then a cutting-room apprentice and I had gall. I think I got the permission of the producer to do it, I'm not sure, but I made my first cut — physically made a cut — a cut in the action — you know, someone using a gun. Then another cut, another angle — the gun in another position. I spent all night in there cutting that little film, then waited for the projectionist to come in in the morning to screen it. I wanted to see it before the editor came in. When he came in and found out what I'd done, he hit the roof and literally tore that little reel apart, frame by frame. I never did see my first piece of work.[10]

Fleischman eventually got into writing and directing. He went to Europe for a year in 1947, but that was after he had married a California film editor, DeDe Allen, who worked on feature films and soon was to become one of Hollywood's best film editors.

He landed his first TV job in 1953, working with the legendary Irving Gitlin, who at that time was CBS director of public affairs on a Sunday series, *The Search,* aired in 1954–1955, which featured university research projects. He was a free-lance writer on three shows before Gitlin hired him as an editorial associate and associate producer.

"He had something up his sleeve when he did it," Fleischman said, "because he left to head up all CBS News public affairs, leaving me twenty-three shows to finish. I had to have four crews out simultaneously; I had to finish this thing in four months and get twenty-six shows on the air."[11]

Gitlin made Fleischman a producer and assigned him the Sunday series, *Let's Take a Trip,* a live remote program for children with Sunny Fox and two moppets going to a new location each week, say from a factory to a helicopter port. Fleischman did 100 shows, one weekly for two years. Later, he worked on *The 20th Century.* He and Al Wasserman were on special assignment, doing four one-hour specials for the series. Fleischman recalled working on one of these, *The Face of Crime,* which was about new approaches to penology at several prisons in the New Jersey prison system. After spending a summer with the prisoners, thus winning their rapport, he was allowed into their group therapy sessions, which were shot from behind one-way glass — then a new technique.

Fleischman was at CBS News a decade, leaving for ABC News in 1964. With Burton Benjamin, producer of *The 20th Century* series, he shared a Peabody and an Emmy. Since then, he has won several outstanding reportorial awards, inclusing two Laskers.*

---

*The years 1965–1970 at ABC News, describing the rise and fall of its half-hour correspondents' round-up series, *ABC* Scope, appears in Chapter 15; documentary reportage at ABC News between 1971 and 1973 has been covered in this chapter.

11 / Av Westin

AFTER 18 YEARS with CBS as mail boy, copy boy, writer, editor, reporter and producer of both news shows and documentaries, and after two years with the starcrossed Public Broadcast Laboratory at PBS, Av Westin came to ABC News in March, 1969, as executive producer of the weeknight and weekend editions of *ABC Evening News*. Back when he had started, *ABC Evening News* was running a poor third, with CBS roughly scoring a 31 share, NBC a 30, and ABC a 12. By 1973, the ratings were running something like this: CBS 27, NBC 27, and ABC 23.

To achieve these good ratings, Westin had done a number of things to the *ABC Evening News*. He stressed pocketbook stories by running items about national economic conditions ahead of Vietnam coverage, a practice his network rivals rarely followed. He ran more stories than had been the rule up to that time, sometimes using as many as ten correspondents in one newscast. He developed vivid graphics, using darker colors and presenting a pertinent quote as a headline or teaser behind the anchorperson as he or she read the story. Primarily, however, Westin used an attitude about TV news to produce his show, an attitude based upon a lengthy memo he had prepared for his staff when he took over newscast production at ABC. He called it "The ABC Evening News Chapter." Much of what he advocated was similar to news practices at the other commercial networks as well as at major independents and Top Ten market stations. But his methods also reveal how TV newsgathering and presentation have become identical with TV news documentary.

Westin said he accepts television as show business, and he sees television news as part of show business.

138

As long as show business techniques can be used to convey information without distorting it, I believe it is perfectly all right. Pacing, in my view, means letting the audience breathe a little between periods of high and intense excitement. A vivid pictorial report of battle actions should be followed by an interlude of less exciting material, enabling viewers to absorb more of the information they are seeing flash by.[1]

The *ABC Evening News,* under Westin's direction, had six distinct segments, if we discount commercials: the lead or story that stands out to the news producers as the day's most important; the second and third segments or the second or third most important stories; the fourth segment, "a wrap-up of foreign or domestic stories that have a certain unity;" the fifth segment, called the Pot, signalized by the anchorperson's catch-all phase: "In other news," and backed up by a graphic showing the world and the legend, "People, Places and Things;" and, finally, the last segment, devoted to a one-minute, 45-second commentary. Allowing for the insertion of six one-minute commercials, the show ran 22 minutes and 29 seconds.

This relative brevity didn't bother Westin, who didn't "hold with those of my colleagues who try to make the nightly news broadcast a program of record encompassing the minutes of the day's developments."[2] He saw TV news as an illustrated headline service, functioning best when viewers used it as an adjunct to newspapers. "In my experience," Westin wrote, "in producing lengthy television news documentaries — some as long as two hours — I found that length did not permit any more than scratching the surface of subjects. If sixty or ninety minutes was not enough to provide 'in depth' coverage, how can five or six minutes achieve it? At ABC News, reports are edited 'short' — often less than two minutes and almost never longer than three minutes." Westin's purpose was to reveal the highlights in each story and, by keeping each story shorter than those of his competitors, try to give his audience a bigger bundle of news.[3]

Westin's success with the *ABC Evening News* convinced ABC management he should head up the ABC News Documentary unit, which he promptly did in May, 1973. He described his new job, which didn't include special events or newsgathering, as being "in charge of taking all the material that comes in and making it into broadcasts."[4]

By this time at ABC, it was felt news and special events were doing okay. Only documentary needed shoring. Until his time, Westin claimed, "the kind of programs they were doing here were essentially either purchased from the outside, like a Jacques Cousteau or Jane Goodall, or they were very non-controversial: Margaret Chase Smith* taking two kids on a tour of the United States — things of that sort."[5]

*Former U.S. Senator from Maine.

Believing documentary can be anything, Westin retained the Cousteau and Goodall fin-and-feathers shows but also developed several others: *Close-up,* a hard-edged investigative series; *Action Biography,* a personality series; *Adventure in America,* which "is beautiful pictures and nice music;" *Americans All,* a series of mini-documentaries dealing with the contributions of minority groups to United States thought and life; and *Scientific Americans,* which would span 100 years of American science.

As we have noted before, investigative TV documentary is a handy means for producing furor. Right from the start, *Close-up* did just that. Twelve hour-long programs were scheduled for 1973–1974, with Westin promising "relevancy" for each. No more wild chases down the Amazon after some rare species of animal. Westin was pushing more familiar merchandise: consumer protection, energy, health and welfare — topics he had mandated for attention on the *ABC Evening News.*[6]

He was given a free hand by ABC top brass to make the new documentary series a success. According to New York *Daily News* columnist Kay Gardella, it was ABC President Elton Rule who called for more investigative reporting right after the Watergate debacle.[7]

"Our philosophical approach to documentary making will be changed," Westin said in 1973. "Heretofore, a documentary unit was a little conclave set apart in the news division that researched its own projects. But we plan to open up the doors and to make use of the 400-plus employees around the world. All will make their contributions to the 12 programs."[8]

Behind the rhetoric lay the real reason ABC News was jumping into documentary: irritation over the way the Emmy committee had handled the selection of nominations for the 1972–1973 season. Westin, along with William Sheehan, then senior vice president for ABC News, wanted something done. Westin said some of the shorter pieces singled out for awards, such as the CBS wheat-scandal report, "were covered completely on ABC News. 'They may have done a good job of packaging it,' he conceded, 'and I won't say they didn't deserve credit. But ABC News, in terms of air time and coverage, did just as well'."[9]

The first *Close-up* program, *West Virginia — Life, Liberty and the Pursuit of Coal,* lived up to Westin's promise that the series would be hard-hitting with no punches pulled, in-depth, informative and clear. If Westin brought anything to the news documentary, it was clarity. Each show — air safety, the fire hazards of new plastic compounds, the flood danger of water "impoundment" by coal-mining companies — had a cohesive pattern, similar to methods he used for the *ABC Evening News,* only refined and purified. Cyclops wrote in the New York *Times:*

> . . . first a disaster; then an inquiry into the causes; then a demonstration that it can happen again; then a confrontation with the bureaucrat who should be, but isn't, doing something to remedy the

situation. (Usually, ABC's Jules Bergman does the confronting; he is an avenging angel who does his homework.) Finally, a morose wrap-up.[10]

Gradually, the series developed its own style. Emphasis on clarity was there from the start, putting forth the prime news element of the program right before the viewer in words he not only would understand but would perk up over. Its use patterns the story of the horse trainer who would approach an unbroken colt and hit it sharply on the nose with a length of two-by-four, explaining, "First, you got to get its attention." Here is ABC News' attention-getting method in action on *Close-up*'s *IRS: A Question of Power* (1975), produced and written by ace investigative reporter Paul Altmeyer, narrated by Tom Jarriel, and reported by Altmeyer and Brit Hume.[11] Tom Jarriel is speaking:

> If you're a taxpayer, seeking assistance from IRS, a word of caution. IRS won't back up its own advice . . .
>
> WHY?
>
> This car, belonging to this couple was seized by IRS. It was all a mistake. It took the couple eight months and cost over 1,200 dollars to get the car back . . .
>
> WHY?
>
> IRS demanded this couple immediately pay 119,000 dollars. It was all done with the power of something called jeopardy assessment . . .
>
> WHY?
>
> If you think your income tax return is a confidential matter between you and IRS, you're mistaken. It isn't . . .
>
> WHY?
>
> IRS gets letters, some of them anonymous letters written by IRS employees. They're called "squeals" and they can trigger audits . . .
>
> WHY?
>
> In the next hour, ABC News will attempt to answer these questions as we investigate IRS, one of the least examined and most powerful institutions of our government.

The documentary was structured to show off the IRS's immense power through a series of interviews between Altmeyer and Hume and urbane IRS Commissioner Donald Alexander intercut with graphic accounts of the agency disclosing that it was three times the size of the FBI, possessing 74,000 employees, including 13,000 investigative agents; and revealing that its agents can go after someone without going into court — in fact, they prefer the freedom of operating outside a courtroom's rules because they can make up their own rules as well as use such techniques as "the scare, innuendo, and the threat of severe or embarrassing punishment."

IRS: A Question of Power drilled so deeply into the average tax-payer's problems with the agency that Arthur Unger, TV critic of *The Christian Science Monitor,* wrote right after the program first played:

> ABC News *Close-up,* which has earned a reputation for invaluable service to the American public with its superb series of exposés, had added still another oak leaf cluster to its public service award by calling attention to a situation which Washington officials seem determined to sweep under the bureaucratic rug. . . .

Close-up went its muckraking way, sometimes featuring " 'talking heads,' those eye-glazing shots of the faces of reporters and interviewees . . . jowls quiver, lips tremble, and eyebrows arch as startled bureaucrats and corporate chieftains suddenly suspect that they are being set up for the kill.'' [12]

Soon, too, the series was giving ABC News what it wanted: awards and the prestige of being a winner. *Close-up* won the coveted Peabody, Emmy and Dupont awards, collecting 14 in all. Marvin Barrett, director of the Alfred I. Dupont-Columbia University Survey of Broadcast Journalism, said *Close-up* "has been consistently courageous and the most outspoken series of TV reports since *See It Now.*" [13]

Often unsponsored, *Close-up* was costing ABC $2.4-million a year by 1975. But it had a respectable audience of from seven to twenty million viewers and it saturated ABC News with long-awaited prestige.

"Every *Close-up* wins an award or gets a good review; our lobbyists in Washington run to every congressman they can find with the clips," a pragmatic ABC executive said at the time. "That's so the next time a congressman starts screaming about sex and violence on TV, we can point out that they provide the money to do all those wonderful documentaries.'' [14]

More directly, *Close-up* had 11 out of the first 18 programs produce ameliorative action on the part of federal, state and local governmental agencies. Likewise, Westin could trace similar action in the private sector to the series. "So we are having an effect," he said. "You assume immediately that a documentary, by and large, is watched less by the general public than anything else, especially if you use the ratings as your criterion. Then who is watching? . . . Probably some of the general public, just too lazy to get up and change the dial. But I think those who do watch regularly are probably the opinion leaders. So it's a select audience." [15]

Then *ABC Evening News* ratings began slipping downward again. From the fall of 1974 to February 1975, the show's audience dropped from 23 percent to 19 percent, compared to 27–28 percent for CBS and NBC. In April, 1975, Sheehan again called on Westin to take over production of the evening newscasts while still continuing supervision of ABC's documentary unit. [16]

According to Richard Zoglin in the New York *Times:*

> When Westin returned to the *Evening News,* he instructed his correspondents to make the question "What does it mean?" the

guideline for all news reporting. The goal, he said, was to get away from the empty "here they come, there they go" type of story — to get at the story's significance, its relevance to the viewer. (For a while this took the form of correspondents concluding their reports with the rhetorical question, "What does it all mean? It means that . . .").[17]

By January, 1976, Westin's efforts to push the *ABC Evening News* back up to near parity with its rivals had failed. Les Brown of the New York *Times,* wrote:

It had averaged 22 percent of the audience in 1973 and 1974 and dropped to an average of 20 percent in 1975. For the last three months of the year, the average dropped to 18 percent.[18]

Some broadcasters figured that a rise of one percent in a network's evening newscast rating was worth about $1-million in 1974 advertising revenue, since that show is the crown jewel in the daily news programming schedule.

Ratings, as always, were important. To bolster the *ABC Evening News,* Sheehan, with Westin's approval, brought in Steve Skinner in June, 1975, as senior producer, responsible for the daily selection of stories.

According to Brown, Skinner's news experience was earned at stations specializing in "eyewitness news," so-called "happy talk," which interlaced lighthearted chatter with the delivery of news items. Skinner had been news director for WABC-TV, New York, and later, for KGO-TV, San Francisco.[19]

Brown reported in the *Times:*

Soon after Mr. Skinner joined the network, Mr. Westin, his immediate superior as executive producer, began to complain openly to colleagues of what he saw as the new producer's lack of experience and of what he considered faulty news judgment.[20]

Even earlier, according to ABC sources, in May of 1975, Westin was annoyed that ABC had cut the budget for documentaries. Brown continued:

Although television profits were good then, the news budget was reportedly cut because ABC's recording and amusement park divisions were doing poorly. . . .

"Westin was appalled that Sheehan let the documentaries be sacrificed without an argument," a veteran ABC newsman said. Later, under pressure from a number of affiliated stations, ABC announced the *Close-up* documentaries would be returned from the austerity schedule of seven to the full complement of twelve next season.[21]

Despite this, Westin quit. Succeeding him was Marlene Sanders, a former correspondent and documentary producer, who had been responsible for several of the award-winning *Close-up* programs, including *Women's Health,*

A Question of Survival and such others as *The Right to Die, Prime-Time TV: The Decision Makers* and *Lawyers: Guilty as Charged.*[22]

According to *Variety*'s Bill Greeley:

> When 21 persons, including four producers, were fired from the *Close-up* unit and the series sliced from twelve to six hours a year (sic), all sorts of reasons were given for the cutback, ranging from expensive political coverage ahead to making up losses in ABC's record division. But it's apparent that the show is just another victim of the prime-time ratings race.[23]

Much of the remainder of Greeley's story deserves quotation:

> Even though the network has decided to restore *Close-up* to its original schedule of 12 hours a year, such forthcoming subjects as "Divorce: The American Way of Marriage," "What Happened to the American Dream?," "The Labor Movement in America" and "Childbirth" would seem to be in weak contrast to such previous *Close-up* investigative efforts as "Fire," "Oil: The Policy Crisis," "Hoffa," "Crashes: The Illusion of Safety," "IRS: A Question of Power," "Washington Regulators: How They Cost You Money," "The Paper Prison: Your Government Records" and "The CIA." The oil show stands as the toughest assessment of the energy crisis on television. The hour investigation of the CIA stands as the only in-depth treatment of the intelligence scandal produced by United States television.
>
> By any standard, the show has shifted a long way from the purpose as outlined by ABC president Elton Rule in a speech at the affiliates convention in May 1973: "If there is anything to be learned from the exposure of Watergate and its widespread ramifications, it is that what is needed is more investigative reporting, and a more resounding affirmation of the principle of the separation of government and a free press. For our part, we intend to expand our activities in the investigative area, as evidenced by the 12 one-hour ABC news documentaries announced . . . by Elmer Lower and Bill Sheehan."
>
> It was a striking declaration from the company that had earned itself the label the Nixon Network, and which in the past had let sponsor 3M dictate telementary policy.
>
> Anyhow, insiders believe the *Close-up* softening and diminishing began at a meeting attended by then *Close-up* chief Av Westin, news prez Bill Sheehan, ABC-Television president Fred Pierce and others. The meeting was held last year in the wake of a disastrous rating season for ABC, and Westin was told of the impending cutbacks in staff and air hours. He objected strenuously, and was even supported by the sales side in his protest.

Soon after, Sheehan called a meeting of *Close-up* producers. He talked of "impact," which some construed as a euphemism for ratings, and indicated it didn't make much sense talking into an empty barrel.

Sheehan reeled off some of the show's depressed ratings, ranging from a high of 15 for "Fire" and a low of 7.1 for "Food: Green Grow the Profits." Subjects of "wide appeal" were called for.

Most *Close-up* producers agreed that the series subsequently reached an absolute low on "The Weekend Athletes," which dealt with the perils of tennis elbow and jogger's heel.[24]

Westin had said in November of 1975:

Documentaries tend to get cut back in time of financial stress because they're the kind of program that requires almost a total cash outlay. The money has to be paid up front, the programs rarely earn back their costs and they have negligible rerun value.[25]

By late January, 1976, he had resigned at ABC News — ten years after his mentor and colleague in documentary, Fred W. Friendly, then president of CBS News, had resigned his post, and largely for the same reason: to protest commercial considerations taking complete supremacy over the selection and production of pertinent and superb TV news programs.*

---

*At this writing (1979), Westin is back at ABC News, working for News Chief Roone Arledge, but he is no longer responsible for ABC News documentaries. Marlene Sanders, now at CBS News, was succeeded by Pamela Hill, Fred Freed's widow, who is now wife of Tom Wicker, the national affairs columnist for the New York *Times*.

12 / The Reasoner Report

It WAS THE FINAL moments of the show and Harry Reasoner was doing the close:

> . . . never before have I been connected with an enterprise which was so much a producers' show . . . I don't know whether you watch the thing that they put at the end of the broadcasts telling who worked on them. Tonight I wish you would, with me. They've been a hell of a good group.[1]

The Reasoner Report, ABC News' try at contending with *60 Minutes* and the television magazine format, was over. It was June 28, 1975, and Harry Reasoner had taken his viewers through segments from several past shows "which were amusing and infuriating, imaginative and investigative." *Report* had been on the air since February 24, 1973, at first consisting of three pieces of equal length, but later dwelling on only two stories per program.

The series originated out of New York at 6:30–7:00 p.m. on Saturdays. Like *ABC Scope,* it was weekly and only a half-hour long. Unlike *ABC Scope, The Reasoner Report* was a producers' series, as Reasoner has pointed out above. The spark behind its generally excellent stories was executive producer Al Primo and his associates. Primo tried to inject the *Eyewitness* concept into the program, an idea which he claimed to have originated when he was news director of Group W's KYW-TV in Philadelphia. Formerly, newscasts had an on-air cast of three: news anchor, sports announcer and weather forecaster. All other materials emanated from the anchor desk. Primo changed that, allowing each reporter to deliver his own story rather than just turn it in for the anchorman to narrate. This approach made for an informal, convivial flow of news items. When carried to extremes, however, *Eyewitness News* has been branded as "happy talk," and can easily become a bore.

Essentially what Primo wanted for *The Reasoner Report* was a good prime-time slot and a show that "put people in the news."

Reasoner's role, other than serving as host, was to supply a weekly "essay" similar to those he and Andrew Rooney had put together for CBS News. He took off one night a week from his ABC News evening newscast to write his weekly slot for *Report,* aided by a writer assigned to the series plus whatever help others at ABC News could offer.

Examples of what Reasoner liked to do were stories about stewardesses; on being a middle-aged man; a discussion of his mail; challenging former tennis star Bobby Riggs to a tennis match after Riggs, 50, defeated champion Margaret Court, 30; and doing commentary on President Nixon's justification of the bombing in Cambodia.

The series' stories were "soft" only when necessary to accommodate Reasoner's wry style. Consistently, the show covered newsmakers, people with something to offer viewers, and topics of direct interest to adults, or stories such as: Barbara Jordan, Texas' first black congresswoman; photographer Ansel Adams; and a look at The Sixth Annual World Series of Poker in Las Vegas.

John J. O'Connor, who said the series "was good; occasionally, excellent," believed it failed because only 75 percent of the ABC-TV affiliates carried it. Of those, at least a third delayed broadcasting it, something not always sensible to do with news. As a result, it never was seen in many major cities, such as St. Louis and Boston.[2] Moreover, ABC-TV didn't back the program by giving it a better prime-time slot than the Saturday night supper hour.

13 / Martin Carr

MARTIN CARR HAS the distinction of having worked in theme documentary at CBS News, NBC News and ABC News, where he respectively produced *Hunger in America* (1968), NBC News *White Paper: Migrants* (1970) and *The Culture Thieves* (1974).

With these productions, along with several others of equal quality, Carr has won four Emmys, three Peabody citations, and two Alfred I. du Pont-Columbia University awards.

Other documentarists have moved from one network documentary unit to another — Andrew Rooney and George Vicas were also at ABC News in 1972 and 1973 — but none has worked at all three so successfully as has Carr.

He is best remembered for *Hunger in America,* a classic social documentary that zeroed in on the hungry poor living in four areas of the country: San Antonio, Texas; Loudon County, Virginia; Navajo desert lands in New Mexico; and Halicon County, Alabama. It does this to point out the incredible theme that people starve in America, going hungry because they have become too helpless to help themselves.

This theme appears to be all the stranger juxtaposed against the glitter and posh of a San Antonio art exhibit and the despairing poor living nearby in the city's Mexican-American slums. According to narrator Charles Kuralt, 100,000 people go hungry in America every day. In San Antonio, children fail to function effectively in school because they lack milk and meat for their meals. The poor get little help from surplus commodities, since they are not the essentials needed for a good diet but only those products that the government wants to get rid of. Hunger for these people and the others visited by the program's cameras causes other dire effects: 11-year-old girls take up prostitution; premature babies are prevalent, by-products of malnutrition; racist attitudes afflict slum fathers: "They just don't want to work," claims a county commissioner.

Trappings of wealth are everywhere in Loudon County, Virginia, except in the slum shacks of the rural poor, where protein-scant diets slowly wear down families to a state of abject helplessness. Only sexual intercourse alleviates their miseries. For these rural women, giving birth is the one process they can positively perform.

Lack of wholesome food incapacitates the others, too. Desert Navajo tribes also subsist on largely starch diets. Meat is eaten once every two weeks. In Halicon County, Alabama, blacks buy food stamps on a $3.00 daily wage. Often the stamps cost too much, which results in their eating of meals continuously made up of chicken and rice.

Beside such contrasts between those who eat well and those who don't, Carr uses the technique of having a local person, one who is known to the interviewee, talk on camera to the starving poor. Father Ruiz, for instance, interviews San Antonio high school boys who can't afford to buy school lunches.

Naturally *Hunger in America* shocked the public. It caused the Department of Agriculture and the Federal Communications Commission some warm moments, too, which I shall discuss later in Chapter 18. (It covers several cases of this primal conflict in American television documentary between the individual and authority.) Suffice it here to say CBS News succeeded in alerting middle- and upper-class adult Americans to the existence of hunger amid plenty.

The several examples that Carr cites in his program may not be representative of hunger in America, but one must admit they reveal the extent and scope of the problem he undertook to explicate. "Food is a human need. It must become a human right," intones Kuralt, as he closes off the program.

Later, while at NBC News in 1970–1971, Carr would take up this same theme of helplessness with *This Child Is Rated X*.

All of Carr's work has been in theme documentary. Typical was his 1966 CBS News production *The Search for Ulysses,* a program with the same thematic pattern as *The Mystery of Stonehenge* and *The Italians*. Carr was trying to use an expert to uncover the truth about some past chain of events or to verify a theory. In this instance, his expert was a contemporary British historian and explorer, Ernle Bradford, who substantiated that "Ulysses was a real man on a real journey to real places" by searching out the very islands and lands described by Homer in *The Odyssey,* wherein Ulysses, after the end of the Trojan war, sets out for home on a voyage which he expects to take ten days but which, instead, takes ten years.

Kuralt, Carr's reporter, aided by actor James Mason speaking Homer's words, shares narration with Bradford, who speaks throughout most of the program. This again is the Carr technique of letting those most knowledgeable do the reporting whenever possible.

Because so much talking is necessary in the theme documentary, music and film must be equally effective to keep the production moving along. This is especially so where film scenes in *Ulysses* prove the accuracy of Homer's words:

Mason (Homer): When the fresh dawn came and lit the sky, we found our-selves in a safe harbor with a beach gently washed by the waves. It is a luxuriant island and the home of innumerable goats. . . .

Bradford: The Odyssey might be describing Favignana.* For Favignana used to be called Aegusa — Island of Goats — 2,000 years ago. . . .[1]

While this narration by Mason and Bradford continues, Carr's camera takes in the gamboling goats on ancient Favignana, scales a mountain and peers across the strait, evoking the presence of Ulysses.

While deeply sympathetic with his subject matter, Carr also understood the exigencies of working in commercial network television documentary. He realized the many tyrannies which the ratings system imposed and which the flood of hyped-up entertainment shows inflicted upon a producer trying to show an audience inured to show biz gimmicks the realities of different phases of American society in the late sixties and early seventies.

By the time he had arrived at NBC News, American journalism had al-tered. The line between fiction (at least, writing techniques used in fiction) and reportage was becoming fashionably blurred in the print media. (See Truman Capote's *In Cold Blood,* a journalistic novel; Tom Wolfe's hyperbolic *The Electric Kool-Aid Acid Test;* and Norman Mailer's scintillating tour de force in parajournalism, *The Armies of the Night*.) But TV journalists had their own set of problems, which the new, subjective print journalists were doing nothing to allay. The resources of the television journalist entailed a greater obligation to guard against unconscious bias. Every technical decision — lighting, camera placement, music, the exigencies of the editing room — added to the problem. Bias could be introduced simply by zooming in on a subject at the proper, or improper, moment — while his hands were twitching or his forehead was beading up with sweat.

"Anyone who grants a producer an interview puts himself in the pro-ducer's hands," Reuven Frank observed. "If the interviewee is, say, a politi-cian with a professional smile, he's going to show this smile to the camera. If the producer keeps the camera running after the interview, and the smile sud-denly wipes away, and the producer keeps this in, he's made a definite state-ment about his subject — and he's been guilty of dirty pool.

"A good producer is 'responsible,' not 'objective'," Frank goes on. "Good work grows out of the producer's subjective ideas."[2]

Martin Carr also realized there was no easy answer to the bias question.

---

*Largest of the Egadi islands just off Sicily's westernmost coast.

He said, "As an honest filmmaker, I cannot 'cast' my documentaries. I cannot deliberately choose only those people whose manner and appearance will reinforce their message."[3]

With *Migrant,* despite threats of violence from growers and local officials, Carr detailed the plight of migrant workers, documenting their complaints. He was returning in 1970 to a topic Murrow and Friendly first used in the early sixties (*Harvest* of *Shame*).

Then, again in 1970, he willingly undertook two studies of American social problems: juvenile justice and alterations in our rural life.

Using Edwin Newman as his narrator, Carr looked at the state of juvenile justice in America in *This Child Is Rated X.* Of the 188 prime-time specials broadcast in the 1970–1971 season, *Child* was ranked 104th, earning an audience share of 27, an exceptionally high figure for such a meaty subject. The documentary opens with a series of talking heads, children intermixed with probation people, then moves to Cook County Jail, Chicago; the Elgin State Mental Hospital; an offenders' school for boys and another for girls in Indiana; and to another pair of similar schools in Texas. A muckraking documentary, this one has a sequence at the Elgin Hospital showing two boys who had been tied to beds for 77 hours to prevent them from partaking in homosexual acts.

Later in the program, a humane judge, Horace Holmes, of Boulder, Colorado, counterbalances this scene of the boys and sets the theme for Carr when he says, "Everybody we don't like, we can't get rid of."[4]

Carr was even more effective with his *Leaving Home Blues,* which gave him full play to develop his preoccupation for watching Americans on the move, usually desperately. This time it was a report on a vanishing rural America where the migration from rural to urban areas is a forced one stemming from lack of work. Narrated by Edwin Newman and Garrick Utley, the program has three sequences: Nebraska farmers; the townsfolk of Scotland Neck, North Carolina; and the cheap labor cycle undulating along the Texas-Mexico border.

Carr's award winner at ABC News in 1974, *The Culture Thieves,* investigated the illegal traffic in valuable antiquities — the looting, smuggling and destruction of much of the world's civilized past. (I shall mention this *Close-up* production again in the Introduction to Part III: Reporters.)

Summing up Carr's work, I'd say his documentaries are wonderful visual tracts that keep pushing at you in scene after scene, demanding your involvement, your continuous response. Carr has such straightforward methods for making his documentaries, you would think his results might be banal. But they never are. He knows how to establish authority, believability and compassion without resorting to gimmicks such as slow-motion sequences, freeze frames or the use of stills. He places a great deal of emphasis on authenticity, despite charges leveled against him for opening *Hunger in America* by showing a dying baby, which critics said wasn't dying at all. Carr moves from reported facts, handed to you by someone who knows what he is talking about, to a visual revelation which substantiates everything you've already been told. He directs your response by giving you visual experiences that stand out so strongly, you no longer need the words of the narrator or others. To do such things with words and film or tape takes a real master.

Part Three / REPORTERS

Introduction

THIS PART IS SHORT because discussions abound elsewhere concerning documentary reporting. One needs only to refer again to Chapter 1, for instance, and its explanations of actuality and television news generally, or to all of Part IV: Events, to find numerous examples of the TV broadcaster's ways with the documentary.

Before getting into specific examples of documentary reporting, let me name several problems the documentary reporter often faces entirely on his own. In a sense, they are really part of one big problem: how does one go about reporting a documentary? For doing a documentary is quite different from reporting a newscast.

The major obstacles facing a reporter preparing to do a documentary are:

1. Being manipulated by news sources.
2. Putting together a program based mostly on what's available visually in film or on videotape.
3. Contending with a lack of balanced or adequate information.
4. Facing the need to organize a program dramatically.
5. Avoiding reenactments.

Consider the first problem, being manipulated by news sources. Back in 1971, anchorman John Chancellor and an NBC News film crew produced a news special, *December 6, 1971: A Day in the Presidency,* which was telecast at 7:30 p.m. EST on December 21st of that year. The "day in the life of" format was and is quite commonplace in news documentary. So there was the need to say something fresh and insightful. What NBC News wanted to do was

153

update the ongoing White House saga, this time concentrating on "President Nixon, his family, his advisors and his various visitors." NBC News hoped to get a truly inside view of the Nixon White House. Unfortunately, the President, not NBC News, really controlled the resulting program. Whenever conversations took a confidential turn, network cameras were ordered away. The result: constant manipulation by the President simply because he allowed Chancellor to see and hear only what Nixon wanted him to. Most news sources, if they can, also try to exert this kind of control.[1]

The television documentary reporter's second obstacle, handling only materials that are readily available, has been succinctly expressed by NBC News correspondent Edwin Newman:

> What makes up news programs should be determined by what has happened. . . . In television production there tends to be great emphasis on the footage. What have I got? I've got two minutes of this, so I'll use that, and I've got three minutes of that, so I'll use that. You're very often not governed by what the story is.[2]

The third difficulty in many ways is the most important: contending with a lack of balance or adequate information. One might think this problem is just like the one defined above by Newman, only grown larger. But it differs, I believe, in the control which the reporter exerts directly over the material rather than his just doing something based only on what's available. Usually, when reporting an event for television, you immediately confront two conditions: (1) how are you going to get across the editorial context — the opinion aspects — of the event?, and (2) what extensive research is required to relate past events to the present story? Failing to cope with these often results in problem number three for the TV reporter, i.e., presenting a story lacking balance and facts.

Karl E. Meyer once acted as a consultant to ABC News when an *ABC Close-up* documentary, to be called *The Culture Thieves*, was being produced. Based on his book, *The Plundered Planet* (published by Atheneum), about an investigation of the illegal trade in stolen antiquities, it eventually was shown on May 30, 1974, at 8:00 p.m. EDT. Meyer, writing later as a *More* magazine contributing editor, said of his experiences:

> Our show, like so many documentaries, turned out to be a picture-postcard album. Everything looked as it should, and not a viewer could have his preconceptions jarred. Nor were the interviews "difficult." They were short, they were snappy, they were effulgent with "television values," i.e., pith, conflict, human interest. The show was adjudged a success; it got admirable reviews and was nominated for an Emmy. But somehow, in the process, the entire point of the program got lost.[3]

Meyer indicted *The Culture Thieves* not only for ABC News being unable to resist "the possibly more insidious temptation of buffo" (the title was the handiwork of "the ad salesman, not the producer"*) but also for evading the omnipresent need to balance and inform.

Meyer found other faults with *The Culture Thieves*, but what I wish to stress here is that he was accurately expressing the anxieties a talented writer necessarily faces whenever he associates with commercial network television documentarians. When one is primarily a writer, one is more apt to respect words rather than sections of film or tape, to honor facts rather than opinions and arguments, to stress thematic precision rather than materials which will cause predictable emotional reactions amongst viewers so that their interest in the program will be sustained as long as possible.

I still would not rule out the use of the dramatic in documentary as long as it remains secondary to the reporter's prime job: making himself clear and understandable, even at the risk of being a bore. Drama has its place in documentary, but only when it's secondary to the truth.

CBS News producer John Sharnik has said:

> If you're looking for a model in some other medium for the documentary as it is mostly done nowadays, as it is mostly required nowadays, I'd say it's the magazine article.
>
> And the documentary has to have a form to it. The big trouble that people have when they move into the documentary from any other side of television — say, the news, where they may be terrific craftsmen with film and may know their way around the whole field of journalism — is documentary's form. It defeats them. They really don't know how to organize dramatically. They also don't have the sense of leisurely developing the atmosphere of a person or milieu — the home, the family relationships — the kind of thing you do when you're doing a magazine piece. You have the time for an adjective, a metaphor or a figure of speech. And you set scenes. You don't come in right tight to a close-up of the President standing at the lectern. You try to have a camera on him in the wings, where he's adjusting his tie and maybe chatting for a minute beforehand with his press secretary, saying, "Listen, how do I handle this item?"[4]

Sharnik isn't talking about PR hype nor is he advocating implying rather than directly saying something. He is backing up Don Hewitt who once said, "People identify with people. Television is best, not when imparting information, but when you let people share in an experience."

We have to keep remembering, however, that television news and theme documentaries are not coded messages; they are pictures. Maybe some of the creative processes that go into writing a feature article are the same as those for creating a documentary, but still, a television documentary is a completely visual message, aided by sound narration. To understand it, then, I think a

---

*The producer was Martin Carr. Meyer presents a wonderful glimpse of what faces a writer who helps adapt his own book to the TV-documentary world. See "Candy Telegrams to Kiddyland," *More*, Feb. 1975.

viewer only has to give it the same amount of attention as he does ordinary conversation.

The last of the television documentary reporter's problems with reporting the documentary is the problem of reenactment. Of course, reenactment has no place in documentary reporting, but it pops up just enough to cause trouble. In January, 1974, ABC-TV ran a disclaimer before and after the showing of a theme documentary, *Journey to the Outer Limits,* "about a climb up the Santa Rosa peak in the Peruvian Andes by students from Colorado's Outward Bound School."[5] The network wanted to be sure viewers understood that it took no responsibility for footage that might possibly not be actualities. One reason network news staffs insist on producing their own film and tape is to avoid the chance that an independent producer-reporter has employed reenactment at some point in his production.

Still, reenactment is difficult to avoid. Often it is a matter of definition as to whether footage has been "doctored." Often the "arranged scientific experiment" comes close to outright staging. Critics usually single out theme documentaries especially for appearing to use such a device. Yet Marshall Flaum, ABC-TV producer for several Jacques Cousteau and Jane Goodall specials in the early seventies, has said nothing on his series was staged for dramatic purposes. Flaum, who has worked for David L. Wolper Productions and *National Geographic* in the past, has said:

> From experience, I know how careful the outfit is about any falsification. For instance, I recall doing a Jane Goodall special for them. There was a dead scene where the animal behaviorist was seen on the beach with a native fisherman. I dubbed in a simple exchange dialogue in Swahili between the two.
>
> The Swahili came from another part of the sound track we had recorded for the program. It simply had Miss Goodall asking the native, "How are you today? Did you do better than yesterday?" When I showed it, the people from *National Geographic* asked specifically if the scientist said those words at exactly that time. I admitted I simply dubbed in the words she said somewhere else during the filming to remove the dead feeling on the screen. It was removed and when the documentary was finally shown it appeared with no dialogue, just dead air.
>
> The only recommended methods are legitimate techniques of filming. You know the story that you are looking for based on research, so the next step is to find it and film it.[6]

All these problems carry with them overtones of the producers' and editors' jobs. But there still are plenty of other chores the documentary reporter faces: interviewing; print influences on documentary reporting; the side effects of Public Television's public affairs reporting upon commercial network news staffs; the pitfalls of instant analysis; the perils of possessing a charismatic on-air personality; dealing with strong audience reactions to documentaries; bending to advertising pressures; handling direct complaints to the Federal Communications Commission about documentaries; and finally, coping with editing, especially the rearrangement of questions and answers when a news documentary interview is being put together on film or tape in a way that the reporter honestly believes results in economy, clarity and dramatic focus.

14 / NBC News, 1966—1975: More on TV News Magazines

A NEW DOCUMENTARY FORM — the magazine news show — appeared early in 1969 at NBC. The hour news documentary was broken up into several distinctive stories, presented, and sometimes produced, by regular anchor-correspondents. The stories were a journalistic mishmash, centered about topics of major news interest, backgrounders about anything current — people, problems, places — and saucy put-downs of anyone suspected by the show's producers of trying to rip-off society. A similar format, *60 Minutes,* had been launched by CBS News in the fall of 1968. It ran an hour every other Tuesday and featured Mike Wallace and Harry Reasoner. NBC News' entry, *First Tuesday* was two hours long, anchored by Sander Vanocur, and featured other NBC News correspondents. It competed directly, except for every third week, with its CBS counterpart. Despite such head-on-head programming, both did well, relegating an ABC musical comedy, *That's Life,* to the ratings cellar.

Antecedents for the magazine news shows are fairly evident. Les Brown, in his brilliant study of the TV industry, *Televison: The Business Behind the Box,* claims Fred Friendly really broke the ground in 1966 when he created the Public Broadcast Laboratory for Public Television, which was supported by the Ford Foundation and dedicated to producing a two-hour weekly "news magazine of the air." The PBL effort lasted two years. "Ironically," Brown reported, "it had a greater influence on commercial television. No sooner had it faded away than both CBS and NBC adopted its magazine format, CBS for the biweekly *60 Minutes,* NBC for the monthly *First Tuesday.*[1]

Credit for the TV news magazine shows also should go to the news magazines themselves. *Time, Newsweek, Business Week* and *U.S. News &*

World Report contained bright, crisp writing; numerous illustrations and charts; and an editorial layout that always gave the biggest play to what their editors felt would interest readers the most. Don Hewitt, producer of *60 Minutes,* claims that that program's real parent was *Life* magazine, whose basic editorial tenet was blending words and pictures to appeal to as many people as possible. According to *Broadcasting* magazine:

> In 1968, when Mr. Hewitt "invented" the television magazine format . . . (documentaries of) all three networks were drawing the same ratings — low. But, he figured, there were the "same documentary freaks out there" for each program, and if he went "multi-subject" and made it attractive as Hollywood presents fiction, we would double the ratings.[2]

Also not to be discounted was TV news' ability to replay an event. If the viewer missed a day of the fighting during the 1967 seven-day Arab-Israeli war, let us say, he could always tune in for a rerun. In a sense, the new TV news magazine program was a compilation — in fresh terms — of the week's or month's or even year's best stories.

Still another factor favoring the advent of the TV news magazine format was the inability of the regular network and local station newscasts to take the time or trouble to "explain" people or stories. After all, the big advantage the news magazines have over their daily newspaper competition is a peppier style and an ample supply of details in a story. TV news had to see this possibility sometime and it came about first at CBS.

By the summer of 1969, *60 Minutes* and *First Tuesday* were directly competing. Essentially a collection of small-d documentaries, each 15 to 40 minutes long, *First Tuesday* was produced by Eliot Frankel, who also would produce its successors, *Chronolog* and *Special Edition.* The magazine news format has continued to remain a fixture in the NBC schedule. Its latest embodiment was *Weekend,* created and initially produced by Reuven Frank.[3]

Reviewing the premier program of *First Tuesday* for *Newsweek,* Harry F. Waters said:

> The best of the bunch was the world's longest surviving heart-transplant recipient, emerging as a medical celebrity so unpretentiously earthy that even NBC's Sander Vanocur momentarily lost his glower. Had the operation ended his sex life? "I was able to resume twenty days after leaving the hospital," grinned (Dr. Philip) Blaiberg, while, on an adjoining couch, his attractive wife nervously plucked at her dress button.[4]

On the February 4 program, Tom Pettit produced a unique, well-made 50-minute investigation of our chemical-biological warfare program, "CBW: The Secrets of Secrecy." It would win Pettit an Emmy. To keep viewer interest aglow during its two-hour span, *First Tuesday* often alternated hard news with soft. In April, it played Tchaikovsky's *1812 Overture* while a French count's hunting party slaughtered hundreds of pheasants.[5]

The July 1 program had another Emmy winner, "Voices on the Inside," produced by Len Giovannitti and Rafael Abramowitz. The show itself also was cited, as was its rival, Hewitt's *60 Minutes.*

First Tuesday became *Chronolog* in 1971, but continued its two-hour format under the continued direction of Eliot Frankel. The program looked at domestic stories as well as any worthwhile news event: Stanford University students role-play being guards and prisoners; war-ravaged East Pakistan; Chairman Mao's thoughts sung in a children's pageant. Often, the two hours were tedious, especially when one story was markedly superior to others on the same show.

For a while, NBC's news magazine was called *Special Edition.* Then, after alternating with the traditional series *NBC Reports* throughout the 1973–1974 seasons, it became known as *Weekend.*

It also became the one ray of light in the generally overcast sky at NBC News. In 1975, *Weekend* performed with consistent quality of content. Starting in the fall, the show was to be on the first weekend of each month at 11:30 p.m. EST, with the remaining weekends filled by the late-night variety series *Saturday Night.*

A typical program, anchored by Lloyd Dobyns, one of TV news' best presenters, was telecast on May 15. It had a lengthy story on "The Reverend Moon's Army: Marching to the Name of God," produced by Jim Gannon, who had come up through the news ranks at WNBC where he did a number of *New York Illustrated* documentaries. A Gene Shalit interview with comedian Mel Brooks was also used, as were stories on male go-go dancers and country music aspirants losing out in Nashville.

Weekend was much more leisurely than *60 Minutes* to which, inevitably, it was compared. As Al Perlmutter expressed it:

> It's not *60 Minutes* by any means. *60 Minutes* is much more serious
> and staid in its approach. Well, it's Dan; it's Mike; it's Morley
> . . . *Weekend* has satire, some fun, and it has some serious, substan-
> tive material in it. But again, it's a different show. I don't think it's
> an answer to anything — just NBC's way of doing a magazine pro-
> gram at this particular time."[6]

Another 1975 development at NBC News was the use of tape for documentaries. Other networks had done the same thing recently — especially PBS. NBC used two-inch videotape for its first taped, regularly scheduled prime-time documentary, *A Country Called Watts,* produced by Tom Tomazawa. Shown on June 29, it was a special update on Watts and the fiery terrors that afflicted that Los Angeles area in 1965. (See *Terror in the Streets,* an NBC *White Paper,* produced by Al Wasserman). Despite the use of tape, the program broke no new ground by offering more accessible, more immediate or more intimate visual coverage. It remained the fact-filled, fast-paced, reporter-dominated TV news hour documentary so prevalent then at NBC News. Still, the outlook for tape being widely used in future documentaries appeared good.

15 / ABC Scope, 1965—1970

ABC NEWS DESCRIBED *ABC Scope* as "a weekly presentation examining the world's fascinating people and places, crises and curiosities. ABC News correspondents — at home and abroad — whose special background and knowledge are pertinent to the story told anchor the program."[1]

It ran at 10:30 p.m. for half an hour on Wednesdays through August, then was shunted to the same time period on Saturdays. Bob Young, the *ABC Evening News* anchor man, and commentator Howard K. Smith usually narrated the series, although Jules Bergman and Frank Reynolds worked an occasional assignment along with the rest of the ABC News correspondents corps. Along with those already mentioned, the people who produced the series included Stephen Fleischman, Sandy Goodman, Harry Rasky, Jim Benjamin, Graham Grove, Dick Goldberg, Hal Wallis, Ernest Pendrell and Nick Webster.

ABC Scope was strong on news. It had the ability to pick and choose stories because of its half-hour length. This meant, on the average, it had to account for 22 minutes and 30 seconds of reportage. It kept the correspondent in the foreground, either as anchor-narrator or while the individual correspondents' reports were being screened. Moreover, the series was able to use sidebars, interviews and commentary pertaining to that week's particular lead story. Topics either hard or soft, spots of news or human interest features, ranging from "Heart Attack" to "Television Moscow Style" to "A Conversation with Brigitte Bardot," ran regularly. They always were pertinent or highly popular.

On February 5, 1966, *ABC Scope* became *ABC Scope: The War in Vietnam*. The series turned its attention exclusively to the war in Indochina, where it considered not only weekly tactical updates but also included such sidebar

162

angles as interviews with American pilots, North Vietnamese officials and Saigonese bureaucrats. Howard K. Smith took over one complete show, in which he expressed his opinions about the war, but they never took hold with the politicians or the public.

In August of 1966, the series ran a three-part series, *Key to Victory,* consisting of "Know the VC," "Hearts and Minds" and "The Rice Roots." These programs were among the best video reportage to come out of any American commercial network news organization; yet, again, as in the case of Smith's expression of his personal insight about the war, these three documentaries failed to ignite much reaction in one way or another back home.

The series continued throughout 1967 and 1968. Nothing like it appeared in 1969, but it returned in 1970 in its original format as *Now* and lasted throughout that year; at that point, the series finally dropped out of sight for good.

To illustrate its quality and timeliness, here are 17 *Now* programs produced in 1970, all of which were hard news. They were:

The Black Panther Phenomenon, April 13
Missing in Randolph (Death in Vietnam), May 18
Women's Liberation, May 25
The Palestinians, June 1
The Kid Next Door Smokes Pot, June 8
The Precious Years (Pre-School), June 15
Alaska: The End of the Last Frontier, June 22
Straight from the Heart (the So-called Silent Majority), June 29
Vietnam: Topic A, July 13
Poisoned Earth, July 27
Help, August 3
Eye of the Storm, August 10
We Have Met the Enemy and It Is Us, August 17
Nader's Raiders, August 24
Unions and the Blacks, August 31
Death Be Not Loud, September 7
POW'S Next of Kin, September 14

Customarily, the programs appeared in those weeks when watching television in America was at its nadir.

When bracketed with the theme documentaries of Secondari or of other major series producers at ABC, such as Cousteau, these brief but effective news shows deserved much better than they got from the network, which generally gave them poor show dates; from the public, which took small or no notice of them; and from media critics, who, by appreciating the background and insights the ABC News correspondents continually offered, at least might have speeded up the coming of the nightly half-hour network newscast. Perhaps the lack of a dominant anchor personality hurt the series. It's regrettable such good reporting didn't do better. The stigma of being associated with a network perennially cast as a chronic loser didn't help the fortunes of *ABC Scope*. It just goes to show that, although a network is weak in one area, it need not be so in another. But sweeping audience judgments about programs are commonplace. Hence, if a network's entertainment programs are down in the ratings, it must follow, so are the ratings of its newscasts and documentaries.

16 / CBS News, 1971: Interviewing

THANKS TO THE INTERVIEW, the reportorial relationship is essentially between reporter and source, not reporter and editor. A symbiotic relationship, ineluctable and fruitful, it is best motivated by a common frankness so that the public — readers, listeners and viewers — truly learn something.

Interviewing a source, usually by phone, always has been a basic tool for the print reporter. Most print stories are a composite of several brief but effective interviews with various authoritative sources. News broadcasts are different: they convert interviews into actualities or sound or video bites. An actuality tries to resurrect exactly what happened so that — filmically — the events appear to occur again. Of lesser importance and verisimilitude are sound or video bites, the broadcaster's version of the print reporter's use of direct quotation. All the viewer gets from the sound or video bite is a quick statement from the source, never the essence of a story — an aspect, vivid perhaps, but still only a fragment.

What about the magazine technique of using the interview to frame a story directly? Rather than let the broadcast reporter incorporate visual and sound recordings into his report, why not run the actual questions and answers themselves? CBS News has favored this program structure much more than the other network news divisions. Perhaps this is due to Murrow's work on *See It Now* and *Person to Person,* the latter an interview program. Perhaps it's due to CBS's proclivity for isolating star qualities in both its entertainment and news personalities, then allowing them, at least in the case of the journalists, full sway to use their talents openly and abundantly in interviews as well as in newscasts and documentaries. More than its rivals, CBS News consistently had

165

dwelt on *why a given story occurs*. Its people have never been comfortable just reporting bare information. CBS News also has demonstrated a shrewd awareness of how forthcoming publicity will affect a particular news event, especially when that event may be perking along in its hazy incipient stages. Again, this is a quality Murrow learned while reporting from wartime Britain in the early forties. He came to understand that drama in an interview resulted from a vivid interplay between an authoritative but appreciative reporter and a knowledgeable, sincere source discussing a supremely newsworthy event. Neither, to be really effective, *must ever hedge*. A Murrow interview was a lesson in moral uplift: both reporter (who really was the public's host) and the interviewee (who actually was the public's guest) were on their best behavior in order to achieve the most scintillating results. A Murrow interview had all the hallmarks of good conversation. It might not always be clear, concise or even important, but it revealed qualities about the interviewee that were wonderfully interesting and arresting.

With the exception of Mike Wallace, who *suspects* his sources and grills them accordingly, most CBS News correspondents and reporters follow the Murrow standard. Here are two examples: Walter Cronkite interviewing two interesting sources with extremely good stories to tell.

First, Cronkite's use of the nightly news September 25, 1971, to talk to New York State Corrections Commissioner Russell G. Oswald, who had ordered the Attica prison insurrection put down with force. As a result, 40 men died, about 41 were wounded and "another 300 . . . had some bruises." Cronkite was talking to a man he described as having to "live with the fact that he presided over the bloodiest prison confrontation in United States history." [1]

Cronkite: Polarization seems to result from every crisis we have in this country these days and this crisis at Attica has polarized society again. There's a very large group over on one side that says get tougher with the prisoners, why do we let them do any of these things, the other says let's reform the penal system and get it done tomorrow. Which side do you think will prevail?

Oswald: Well, I'm a pragmatist and I feel that if you could say get tougher with prisoners and to hold prisoners that way and turn them out better people it might be alright (sic) to say get tougher with prisoners. But I say that doesn't work as well as the other approach. And I say to treat them firmly, fairly and decently and to me that's not being a liberal.

Earlier in the interview, Cronkite brought up the matter of the hostages' "cut throats," which later proved to be untrue.

Cronkite: . . . how did that thing get started?

Oswald: Well, I've tried to reconstruct that myself. I would say now at the outset that my own department on occasion did not report as well as we might have. It was under tremendous tensions, tremendous pressures, people were reporting at all times, no time to verify, the press was interviewing almost anyone who came out of the institution who looked like an official or an unofficial visitor there.

There was a story put out by a guard that throats had been cut; there was a story put out by a police sergeant that the throats had been cut; I believe that one of my staff said that throats had been cut. Someone said I said they had, and so far as I know, no one has been able to prove to me that I did; I hope I didn't. One thing that I told them was that I saw a sniper from the State police who told me that a man was pulling a knife across this inmate's throat was begun (sic) and that as he pulled the knife across the throat he had about this much of the back of him showing and he felt that he had to get him and that man came into my office thereafter and was shown on TV as you may know. His throat wasn't badly cut. Now this . . .

Cronkite: You meant a hostage, you said an inmate . . .
Oswald: A hostage.[2]

A second example is the Cronkite interview in June with Daniel Ellsberg, the former Defense Department aide who had supplied the New York *Times* with the Pentagon Papers and who had helped write the study that "showed government leaders had held Americans in as much contempt as they did the Vietnamese allies."[3] A News Special broadcast that same evening at 10:30 p.m. also featured the Cronkite-Ellsberg interview, which had been recorded June 23 at a secret location. In it, Cronkite introduced Ellsberg as "the man most frequently suggested as the source of the Pentagon documents."[4] Ellsberg, obviously intelligent and articulate, spoke earnestly at the start of the interview for a couple of minutes, saying in part:

Ellsberg: I was struck by the cover of *Newsweek* here. I refer to this super-history of Vietnam — a map of Vietnam with the faces of important people who effected that secret history of Vietnam. You notice they are all Americans. Every one of them. That reflects accurately the way the history of Vietnam emerges from those studies — that is, from the internal documents to the United States.

It affects the way the Vietnam war is seen from Washington, as to who matters and who doesn't. And there is great realism in that, actually. . . .

The war has been an American war and there is certainly realism to the way that it's been reflecting the actual attitudes of the people making the decisions.

. . . I came back then with this sense, an additional sense, of concern then about what we were doing to the people of Vietnam as well as what was happening to this country. . . .

Cronkite: . . . It's a black history as it's been drawn so far. Are there any heroes in it?

Ellsberg: I think that a man I read about named Bernard who put his rifle down to the ground at the risk of his life and refused the orders of his superior commander to fire at civilians at Mylai. He's a hero.

Cronkite: You don't find them at a higher level?

Ellsberg: That's a hard question you've asked me. I hate — I hate not to find it easy to answer. I hate as an American not to find it easy to answer. Looking at the record, it seems hard for me to find men who have lived up to the responsibilities of their office in terms of not only of what they did but of what they could have done, what they should have done, given their feelings.

    . . . Americans now bear major responsibility, as I read this history, for every death in combat in Indochina in the last twenty-five years. . . .[5]

Ellsberg made it clear he was troubled by differences between information he knew was in the 47-volume, 7,000-page secret study — the Pentagon Papers — and what the government was telling the American people.[6]

The Cronkite newscast wasn't the only CBS program using newsmaker interviews rather than stories (Cronkite also interviewed West Germany Chancellor Willy Brandt October 27 and Britain's Prince Philip on November 19 and 21). The *Morning News* featured John Mitchell on February 17 and 18, concerning the Pentagon Papers law suits against the press; August 28 saw Richard C. Hottelet interview Egyptian Foreign Minister Mhmoud Riad; and in December, GOP spokesman George Bush appeared. But all these lacked the power of the Oswald and Ellsberg stories.

In April, Eric Sevareid's powers as a broadcast journalist were severely tested when CBS News, probably with a prescient eye cast ahead to the forthcoming Bicentennial, inserted the redoubtable commentator into a Perry Wolff-produced *Conversation with Lord North,* telecast on April 6 and starring British actor Peter Ustinov, complete with wig and eighteenth-century costume, as George III's prime minister during the American Revolution.

It was the first in a series to be about that revolution, covering the years 1770 to 1783. Since it was complete reenactment, it wasn't a good showcase for Sevareid's exemplary talents as an interviewer. I cite it here only to show how the interview can be abused even with the best of intentions at hand. Good interviews depend on strong, substantial news hooks. *North* obviously lacked this.

No look at the art of interviewing as it applies to broadcast news and documentary is complete without including the work of Charles Kuralt. Not only is he one of the best narrator-reporters in TV news documentary, but he is on a perch all his own, possessing the ability to grab and retain the viewer's attention, yet never offending him by being overly callous or obstrusive. If any broadcaster has the common touch of personable humanity, it is Charles Kuralt. Nowhere does this deft quality appear more palpably than in *On the Road,* which began in October of 1967, and which sticks to some aspect of individuality as its recurrent theme.

Kuralt joined CBS News as a writer in 1956, was assigned to the news assignment desk in 1958. The first host of *Eyewitness,* a news series, he later went to Rio de Janeiro as CBS News Chief Latin American Correspondent. In 1963, he was named Chief West Coast Correspondent and held that job until 1964, when he returned to New York news headquarters. He was and is preeminently a reporter.

Part of the effectiveness of *On the Road* is the "lead" Kuralt writes to set the stage for an interview. "Americans ate forty billion hamburgers," he will say in that homey, North Carolina baritone, "in the last year, give or take a few hundred million, and 'on the road' you tend to eat more than your share. You can find your way across this country using burger joints the way a navigator uses stars."[7]

Or:

Full moon over Texas and a school bus rolls along a lonely road in the hill country, a road that leads only from Cranfills Gap to Iredell. At the wheel is J. F. White, who made his fortune in oil. His passengers are young, silent and grim, facing what they consider to be the most important night of their lives. What's happening here is that Coach White is driving the Cranfills Gap Lions to Iredell, where they will play for the district's six-man football championship.[8]

His copy sounds at first like a letter — plenty of facts about what it is like in Idaho or Minnesota or the Florida Keys. But there is more to his writing than that. Kuralt always is aware of what Time and Change (they must seem to be actual personages to him) are doing to the individual or place he singles out for attention.

Here is the conclusion of "a chat" with Alaskan Tiger Olson who "prospects, hunts, fishes and, as he's done every morning since 1918, cuts the wood to make his breakfast coffee."

Kuralt: Are you in favor of it?

Olson: I am not in favor of that whatever. I believe in keeping Alaska the way it is.

Kuralt: When Tiger Olson goes, he won't leave much — an ax and a chopping block, a water bucket and a pipe he laid to bring the water down from a mountain spring, an old boat beyond repair, a string of cork floats hanging on a tree. If you measure a man by how much he has earned or saved or built or paved, you might think of him as a failure. But in Tiger Olson's world, all . . . the failures are dead and gone.

He survived.

There may someday be apartment buildings on his cove, pouring sewage into his water. He won't survive long enough to see that. That's just as well.[9]

Kuralt walks a thin line between sentimentality about his subject, a person who, in his own right, comes across on camera as strong and unique, and catering to the eccentricity in a person who has lived too far from others to accept the usual accommodations to the stresses, strains, compromises and civilities which come, mumbo jumbo, with the lives most of us lead. Somehow Kuralt manages to retain a tasteful balance between these two ways of living by sticking to concrete details and reporting exactly what is out there before him, and by understanding, way before it hits the viewer, what kind of impact his questions and their consequent replies are going to have on us. Like the Roman poet Horace, and our own Robert Frost, Kuralt dwells on the rude pleasures of nature and nature's children. We never see too much of the kind of world in which most of us dwell. That fact may well explain his hold on us.

As he has said, "Every place looks and feels and sounds and smells like every other place. We stick to the backroads where Kansas still looks like Kansas. And Georgia still looks like Georgia. Where there is room for diversity and for the occurrence of small miracles."[10]

17 / CBS News, 1971:
Clashes with News Sources

On November 3, 1969, Richard M. Nixon addressed the country on television, making a major statement about Vietnam. The President offered no concessions to Hanoi — or to the anti-war movement at home — and no fresh hopes for peace in Paris. He hinted, in fact, he might step up the fighting. That same night, Dean Burch, a close friend of the President and formerly active in Arizona Senator Barry Goldwater's 1964 bid for the presidency, as new head of the FCC, personally telephoned NBC President Julian Goodman, ABC President James Duffy and CBS President Dr. Frank Stanton to ask them for transcripts of their respective commentators' remarks about the speech.

Burch's unprecedented request was ominous. It signaled that new hostilities were about to break out between the government and broadcast journalism.

What Burch was seeking was an accounting of a practice called instant analysis. After the President made a television speech, network correspondents picked up on it and discussed it, usually repeating what was said so viewers understood it. John Chancellor, a preeminent practitioner of instant analysis, once explained how it worked.

(There was) . . . Nixon's sudden midday appearance . . . when he read a carefully worded statement of the agreement with the Russians to move ahead on the limitations of strategic nuclear arms. The statement had to be identical with the one issued in Moscow, which meant that, like most diplomatic language, it had a sort of Delphic quality about it. It had to be analyzed and explained — immediately — and that was just what we did. When we engage in that kind of instant analysis, or talk about Henry Kissinger's secret mission to Peking, the White House is all smiles. But when we say that the President ducked some questions at a news conference, there is a certain amount of glaring the next day. In that sense, the President's men are very human.[1]

Such uneasiness about public discussion of their actions has not been untypical of American presidents — especially since the Kennedy Administration, when TV cameras became unblinking monitors of what was going on. In fact, President Kennedy — the idol of the press — once asked it to ask itself: " 'Is this news?' All I suggest is that you add the question: 'Is it in the interest of the national security?' "

The right of the press to speak out usually has been tempered by commonsensible precautions, especially in broadcast journalism. The same precautionary contingencies lie on the side of the government as well. Usually, in any clash, neither side wins or loses. Only stalemates result, with the public, hopefully, maybe the wiser for it all.

In broadcasting, the urge to report is often tempered by several gatekeeping proclivities germinating within a broadcast news staff. The desire, first of all, for maintaining and increasing its own prestige within the community it serves; second, the urge to respect the mandates of the Fairness Doctrine to air both sides of an issue; and third, the need to incorporate the opinions of various distinct groups within its general audience, some of which are formal, such as government officials, and some of which are informal, such as the Society for Prevention of Cruelty to Animals. All these in turn are tempered additionally by either the lack of an audience for a certain news subject or the unwillingness of a reporter to do a certain story. Other factors are costs, time limitations, fear of angering others or an unwillingness, quite plainly, to enter the dismal bogs of political rhetoric, trying hopelessly to delineate differing opinions and prejudiced viewpoints.

News broadcasters, then, thought they had controllable choices when Dean Burch asked to see the network commentators' remarks about the Nixon speech. As far as instant analysis went, they did. As far as reporting and editing the regular nightly newscasts and live News Specials, they did. Only in two other areas were they to find themselves in trouble: dealing with the on-air personalities of their correspondents and dealing with reactions to their news documentaries.

One reason correspondents' personalities turned out to be a problem was that broadcasting always has had a peculiar effect on two broad categories of people. It can take some people and enhance them so strongly that they make an instant, smashing impact on audiences. Numerous entertainment stars have benefitted from this phenomenon. Comedian Flip Wilson, for one.

Broadcasting emphasizes another group of personalities in an entirely different way. Rather than create a sudden brilliance that soon wears thin, camera and microphone combine to bring on this second type of personality so slowly that, as time passes, the personality is burnished into becoming a regular, acceptable guest in the viewer's living room. The late Ed Sullivan exemplifies this process.

These two effects occur as well in newscasting and reporting. Dan Rather illustrates the former type, Walter Cronkite the latter. CBS probably had to take Rather off the air for a while after Watergate to reduce the irritability his on-air personality quite unintentionally had been producing.

Documentaries also have these same hare and tortoise qualities and either can be highly irritating and explosive on onset or can be completely innocuous and nearly soporific. Seeing the documentary in its activist role, Harold Clurman has said:

> When our own documentaries draw attention to a social problem, they almost always insist or imply that the problem is an anomaly in our society which could be eradicated if people were a little less complacent. The viewer may even join a process which starts with working up feelings of outrage and shame, and includes forming a public pressure group, placing ads in the Sunday *Times* and possibly celebrating the passage of legislation. The problem may remain, of course, but we still associate documentaries with reform in action.[2]

But for every potentially abrasive documentary, there are dozens that are scarcely memorable or deserve to be. At this point, it's well to emphasize that in 1971 the stimulus-response tie between the American people and their complex and penetrative media system was extremely sensitive. What happened at Kent State University, for example, after four white middle-class students were shot, is indicative of this relationship. Daniel Bell wrote in *Encounter:*

> In 1970, the shooting of the students on the Kent State University campus within 24 hours produced strikes on some 400 college campuses, involving over 3 million students. None of this was centrally organized; it could not be. What one saw was a common emotional reaction, spread almost instantaneously by contagion. In short, the loss of insulating space makes the United States vulnerable to the kind of mobilization politics that has been a feature of ideological conflicts in European societies in the nineteenth and twentieth centuries. And, as traditional party structures continue to erode, and television and rapid transportation allow political candidates to come forth quickly, we have the basis for a volatility of emotions, the accentuation of demagoguery, and the possibility of plebiscitary democracy — though not Caesarism, for the United States polity is too complex, and interest groups too diverse for that — as the coming modes of politics in the country.[3]

By "insulating space," sociologist Daniel Bell meant a relative isolation between a violent event and its eventual receptors, plus lack of immediate spill-over effects or trauma being transmitted from the event to areas beyond it.

The Kent State phenomenon admittedly has nothing to do directly with TV documentaries except when we address ourselves to the hypothetical situation where — say a year later — we decide to produce an in-depth study of that calamity. Knowing how explosive it had been as a news story, how would it be as an investigative opinion piece? Would its audience react in the same way as students reacted to news of the original event? No one can say with certainty. One has choices about how to deal with audience reactions, as do the news divisions of the networks. One can ignore the subject. Or one can do something: take a stand to either defend or attack. Or — following a third option — one can do something, but water it down either by presenting both sides in perfect balance or by offering a very hazy picture of only one side.

Eugene McCarthy, former United States Senator from Minnesota and an independent candidate for President in 1976, has said:

> There are, I think, at least four rules of selection which the media can and should apply. First, if someone is talking or writing nonsense, there is no obligation to spread the word. Second, if someone is talking nonsense and having an effect, the press has, I believe, as a monopoly or near monopoly, an obligation to report the nonsense. It can and should challenge it with counter-information and analysis. Thus I think the press and the electronic media had an obligation to report, as they did, the campaigns of George Wallace. Third, if someone is speaking sense and having an effect, there is obviously an obligation to report it. And fourth, if someone is saying things that do make sense, and that have relevance to current problems, even though there is no immediate evidence that what is being said is having any significant effect, these things should be reported. It is in this fourth case that the failure of the press is most evident.[4]

Even so, after perusing such choices, there's still another condition with which the documentarian, at least, must contend: when news documentaries get off news subjects and onto an arbitrarily selected topic and then that topic is glazed over without benefit of clear analysis, the results often quite unintentionally end up spouting public relations for somebody. This condition is one of the hair shirts the theme documentarian wears.

Faced with such options, what did CBS News do? Facing potentially enormous public reactions, what choices did it make?

In the case of *A Conversation with Eric Hoffer,* CBS News followed up what many felt wasn't so much a conversation as a tirade with a symposium of Hoffer critics. In the instance of *The World of Charlie Company,* the network repeated the broadcast so that a bigger audience could see it (the original telecast was blanketed by a rival network's coverage of the Annual All-Star Baseball Game) or so that those who first looked at it could see it again. In the case of *Hunger in America,* Salant's staff repeated the program but edited the introduction and close so as to expose and update criticism of the program and the network's defense of it. With *Sixteen in Webster Groves,* CBS News actually recorded reactions to the program by participants and then followed it up with a second production, *Webster Groves Revisited,* based entirely on the reaction footage. More recently, the news division has been using a new technique which helps boost its reputation with affiliates by holding ''feedback'' press conferences at various CBS radio and/or television stations around the nation, which sometimes feature Cronkite, Salant and any number of their confreres.

Aside from these methods for handling audience reactions, there were distinct instances where not only was the general audience reacting but so was the government and its political agents.

One ironical high point was the CBS News Special, *In the Pay of the CIA: An American Dilemma,* broadcast on March 13, 1967, produced by Les Midgley and narrated by Mike Wallace, which was about the use of Radio Free Europe — obstensibly funded by the American public — as a CIA propaganda service as well as about dummy foundations set up by the CIA to channel money into real foundations and thence to students, labor unions and social workers.

Actually, CBS News could have included itself in that roster. E. K. Mead, Jr., CBS vice president for corporate relations, admitted in 1977 that ''CBS shared responsibility for the company's cooperation with the Central Intelligence Agency in the 1950s and 1960s.''[5] Earlier, Salant, in an interview in the Los Angeles *Times* on May 27, 1977, said, ''CBS had cooperated with the CIA twenty or so years ago by allowing agents to monitor news reports coming into the studio and by letting them have outtakes (film never used on the air but still retained in newsroom files) and blowups of new film.''[6] Salant said he ended the CIA ties when he learned of them shortly after first becoming President of CBS News in 1961.

In 1966, CBS News voluntarily passed up $250,000 in sponsor money rather than take a chance that a *CBS Reports* documentary, *I.O.U. $315 Billion,* about whether Americans were overextending themselves financially, might be embarrassing to IBM.

Salant wrote to Dean McKay, IBM vice president of communications, and advised him that the program dealt ''directly with, and may directly affect, the sponsor's business interests'' because it involved ''major IBM customers.''[7]

Bucking the CIA and corporate clients weren't the only reactions confrontations CBS News has faced. On January 4, 1966, the news division televised the theme documenatry, *The Volga,* in spite of indications that it ran the risk of reprisals from the Soviet Union. Fred Friendly, then CBS News president, was visited by a Soviet embassy official from Washington and a member of the Soviet State Commission on Radio and Television, who specifically objected to the documentary's reference to Lenin as one part God, one part politician and one part Boy Scout. "Their greatest objection . . . was to Lenin's being coupled with a Boy Scout," Friendly admitted.[8]

In June of that same year, Salant said he "goofed" in permitting a staff correspondent, Harry Reasoner, to appear in the documentrary *Wall Street: Where the Money Is,* which was produced by an outside firm, David L. Wolper Productions, and broadcast on June 4.

Salant also was upset because some segments of the program had been submitted in advance to participants for their approval — a breach of journalistic ethics, he said, although Wolper's organization disagreed.

Salant said that legally he couldn't bar the program, sponsored by Xerox, which discussed stocks and bonds, but he said he intended to announce at its outset that some participants had been granted rights of approval.

According to Alan Landsburg, vice president of Wolper Productions, none of the documentary had been edited at the request of the participants. Both the Securities and Exchange Commission and the National Association of Securities Dealers had previewed the script.

Some brokerage houses had bought commercials adjacent to the program on stations throughout the country; others, such as Bache & Company and Merrill, Lynch, Pierce, Fenner & Smith, Inc., had purchased newspaper ads calling attention to the program.

Because Xerox and Wolper had proposed using a famous entertainer rather than a newsman as the program's narrator, Salant considered three proffered names. "I turned them all down because I don't want comedians narrating a journalistic effort. I suggested they get John Daly, but they struck out. In desperation I finally had to supply somebody, so I told them to use Harry Reasoner."[9]

WTTC-TV, Hartford, canceled the March 14, 1967, *CBS Reports: Saigon,* although 144 other CBS outlets did carry the Beryl Fox documentary. As a result, the station was picketed, flooded with phone calls and was the object of direct complaints to the FCC.

After seeing the program, about the Vietnamese war's effects on the South Vietnamese capital, WTTC-TV's owners, executives of Broadcast Plaza, Inc., a subsidiary of the Travelers Insurance Company, decided to cancel the program, replacing it with two Danny Thomas reruns. "We felt the program presented a distorted view of the American purpose in Vietnam," Kendall Smith, WTTC station manager said. ". . . the documentary dwells on the seamy side of life in Saigon while failing to tell of the good work our troops are doing for the people of that city."[10]

With the production of *The Selling of the Pentagon,* CBS News was honestly trying to follow Senator McCarthy's fourth precept: discussion of the sensible, relevant but not yet discernibly important subject. Virtually all information used in that documentary had been made known earlier and in fuller detail in newspapers and magazines as well as in Fred Cook's book, then ten years old, *The Welfare State,* and in *The Pentagon Propaganda Machine,* a book recently completed by the then chairman of the Senate Foreign Relations Committee, Senator J. William Fulbright.[11]

What happened after this information was processed and molded into a television news documentary provides us with a classic case study of audience reactions. All CBS News did was revive these same facts. Nothing extraordinary was in mind. Salant had been watching NBC's *First Tuesday* a year or so earlier and had been struck by a segment of it which had been filmed by the Atomic Energy Commission.[12] "Well, my God, does the AEC make its own films?" he thought. "Who said they should do this, and how much of it is going on?"*

The documentary, first telecast on February 23, was to have been an examination of Pentagon public relations activities, including filmmaking, VIP tours, fire-power displays, air-power exhibits and speaker programs, as well as efforts to use the media to present the Pentagon's objectives. Congressional Correspondent Roger Mudd was the reporter; Peter Davis, the producer-writer; Perry Wolff, the executive producer; and Dena Levitt, the film editor. Cameramen were William Wagner, Walter Dombrow, James Kartes, Robert Clemens and Richard Francis; soundmen were Richard Wilhelm, Larry Gianneschi, Richard Peepe, Leonard Zuck, Richard Wiggins and Joel Dulberg.

The program was a vivid eye-opener. Congressman F. Edward Hebert, chairman of the House Armed Services Committee, said it was "one of the most un-American things I've ever seen . . . on the tube, the greatest disservice to the military I've ever seen on television, and I've seen some pretty bad stuff." Defense Secretary Melvin Laird labeled it an unprofessional job of reporting. Vice President Agnew called it "a subtle but vicious broadside against the nation's defense establishment." Congressman Harley O. Staggers said "his special investigating committee would look into the whole field of TV news reporting to see how much of it is staged but made to look spontaneous."[13]

These were responses from politicians. The public appeared overwhelmingly to approve the documentary. But since the politicians were the ones who could apply regulatory pressures, CBS News ran *Selling* again on March 23, carefully researching the program's audience response. It learned that 14,-100,000 saw the second run, compared with the 9,600,000 who saw the first. 171 stations carried it, 6 more than had carried it the first time. CBS Research also claimed "in the five cities with CBS-owned TV stations, 2,064 telephone calls were recorded in favor of the broadcast and 890 were critical of it."[14]

Following the broadcast, the remarks of Hebert, Laird and Agnew, as culled from statements, appearances and news conferences the three men had

---

* See Martin Mayer, *About Television* (New York: Harper & Row, 1972), pp. 254–68. Mayer has said, "Few episodes in the tangled history of news broadcasting have been so generally discreditable to so high a proportion of the participants as the fuss attendant on *The Selling of the Pentagon.*"

held since the first telecast, made up a 15-minute critical reprise which Salant
then concluded with his own short statement.[15]

On April 18, CBS News devoted still another hour to "discussion of the
substantive issues" raised by the program. Salant said:

> I would note that no one in the government requested time to reply
> to the original broadcast. We are presenting the broadcast because we
> feel that a continued discussion is in the national interest. The discus-
> sion will not deal with the specific criticisms leveled at CBS News'
> editing techniques employed in the original broadcast, which are a
> matter of controversy and under official investigation.[16]

The program was scrupulously balanced. Four experts on Pentagon affairs, equally divided pro and con, were present: Senator J. William Fulbright;
Adam Yarmolinsky, a member of the Defense Department under McNamara
and a Pentagon public affairs critic; Arthur Sylvester, former Assistant Secretary of Defense from 1961–1967; and Brigadier General S.L.A. Marshall
(Ret.), military historian and syndicated columnist. George Herman anchored
the broadcast, which was overseen by Executive Producer Burton Benjamin.

By May, Colonel John A. MacNeil of the United States Marine Corps
had filed a $2-million libel suit against CBS and the Washington *Post*, which
then owned WTOP-TV, the D.C. outlet for CBS. He charged CBS "willfully
and wantonly" rearranged a film of a lecture he delivered in Peoria, Illinois,
with the result that he appeared to say what he did not say. The colonel said
the documentary made him appear to be an officer deliberately disobeying service regulations, that he appeared to be on a junket "crisscrossing the country," that he appeared to be propagandizing for the Caterpillar Tractor Company.

Another interviewee, Assistant Defense Secretary Daniel Z. Henkin, criticized the network for presenting his statements on the program out of sequence
by rearranging questions and answers. His interview, which lasted 40 minutes,
he said, was boiled down to 2:04 minutes of airtime. Because his letter, refut-
ing the documentary, was so long, Henkin found it necessary to index it.[17]

Still another potential stricture facing Salant was the Fairness Doctrine,
"which requires that on controversial issues both sides be given a reasonable
amount of time" to discuss them. Salant, from the very beginning, had been
sure to "balance" whatever shows in reaction to *Selling* were broadcast. At
the same time, he carefully controlled these productions. CBS News was allowing its opposition to shoot at it but it also was handing out the kinds of guns
and bullets they could use.

It was not a happy time to be a broadcast crusader. Aside from direct
criticism, other methods available to government officials in 1971 for influenc-
ing network policy were suggestion, surveillance and open solicitation. News
departments were forced into lengthy and expensive defenses of their programs.
Affiliates and networks squabbled about how and who presented network news.

Both were kept on edge by the fact that "someone with the power to punish was watching from Washington."[18]

No one deserves plaudits for his behavior concerning the entire episode of *Selling*. Some of the editing was certainly suspect, and CBS News followed up aspersions about its editing with a complicated directive to its news people about editing film procedures that made the news division look even more suspect. Needless to say, neither Congress nor the Nixon Administration deserved commendation.

Salant once had Herbert Klein, Nixon White House communications director, visit him.

> Klein was up here at the Columbia Journalism School for some lecture . . . and he called me and said it was important. He wanted to see me. Well, he sat there and made small talk, and then he reached into his pocket and pulled out what seemed to be the back of an envelope with a lot of scribbling on it, and he said, "The Vice President didn't see that *60 Minutes* segment you did on 'The Young Agnew' but Mrs. Agnew was very unhappy." In that program we explained that Agnew wasn't a very good student; we tried to get his records from high school, but at government request they had been withdrawn. I don't remember whether Klein said Mrs. Agnew had passed her unhappiness directly to him or whether she had passed it on to Mr. Agnew who had passed it on to Mr. Klein. Anyway, he was up to complain about it.
>
> So I said, "We have a letter to the editor segment in *60 Minutes*. If you or Mrs. Agnew or the Vice President want to react to it, we would be glad to put that in the next broadcast." We never heard from them again.[19]

If anyone is to be praised, it is probably Stanton, Salant and Davis: Stanton, for refusing to turn over sources to congressional investigators; Salant, for keeping CBS News on target by continuing to put out hard-news documentaries (*Justice in America,* Part I, ran April 20, two days after the hour-long *Perspective* broadcast); and Davis, for demonstrating a rare talent to write and produce exemplary investigative documentaries. He has written three of the best American news documentaries of the sixties and seventies: *Hunger in America, Selling* and *Hearts and Minds,* a theater documentary about Vietnam.

On May 7, 1971, during the first half of the ceremonies, which were telecast simultaneously from the New York Hilton and Los Angeles Century Plaza hotels, CBS News was awarded two Emmys for documentaries. They were: *The World of Charlie Company* and *The Selling of the Pentagon.*

Part Four / EVENTS

Introduction

UP UNTIL NOW we have been looking at TV news and theme documentaries as they have been used in theory and practice: what they are, how they evolved, who prominently developed and applied them from 1965 to 1975.

Now we must look at them in a still wider context. We must ask just how they related to the big, important stories — ones that ran continuously for days, weeks, months and years.

There is a danger in reviewing a decade solely in terms of one particular form of news: we can credit that news form, in this case, news and theme documentaries, with powers which they may or may not have possessed. When a hubbub has resulted because of a particular broadcast of a particular documentary, we realize that documentary can strongly influence us. On seeing a certain show, you may have thought, ''Now I wouldn't have known anything about that mess if I hadn't just seen that documentary.'' *The Selling of the Pentagon, Pensions: The Forgotten Promise, The Guns of Autumn,* or the earlier *Hunger in America* — all these documentaries caused strong reactions, ''made waves.'' And if they hadn't been produced and telecast, most of us would know nothing about the issues they explored.

This part — EVENTS — deals with stories *we did know about*. We learned about them through newscasts, live accounts and News Specials. They were big, important, continuous.

If anything demonstrates how widely documentary approaches had permeated into the general process of telecasting news, it is the widespread coverage these monumental stories received.

Small-d, big-D documentaries; newscasts and News Specials, live coverage and mini-docs; whatever name you want to give it, TV documentary was there.

But how effective was it all? How did commercial network news and theme documentaries relate these pivotal events to the American people? What was covered concerning the great social issues of the day? How did TV documentary report Vietnam? President Johnson? Watergate? Henry Kissinger? How well did TV documentary use its tools: talking heads, in-depth interviews; A- and B-rolls played simultaneously to augment scenes, situations, personalities; actualities and videobites; the use of tape, film or live cameras? How effective were they?

This part tries to tell you.

18 / The Despairing Eye

Urban Strife: 1967

THE CBS NEWS HOUR reached its eighth season in 1967 still averaging four programs a month. Most shows either were *CBS Reports* or News Specials, although a new entry — *Who, What, When, Where and Why?*, featuring Harry Reasoner — was scheduled to start August 22. Sponsored by Connecticut General Life Insurance Company, it would consist of ten half-hour and four full-hour programs.

New individual hour-long programs were planned for 1967–1968. One would mark November as the fiftieth anniversary of the Bolshevik Revolution. Others would cover congressional ethics, the United States Post Office, the black middle class, a history of Vietnam ("the broadcast will attempt to trace some of the history of events in Vietnam leading up to the present"[1]), the ministry, Broadway, the new Left, "loneliness," Barry Goldwater's Arizona, the West Germans, longshoreman-philosopher Eric Hoffer's world, Singapore and its prime minister, Lee Quan Yu, artist Andrew Wyeth, actor-politician Ronald Reagan, spies, the State Department, the *Queen Mary*, college football players and even the anatomy of a demonstration, an attempt to spotlight a typical "race" demonstration.

Some of these ideas survived and went on to become outstanding productions. Others never were to make it. One reason was the emergence of past program ideas into final form. Another, the reluctance to abandon program formats that in the past had proved to be good audience lures; such as the Rooney essays or the various "tests." CBS News had discovered the public also liked "literary" theme documentaries. So a viable mix seemed to satisfy just about everybody, although one last consideration also was a nagging concern: the omnipresent need to do as well or better than the news division had done previously. But even that worry was overcome. Looking back at what was finally broadcast by CBS News in 1967, we find that one of the best American television documentaries ever made appeared in that year: Jay McMullen's *The Tenement*.

The Tenement, although obviously cast in the investigative mode, was more than just a hard-news commentary about what it was like to live in a Chicago black-belt slum. Broadcast on February 28, 1967, it was impressionistic, complete with poetical touches one rarely sees on a commercial TV news documentary. According to *Variety:*

> In a welcome departure from the traditional CBS format for the documentary, there was no explicit statement of point, no pat summarizing, no overt urge to take action. The film . . . spoke pointedly enough for itself of the loneliness, boredom and despair of those who live at the socioeconomic bottom of the cities.[2]

I rate *The Tenement* very high. Repeated viewings of it do not bore you. It remains as fresh and as vivid as the day it was filmed. It isn't history, maybe because its subjects, poor black Southern migrants adrift in a northern city, come across on camera — with their strong dialects, simple pieties and open honesty — with an impact that time cannot erase. Equally good, perhaps more important documentaries, such as *Pensions: The Forgotten Promise, The Selling of the Pentagon,* or *The Guns of Autumn* — programs that have stirred up widespread reactions — don't, on successive viewings, hold up in the same way as does McMullen's marvelous commentary on slum life. It has an immediacy in each scene that, though perfectly literal and real, also happily connotes so much more.

The Tenement took eight months for Jay McMullen, assisted by Perry Wolff and Jules Laventhol as executive producer and associate producer, to write and complete. An hour of black-and-white film, it consists mainly of talking heads of the various tenants conversing either with one another, McMullen or with narrator Hughes Rudd. We are at 3823 South Ellis Avenue, where nine families live, composed of 48 children and 17 adults. These people, as Rudd says, "speak for themselves without the interruption of statistics or the views of experts."[3]

We watch the day unfold: at dawn, throughout the morning, hour by hour until 10:00 a.m., when the shouting rag man comes by; on through the afternoon until 2:45 p.m., when the mailman calls, to be followed by the huckstering cries of the watermelon man and a confrontation down front between police and two young suspected car thieves; later, at 10:00 p.m. we see kids out, still standing aimlessly on the tenement front steps.

By enlisting the hours of the day and night, McMullen shows how long and tedious and unfulfilled they were. Each hour punctuated the real day's passage, when actual physical acts took place. At the same time, the passing hours also served to show themselves as the major cause for great blocks of mental insensitivity to expand within each tenant, gradually agonizing and stultifying each tenant into losing touch with life as it really could be:

I never look forward to a new day.
Why not?
It's nothing to look forward to.[4]

In the closing third of the documentary, after we have become acquainted with the building and its occupants (five of the nine families living here in the summer of 1966 were headed by women, only two were headed by fathers[5]), we see a new sequence, based on the change from the dull, hot nothingness of a slum summer to opening day in September at Donoghue Elementary School. It's a frightening time for young tenant Derek Milner, his first school day:

Second Teacher: All the boys and girls are waiting to meet you. Won't you come over and meet them with us?
Derek: No.
Second Teacher: Oh, come on, let's go. They want to meet you. Boys and girls, this is a new little boy. Can you say, "Good Morning, Derek?"
Children: Good Morning, Derek.[6]

McMullen closes with yet another seasonal rite, Christmas, showing scenes of the tenement in snow and cold, which contrast with the documentary's slow opening shots on an early summer morning. Men stand around an oil-drum wood fire, keeping warm. The sequence ends with Mrs. Georgia Johnson, who has lived here for 15 years, moving away in February of 1967. The tenement, it appears, will be destroyed as part of an urban renewal program. Soon, all must leave. Standing in the snow, watching two men load her furniture and goods onto an old truck, Mrs. Johnson, a religious, middle-aged person with a massive, long-suffering face, says: "I'm glad to move to this other place. Has churches all around and that's really what I love. I love churches."[7]

What makes *The Tenement* so fine is the realization we have in watching it that its people are being forced to live so hopelessly, never to know the many pleasures that so many of us take for granted — Christmas gifts, a loving husband or father, an overriding interest in doing one's job satisfactorily.

Reviewing *The Tenement*, Jack Gould said:

The hour was an unalloyed saga of defeat, purposefully disturbing in its social implications but strangely unsatisfactory in its failure to solicit even a trace of opinion or counsel on what could or might be done.[8]

The fact nothing was done or can be done is exactly why the program retains its power. Parts of New York City — at this writing 14 years after *The Tene-*

ment was broadcast — still have hollow husks of buildings standing uselessly empty. Other cities, including Chicago, are not better off. *The Tenement* points out a dead end: some of us, to paraphrase William James, are winners who win big, while the opposite is true for others. It's those "others" at which *The Tenement* unflinchingly looked.

DEATH AND VIOLENCE: 1968

1968, a year beset with contention and strife. Two progressive leaders: Dr. Martin Luther King, Jr., and Senator Robert F. Kennedy were assassinated. Draft resistance, protests by those who considered the draft an immoral system for getting manpower to fight an immoral war, caused conflicts everywhere. King's successor, the Reverend Ralph D. Abernathy, led 50,000 in May and June to a Washington, D.C., encampment called "Resurrection City." In the East, Columbia University students and, in the West, San Francisco State students seized campus buildings, sometimes destroying their interiors, imprisoned administrators and confronted police who tried to stop them. Youth everywhere attacked the system, struck out at all the impersonal, mechanistic, dehumanized qualities they saw pervading society.[9] The Sorbonne riots in Paris, Russian repression of the liberal Dubcek regime in Czechoslovakia, the United States commitment to Israel (similar to Russia's commitment to Czechoslovakia in that both powers would tolerate only forces favorable to their interests), the ongoing American intrusion in Vietnam — all were part of a division between belief in new emerging values and stubborn attempts to retain the status quo. At the very time the world's Western powers were undergoing a cultural revolution, governmental acts often remained distended, intricate, pervasive, inefficient and amoral.

Evidences of this primal conflict between authority and the individual abounded in documentary. The Emmy winner, *Hunger in America,* for example, accused the United States Department of Agriculture of being unwilling to use its emergency powers to bring food to hungry people in any county in America. Broadcast on May 21, the documentary focused, in one instance, on hunger in South Texas, and produced an outcry from then Agriculture Secretary Orville L. Freeman, congressmen from that area and others.

Later, the FCC reviewed these complaints and dismissed them. Freeman said the program's producers charged that ". . . the Department of Agriculture protects farmers, not consumers, and especially not destitute consumers." Freeman said, "This is a lie," that "this department has distributed 7.9 billion pounds of food, at a cost of $1,320,560,000, and another $279.7-million worth of bonus food stamps to needy families."[10]

The FCC commended CBS for doing the program, then declared its interest in it was whether or not it was slanted. Other complaints had charged that a newborn baby shown at the opening of the program was falsely portrayed as having died of starvation, that a sequence in a San Antonio food market was staged and that CBS attempted to induce a San Antonio physician to make dramatic statements about hunger.

The commission discovered that the baby had died of complications of premature birth. Still, Producer Martin Carr and others at CBS News insisted that hospital officials had said death was due to maternal malnutrition.

The FCC had deferred action on renewal of some broadcast licenses held by CBS-owned-and-operated stations but said, in the future, it would not do this "unless extrinsic evidence of possible deliberate distortion or staging of news" was uncovered. The commission found no evidence of this in *Hunger in America*. [11]

As for Freeman's complaints, a congressional inquiry looked into governmental food programs and Congress later voted an additional $200-million to buttress such programs. Reaction to the program, meanwhile, had been so widespread, CBS repeated it on June 16, editing the introduction and close so as to accommodate both the praise and the censure the original telecast had received.

Big city ills were the subject of a three-part series, *The Cities,* produced by Ernest Leiser and shown successively on June 24, 25 and 26. Industrial waste in Cleveland, suburban lifestyles in Crenshaw (a suburb of Los Angeles) and urban racial issues in Brooklyn's Bedford-Stuyvesant were shown, plus various schemes to reconstruct our cities. [12]

Another series, the work of Perry Wolff and Andrew Rooney, *Of Black America,* won an Emmy for its first episode, *Black History: Lost, Stolen or Strayed,* broadcast on July 2. Six other programs followed, appearing mostly in the low-viewing weeks of July and August.

FAMILIES: 1969

American curiosity about British royalty was the basis in 1969 for CBS buying *The Royal Family,* a $360,000 production made for BBC and the Independent Television Network in Britain and sold here and to Canada and Australia at "secret but record prices." Produced and directed by Richard Crawston, *Family* was broadcast on September 20 from 7:30 to 9:00 p.m., sponsored by Sears Roebuck. Anthony Jay's script was narrated by Michael Flanders. Photography was by Peter Bartlett. For a year the crew, working in 75 locations, shot 43 hours of film for the 105-minute program (American version: 78 minutes). The documentary was a public and private look at Queen Elizabeth II as queen, wife, mother and member of the ruling house of Windsor. She was seen feeding carrots from a silver platter to the horse on which she had just reviewed her troops; she then related how she tried to keep a regally straight face at a reception when a footman facetiously told her "Your Majesty, your next audience is with a gorilla." Although her next visitor was an official one, in walked a man who did indeed look like a gorilla and the Queen couldn't hide her laughter. The program was literally an inside view of her various

palaces. The camera followed her to Windsor, Balmoral, Sandringham and
onto the yacht *Britannia*. The Master of the Household was seen supervising a
staff of 200 who tidied 600 rooms and wound up 170 clocks just in the confines
of the London palace alone.[13] Much of the program was devoted to a transpor-
tation theme — a view of the Queen in constant transit — aboard a ship,
seated in a plane, touring in a car, atop a horse.

The year closed with an important CBS News Special: *The Battle of East
St. Louis,* broadcast on December 30. Perry Wolff was executive producer;
Peter Davis, writer-producer; and Hughes Rudd, reporter. It illustrates how a
documentary can exploit a social science experiment in sensitivity training by
becoming itself a more intimate vehicle through the use of cinema vérité techniques, providing visual qualities usually absent from commercial network
documentaries. The program covered a three-day session in May at a YMCA
camp, with 18 hostile blacks and whites — all citizens of beleaguered East St.
Louis.[14]

Rudd stated at the start that what was being tested — though the results
would be difficult to measure — "was the capacity to change: in individuals,
in a community and, by implication, in a society. That's why CBS News went
along to the Battle of East St. Louis."[15]

To gain intimacy the session was split into two small groups. One of
these was made up of a community psychologist; his assistant, Jack Porche, a
former policeman who now works with the Illinois Commission on Human
Relations; Tom Buckley, a rookie just joining the force; Alvin Toldin, who
was trying to be loyal to both the force and the black community; Tom Hunter,
another policeman; and Bill Jeremias, "whom the blacks in East St. Louis
called — with no affection — 'a chunky honky'."

On the community side were Claryce Braddix, "who had mistrusted the
police since her son became a militant, and Bill Luckett, whose bitterness is
typical of every street in every city."[16]

The first day of the session:

Luckett: Did you catch them with the clothes?
Jeremias: The clothes were on the man's arm. They were taken away from
   him.
Luckett: Aw, no, Jeremias.
Jeremias: I still want to know — what good did it do youse?
Luckett: We was mad, man. We had to blow off the steam somewhere. You
   know, 'cause like I said, you can be pushed so far. You know. And we
   knew that the police department had a grudge against us.[17]

On the second day, Claryce Braddix, feeling better toward the police,
was still unwilling to talk about her own protective attitude toward black men.
Members of the group felt she tended to smother the new self-confidence black
men were beginning to assert.

Dye: You know she's in this — she's constantly playing this role of mother. Like one of the guys might have a piece of nap on his shirt, you know, and she walks up to him graciously and takes it off.

Mrs. Braddix: . . . but what my feelings are — I need, I have a very definite need for my black men.[18]

Six months after the sensitivity training session, CBS News returned to East St. Louis in the fall to hear statements that measured the distance between May and December:

Jeremias: At the session we had, I got to know the people down there, I mean they were right in what they were saying. They've got a problem; I've got a problem. We just have to work together to work this out. The days of punching people in the nose for doing something wrong, them days are over. . . .

Luckett: These three days sort of helped me out a little bit, you know, because I saw something that has never been did (sic) before. When I first went to the session, I looked upon Jeremias as a racist pig policeman, but since the session when I see Jeremias, he appears to me as an individual, as a white man to a black man.[19]

AMERICANA: 1971

Charles Kuralt, in addition to his *On the Road* chores, narrated two documentaries about American families in 1971: *Kids! 53 Things to Know about Health, Sex and Growing Up* and . . . *But What If the Dream Comes True*.

Rooney wrote *Kids!*, which was produced by Joan Richman and Vern Diamond and broadcast on January 27. It was largely a failure because although it was enlightened and sensible about "such problems as drugs, dress, health and diet among the young," it treated sex too gingerly and kept its aim "so narrowly middle class as to make it suspect to anyone who is not and some who are."[20]

In November, Kuralt narrated the superb . . . *But What If the Dream Comes True*, with Perry Wolff as executive director and Robert Makowitz as producer-writer. The latter traveled to Birmingham, Michigan, and spent eight weeks with the Greenawalt family — Sam, Jane and their three children. At the time, Sam was the 41-year-old senior vice president of a Detroit bank, "a white Anglo-Saxon Protestant committed to the ethic of hard work and responsibility."[21]

The program really was about suburbia. Birmingham was "a community of peers, living in physical, though not emotional, isolation from the explosive problems of the cities."[22] Like most suburbanites, the Greenawalts did things for their children. Sam worried "about his son not being able to 'relate' to a boy who had nothing. . . . 'One of the reasons we moved to Birmingham was to insulate him in that (sic), but I want him to grow out of it, too'.''[23]

And Jane Greenawalt frankly admitted: ''And now I have my three kids, my husband and I. I'm not conscious of wanting more for myself.''[24]

The documentary was several extended interviews within which the Greenawalts came to life. It climaxed when three black boys from Detroit arrived as dinner guests. Again, emphasis was on giving the children something — ''to give their children their first knowledge of the world outside while protecting them from being hurt by it.'' It pictured a schism all too common in American suburbs and cities everywhere.

AN ESSAY ON THE MAFIA: 1972

In mid-summer, on June 25, 1972, CBS News produced a sparkling News Special: *An Essay on the Mafia,* written and produced by Perry Wolff, directed by Howard Stringer and featuring Luigi Barzini and Nicholas Pileggi. Barzini had narrated *The Italians,* had written several books, including *From Caesar to the Mafia* and, as a member of the Italian Chamber of Deputies, had served on a committee overseeing the Mafia. Pileggi had a magazine piece on Mafia activities running in the June issue of *Life* magazine, was a 16-year veteran with the Associated Press and, at the time of the broadcast, was working on the staff of *New York* magazine.[25]

CBS had preempted *The CBS Sunday Night Movies* to run the *CBS Reports: The Mexican Connection* at 7:30–8:30 p.m. EDT, followed by Wolff's *Essay.*

The theme of *Essay* was to show the Mafia as ''a corruption of some absolutely wonderful virtues of the Southern Italian.''[26] To do this, Barzini talked about Italian-Italians and Pileggi, about Italian-Americans.

The Southern Italian, according to Barzini, resents outside authority and takes care to keep things within his own family. ''These honorable people use the word 'Mafia' to mean an attitude, not an organization. Mafia can mean proud and secretive in the face of authority.''[27]

Thus, Barzini claimed, over two million immigrants left Sicily and Southern Italy for America, clinging to two tenets: only the immediate family could be trusted and the rest of the world would be hostile.

Preyed upon by their own padrones or work contractors, unable to understand English, forced to take the meanest sorts of work, the Italians clung to their ways. Then something happened according to Barzini:

> To all Latins, Prohibition was a Protestant Anglo-Saxon madness . . . here they were, these old men, with a still in the cellar and the people outside Little Italy willing to pay dollars for what cost only a few cents. All it took was organization. And the little organization called the Mafia was in big business in America.[28]

Pileggi picked up the narration to explain to viewers that Americans see the Mafia, not as a group of so-called families informally united by undeclared mutual bonds of self-interest, but as corporations, complete with executives and stockholders. The word "families" best described the Mafia, and as long as the agreements between families held up, all was well, but when they were broken, one violent death followed another in bloody succession.

Much attention was given in the documentary to Joe Colombo. Wolff used an extended tease — that is, cut directly into the footage before making any kind of formal introduction to the program — to detail that day in June, 1971, on Mulberry Street in New York, when the folks in Little Italy were on their way uptown to attend a rally at Columbus Circle to celebrate Italian-American Unity Day. During the tease, the program managed to show the circumstances of Colombo's wounding by one Jerome Johnson, who also was almost immediately shot; it showed some of the Colombo "family" who were destined to die soon after Colombo died; and it ran a long interview (which was set within the attention given Colombo and his fellows), between Pia Lindstrom and an anonymous man who resented her even asking him questions.

> *Pia:* Can you describe anything?
> *Man:* I don't know anything.
> *Pia:* How do you feel about it?
> *Man:* You can't print it. That's it.[29]

Reporter Pileggi told viewers why Colombo was killed. Mafiosi, following the old peasant rules of secrecy and quiet, always spoke carefully in public. According to Pileggi, in 1967, the New York police arrested a number of men at La Stella restaurant in Queens. One man, Joe Colombo, hid his face from the camera. But three years later, in 1970, Colombo "came out from the quiet." The FBI and the press had been harassing Italian-Americans and Colombo wanted his say:

> I have always maintained and said there is no Mafia, there is no Cosa Nostra; and I said that this is only a harassment of the Justice Department, of the Administration and the law enforcement agencies. . . .

Pileggi then spoke:

> In Mafia circles there was consternation. . . . The secret society had been Americanized. The question was, what kind of power was Colombo trying to build for himself? The sight itself was unthinkable to Colombo's peers — Mafia leader standing before 50,000 people in Columbus Circle — guarded by the police. So a year later, the mob shot Joe Colombo.[30]

Barzini, closing off the broadcast, said Americans should pay more attention to the Italian virtues — hard work among them — but more important, the pleasure of simple things: "a glass of wine; dining, not feeding; and the pride of craftsmanship."[31]

BLACK FAMILIES: 1974

Four Portraits in Black, which was telecast on CBS-TV from 9:00 to 11:00 p.m. on April 26, 1974, was a two-hour study of four black families who had climbed out of poverty to varying levels of affluence. It also was a history lesson, lifestyle lecture and seminar on social mobility, appealing to both blacks and whites. Produced and directed by David Fuchs, it was narrated by Correspondent Hal Walker.

"To our minds at least," Walker said, "the major unrecognized drama in black America is the movement from poverty and slums into middle income."[32] Six years after the death of Dr. Martin Luther King, Jr., Walker reported, "Half of all black families have moved from dependence and poverty to independence and middle income." He introduced some of these "upward strivers," but with reminders that poverty still is the usual lot of most inner-city blacks. And, among the middle class, the black father may hold two — even three — jobs, while the wife also works. They are moving up, Walker said, "because the black woman works more often than the white woman works."[33]

The documentary monitored the efforts of Willie and Minnie Mae Collins to break away from the Mississippi "bottomland," which they had left 17 years ago, and to carve out a better lot for themselves. In the words of a CBS News press release:

The Collins family in 1974 lived in a once all-white middle-class neighborhood of single-family homes on small plots on a tree-lined street in Kansas City, Missouri.

When they had gone North, they first tried St. Louis, but the going was so tough that Minnie Mae and the children had to go back home. Willie tried it again in Kansas City. He had a number of jobs by night and did lawn work by day. All through it, he saved five dollars a week. Finally, his family came North again to rejoin him. He got a job working the night shift at the local post office. With his savings, he eventually bought a car, then a lawnmower. The lawnmower was a business investment: Collins started a small gardening and landscaping business of his own. By day he was an independent businessman; at night he was a janitor at the same post office.

Minnie Mae Collins didn't have it easy either. As a young woman, she was a picker in the cotton fields of Mississippi — sometimes carrying 50 pounds at a time: Some 27 years and seven sons later, she had earned a high school equivalency diploma and was studying for her bachelor's degree. She supplemented her husband's salary by working in the local public library.

Willie and Minnie Mae Collins worked hard — they believed in work. Willie says to his son on the broadcast, "You can't get something for nothing. You've got to suffer for anything that's good. Even if it's time, you've got to spend that, too.

"I wish I had the opportunity that you have," he tells his son. "I believe I really could have been somebody." [34]

Walker noted that a national CBS survey of about 2,000 adults showed that college-educated black women were earning about as much as college-educated white women. "But if you take a black man with four years of college," he said, "you'll find that he earns about as much as a white man with four years of high school." [35]

Four Portraits also revealed that long-held attitudes by both blacks and whites still prevailed. "The overwhelming majority of whites," Walker reported, "continue to believe that blacks don't work hard enough, and the vast majority of blacks believe they are discriminated against." [36]

The last half hour was given over to a panel discussion, chaired by Walker: it featured the Reverend Jesse L. Jackson, the civil rights leader who headed up Resurrection City, the shanty town set up in 1968 in Washington, D. C., to dramatize the plight of the poor; Andrew Young, then a Georgia congressman; and Addie Wyatt, director of women's activities for the Amalgamated Meat Cutters Union.

A CBS News memo saw *Four Portraits* as "a comprehensive, graphic study of a completely new and hitherto untouched area" of the black American community. It also estimated that the program would attract 18 percent of the available audience, "thus earning a 9.5 average-minute rating or 6,290,000 average-minute homes." [37]

19 / War

VIETNAM: THE ADVISORY STAGE

LIKE THE MEANDERING Mekong River, war in Vietnam had been nearly endless. For more than eighty years, Vietnam (French Indochina) had been under the colonial sway of the French. That changed abruptly when the Japanese took over in 1940 only to find themselves contending with the wily Marxist, Ho Chi Minh, who was running the League for the Independence of Vietnam or Viet Minh. Later, after Japan's defeat in World War II, Ho was recognized as the legal leader of the Democratic Republic of Vietnam by the returning French.[1]

By 1946, Ho and the French were fighting one another. The latter recalled Bao Dai, a former emperor, and set him up in Saigon as the country's chief of state. Still, the fighting went on until the French were overwhelmed at Dien Bien Phu in 1954 by Ho's redoubtable defense minister, General Giap. That summer at Geneva it was agreed that Vietnam would be divided along the seventeenth parallel — above it, Ho Chi Minh would reign; below it, Ngo Dinh Diem and his family would oversee the bounteous southern regions. Elections in 1956 would decide unification.

But there was no voting. Vietnam became two regimes wallpapered over a common people possessing common traditions that extended back for centuries. Diem, by describing himself as president of the new Republic of South Vietnam, not Vietnam entirely, made a major mistake. In the north, meanwhile, the National Liberation Front (NLF) was formed, vowing to *unite* Vietnam! As Viet Cong guerrillas penetrated southern villages and hamlets, the United States stepped into the international morass left by the French regarding Vietnam.

194

Since Peary opened up Japan to the West, the United States has had an affinity for the Far East. That special relationship, however, was dashed after World War II when China became Red. Public opinion in America over this loss was thereafter always a treacherous shoal for any Democratic president. China was the major Communist power in Asia, and somehow it was our fault for having let it happen. Now, although America "ringed" China from South Korea through Japan, the Philippines and other island bastions in the Pacific, it could not afford to allow another acre of Asia to slip out of its hands. Where the Allies — let us be judicious — had failed to retain China after World War II, where the French had failed to retain Vietnam, America wouldn't fail; it would support President Diem in his efforts to establish a separate nation in southeast Asia. To do so, President Eisenhower set up a Military Assistance Advisory Group (MAAG) to train Diem's troops.

This was the start of America's involvement in Vietnam, the beginning of the advisory phase, when 300 advisors were sent to Diem.

By 1961, the advisors totaled 900. But a new president, John F. Kennedy, found them ineffectual against Viet Cong guerrilla tactics as well as the unpopularity of Diem and his family. So Kennedy pushed the figure up to 3,000.

Still, South Vietnam would not settle down. In 1963, Diem and his brother were murdered on orders from several South Vietnam generals who were encouraged by bitter uprisings against Diem's Catholic party and by self-immolations by Buddhists.

During the next year and a half in South Vietnam, ten governments rose and fell.

Then, in 1964, North Vietnamese torpedo boats attacked two American destroyers in the Tonkin Gulf. The United States ships drove off the boats after being repeatedly attacked. There were no American casualties and only one ship showed any mark of the encounter — a single bullet hole in its bulwark. Yet news magazines back in the States accepted Pentagon leaks about the Tonkin incident without reservation, playing up the PT boats' foray as if it had been a major action at sea.

Lyndon Baines Johnson, Kennedy's successor, asked and received a resolution from Congress giving him powers to "repel any armed attack against the forces of the United States and to prevent further aggression."

Observers thought that they saw what was happening up to this point rather clearly. Hanson W. Baldwin, military analyst for the New York *Times,* saw Vietnam not as just one war but four: a sanctuary war, aimed at alerting the North Vietnamese that we wouldn't tolerate their support and direction of the war in the south; a guerrilla war in the south, which must be won by employing ground troops; a third war to create a stable economic, political and civic environment in South Vietnam; and a final war, Baldwin felt, to win over the opinions both of the American public and of our allies that all the foregoing "wars" were right to undertake.[2]

At the same time, Senator George McGovern, later to be the Democratic Party's presidential standard bearer in 1972, saw a different store of events awaiting the nation in Vietnam:

> I think there will be a staggering loss of human life out of all proportion to the stakes involved. . . . In fact, I think it will be a lot worse; I think that there will be such enormous political instability, such enormous political chaos that indeed we invite a much worse situation than the one that exists today.[3]

Of course, hindsight has proved McGovern largely right. Yet both he and Baldwin spoke the truth.

What took place out there to cause us so many ghastly problems?

Broadly considered, Vietnam was unique for us. We never did declare war formally, and the Tonkin Gulf resolution, although exploiting a minor sea action as extravagantly as the Johnson Administration and the American press would allow, never did take hold upon the public so as to commit everyone to winning the "war." Dean Rusk, along with other Johnson Administration officials, struggled earnestly but unsuccessfully to implant the idea that our honor was at stake in Vietnam:

> There are costs involved in meeting your commitments of honor. There always have been. There always will be, but I would suggest if we look at the history of the last thirty or forty years that the cost of not meeting your obligations are far greater than those of meeting your obligations.[4]

Still another unconventional factor about Vietnam was the North Vietnamese ability throughout the entire conflict to retain sanctuaries in the south, in Cambodia and Laos. There were no stable battle zones, such as existed in Korea, where one army could contend with another army and bring it to heel. Guerrilla warfare abounded in all sectors of Vietnam as well as in its adjoining neighbors. In the early sixties, moreover, Washington was more concerned with Laos, for instance, than with South Vietnam.[5] At the time of the Tonkin Gulf incident, only 163 Americans had died in Vietnam, and the 16,000 American troops serving there were acting as "advisors," not fighting troops.[6]

We Americans really couldn't differentiate the enemy from friends — Vietnamese looked alike. Such a limitation could and did lead our troops to overreact against the innocent while trying to avenge themselves against a largely unseen yet deadly foe.

Moreover, we fought guerrillas with airpower and firepower. We never understood the political power of the NLF. Its troops were not just living in the villages but *under them!* Frances Fitzgerald has observed:

> Landing from helicopters in a village controlled by the NLF, the soldiers would at first see nothing, having no criteria with which to judge what they saw. As they searched the village, they would

find only old men, women and children, a collection of wooden tools whose purpose they did not know, altars with scrolls in Chinese characters, paths that led nowhere: an economy, a geography, an architecture totally alien to them. Searching for booby traps and enemy supplies, they would find only the matting over a root cellar and the great stone jars of rice. Clumsy as astronauts, they would bend under the eaves of the huts, knock over the cooking pots and poke about at the smooth earth floor with their bayonets. How should they know whether the great stone jars held a year's supply of rice for the family or a week's supply for a company of troops? With experience they would come to adopt a bearing quite foreign to them. They would dig in the root cellars, peer in the wells and trace the faint paths out of the village — to search the village as the soldiers of the warlords had searched them centuries ago. Only then would they find the entrance to the tunnels, to the enemy's first line of defense.[7]

In assessing the unique qualities of Vietnam, we must realize that probably the most important factor is that the American public consistently learned only of the horror of the war. It never had any reports or evidence to justify such a war. Unilateral belief always was lacking. College students, ordinarily first-rate draft fodder in wartime, were exempt from serving, thus leaving many of our most articulate youth at home to proclaim, "Hell, no! We won't go!" while men unable to enroll in colleges were sluiced down the Vietnam drain. And, even under the most auspicious occasions, an air of unreality clung to the government's actions concerning Vietnam. As Eric Sevareid said:

I know that Mr. Johnson always refers back to President Eisenhower and President Kennedy as though this were a continuous process without any essential change. It seems to me, reading the documents and statements going back eleven years, that the commitment today [1965] is not only different in degree and vastly so than the original ones, but in kind. . . . We were told over and over and over again until rather recently we would not have American fighting units fighting in the land of Asia.[8]

By 1965, two out of three Americans supported the American military presence in Vietnam, but two out of three of these pro-war Americans thought that the administration was not doing enough to get us out of there and one out of three was afraid that the fighting could erupt into a third world war.[9]

Though undeclared, America had a war on its hands — the first to be fought under the scrutiny of television.

Truth Fragmented into a Thousand Pieces: 1966

One strange aspect of watching the Vietnam war on television was that while it reenforced what we already knew well and familiarly, it also tended to repel us when we saw things which were unknown and unfamiliar. Not just seeing strangers: white, yellow, brown or black. Not just watching vistas —far away and foreign. Neighborhoods are as much a part of our minds as they are actual parts of the world around us, but without being experienced, without our knowing about them, they cannot become neighborhoods. Even though television was an electronic machine that could cut down the miles separating soldier from family and could juxtapose those people who were far away almost instantly on the screen with those near by, it only made a "neighborhood" in our minds when we could truly empathize with what we saw. Too often — and this is still true — all TV did for us, even when we were watching the most memorable footage on a news documentary, was joggle our minds in much the same way looking through a long-forsaken photo album reinstalls our past.

Back in December, 1965, for example, CBS News presented *Christmas in Vietnam,* hoping it would be as memorable and touching in 1965 as had been Murrow's *Christmas in Korea* back in the fifties.

"But even without Ed Murrow, without United Nations sanction, without the air of nobility," wrote Harriet Van Horne, "that usually surrounds any American endeavor abroad, this *Christmas in Vietnam* could have been a meaningful show. But it was inept, repetitive, terribly labored and — until the last heart-tearing scenes when a wounded soldier stumbled out of the clearing — it was all a mottled green bore."[10]

Her reaction is understandable. The set owner was not always equipped to comprehend what was happening on the screen right in front of his eyes. Vietnam was not Korea. America in 1965 was not America in 1955. Although nothing about Vietnam was familiar, "a viewer was struck immediately by the ordinariness of the setting," Van Horne writes in her review. "Before us was a clearing on the edge of the jungle in southeast Asia. But it might have been the backwoods of Georgia or Florida."[11]

Then the TV set began to show you things you had never seen before. Sergeant Jose Duenas talks about his job with CBS correspondent Charles Kuralt: how he "free-lanced" for mines while crawling through the jungle. The mines detonate easily, throwing pieces of sharp steel in all directions.

You meet Sergeant Ralph Bosalet, a Puerto Rican, who speaks about his wife and five children back home in Seaside, California.

Then you are in Seaside, watching the Bosalet children in their living room trimming the family Christmas tree. One of the children, a little girl, says her prayers, asking God to watch over her father.

Back abruptly to Sergeant Bosalet in Vietnam. His platoon has searched out a Viet Cong sniper. Another sergeant stumbles back out of the jungle into camera range, his leg badly ripped open by a mine. He smokes a cigar as medics attend him. But Sergeant Duenas, the "free-lancer," doesn't come out of the jungle. Wounded mortally by a mine, he has been picked up by another aid station where he later dies.

Then Christmas is commemorated at a common service in a roofless chapel as the chaplain blesses his flock:

> And God so loved the world he gave his only begotten Son, that whosoever believeth in Him should not perish, but have everlasting life. . . .[12]

The scenes roll on, involving you yet keeping you more or less a voyeur, a dispassionate witness, unaffected by these strangers swimming so eerily across your home television set. Were Sergeant Bosalet's wife and children too aware of the presence of the camera opulently recording them in their home? Was the camera too remorseless in bearing down unblinkingly on Sergeant Floyd after his leg was mangled? Who was the dead "free-lancer," Sergeant Duenas, anyway?

So far away, so different, so odd was this war when scenes like these were thrust up against the familiar life back home.

Vietnam was so remote geographically, psychologically and ideologically for most Americans that television news departments and the Johnson Administration faced enormous common difficulties in getting the war "understood." *Much of the difficulty was due to the public itself.* It didn't always believe what it read or saw. As early as December, 1965, an Opinion Research Corporation poll revealed that 67 percent of those sampled believed they only sometimes got the truth from the administration about Vietnam, while another 13 percent thought they almost never got the truth.[13]

A number of telecasts came out of CBS News from late 1965 through 1966 to help clarify administration actions as well as to describe what was happening in Vietnam. One of these was telecast in December of 1965. Writing in *Newsday,* Barbara Delatiner reviewed *The Battle for the Ia Drang Valley,* saying, "Despite the fact that most of the special consisted of film snatches previously seen on regular evening newscasts, it did have immediacy going for it."[14] Small wonder. Ia Drang (sometimes called Pleine) was the "fiercest action in Vietnam to date." American casualties in a single week suddenly exceeded "the average weekly rate of dead and wounded in the Korean war — 240 Americans killed, 470 wounded." "The United States is indeed at war," narrator Walter Cronkite reported, "a full dress war against a formidable enemy."[15]

Though immediate and vivid, as Delatiner noted, the broadcast was really handing the American public some bad news, as delivered by Morley Safer:

> Ahead lie even higher casualties — a point that every GI and every general in Vietnam is acutely aware of — a point that many feel has not been fully grasped at home.[16]

The program also tried to clarify the new, unusual tactics being employed by both sides. What appeared to be an attack on a Special Forces camp, "a triangular-shaped outpost in the central highlands held by a handful of American advisors and 350 mountain tribesmen,"[17] turned out to be "a new kind of attack by a new kind of army."[18] Full-scale assault waves by two heavily armed regiments of North Vietnamese regulars tried to wipe Pleine off the map. American air power — ten bombing missions an hour around the clock — tried to stop them, ringing the defenders with a circle of protective "deadly fire." Only when a relief force fought its way in from Pleiku, 25 miles away, was the issue settled.

Safer stressed the uniqueness of this action: "Pleine was the jumping-off point for a new kind of operation against a new kind of enemy. . . ." Air cavalry came into its own at Pleine. Using "Hueys," armed helicopter gunships, the Second Battalion, Seventh Cavalry had marvelous mobility. "When you run out of targets, you change command posts, hit the enemy front and back." [19]

Despite these tactical innovations, the news remained at bottom, bleak. Casualties in Vietnam to date had been heavy. Since 1961 the South Vietnamese had lost almost 27,000. At Ia Drang, they lost 1,000.

Safer continues:

> American casualties up to now have been relatively light, but on
> Thanksgiving morning Americans picked up their newspapers to find,
> beside the usual Thanksgiving picture, headlines announcing that our
> casualties in Vietnam were the highest ever. . . . The toll was three
> times higher than any previous week of the war. [20]

"Combat — death — are still unrealistic to me," said one officer after undergoing Ia Drang. [21]

Confusion stalked this period from late 1965 well into 1966; it was a confusion compounded by several things: our open intrusion into southeast Asia, the effects of massive cultural quandaries at home — civil rights, draft protests, new stresses on the American family, whether black or white, ghetto or suburb — and the spread of a general malaise elsewhere in the world as others overseas watched helplessly as American hubris went its vertiginous way.

"The general idea that America seems to have is that she can run the world," a British woman said on *The Anti-Americans,* a CBS News Special Report broadcast on Tuesday evening, June 7, 1966. Its co-producers, Harry Morgan and John Sharnik, were two of the network's best. It sought to find out if we Americans were doing something wrong; or, as Charles Collingwood put it during the program, was our influence in the world dissipating; were others hating us for what we'd become?

Malcolm Muggeridge, former editor of *Punch* and now a broadcaster, was only too happy to give Collingwood an answer:

> A specter is haunting the American way of life, leisure. . . .
> There is one recourse — sex. In thousands of little identical towns in
> tens of thousands of drugstores, for just a few cents — the ecstasies
> of the flesh are all available, in words or pictures, (in) black and
> white or color." [22]

To help clarify his mind about the war, Walter Cronkite would go to Vietnam in the summer for three weeks to tour South Vietnam battle zones, Saigon and "other focal points in that nation." [23]

Meanwhile, earnest efforts were being made in New York to develop several major interviews for the series *Vietnam Perspective*. It would give the public as much exposure as possible to what the Eisenhower, Kennedy and Johnson Administrations had been up to regarding Vietnam. News officials realized the limitations of brief film clips and cursory reports from field correspondents on the evening newscasts. Documentary treatment, such as Charles Kuralt's report, *Christmas in Vietnam,* also had limitations: actualities and interviews certainly brought vivid incidents into the home — but they often failed to answer just why were we over there and increasingly taking on a fight between two factions of Vietnamese?

Jack Gould said of the CBS approach:

> The CBS series of quiet hour-long interviews with major administration officials on the Vietnam war has been a fine undertaking. The programs have been among the clearest expositions of the government's policies.
>
> The format used by CBS has been a welcome change from the usual discussion where one opinion is always instantly counterbalanced by an opposite view.
>
> The cause of balanced presentation of controversial matters is not invariably best served by a crossfire within a single program. It is often better realized by allowing one position to be thoughtfully elucidated without immediate contradiction and dealing with the contrary view at another time. In covering the Vietnamese issues, the TV objective must be information and education. [24]

For a long time, the American public failed to realize that the Vietnam war was an administration war, not a conflict sanctioned by a congressional declaration nor even buttressed by a massive uniform public opinion favorably disposed to it. This Asian war was a conflict instigated in Asia, but certainly engineered in Washington. As such, its direction was presently dominated by President Johnson and his men. Of Johnson's advisors, Dean Rusk, Secretary of State, and Robert McNamara, Secretary of Defense, served as the most forceful, articulate spokesmen.

What the administration said and when it said it, as well as what and when it failed to speak, were root features governing press coverage of the war — and there's more to be considered about these points. Suffice it to say that much of the confusion about the war and about our role in it was inevitable.

In 1966, CBS News was doing all it could to make Vietnam meaningful to its audiences. To cite an instance, it had preempted its excellent Arthur Barron documentary *Sixteen in Webster Groves* to broadcast the Special Report:

The Councils of War, telecast on Tuesday, February 8, at 10:00 p.m. EST, and featuring Cronkite, Marvin Kalb, Peter Kalischer, Roger Mudd and Eric Sevareid. Kalb and Kalischer had covered the Hawaiian meeting between President Johnson and the South Vietnamese leaders. Reporting from Washington were Sevareid and Mudd, who had been covering the Senate Foreign Relations Committee cross-examination of General James Gavin, advocate of the so-called enclave theory.

The formal result of the war council in Hawaii was a Declaration of Honolulu, wherein President Johnson and the Saigon leaders pledged to defeat the communists and to develop a better life for the Vietnamese people. The declaration stressed economic aid and social reforms; it ignored military policies almost in toto.

Near the close, Cronkite asked Sevareid what effect the Honolulu conference would have on "the senators who are so doubtful about the course of events."

Always the cerebral presenter, utterly devoted to the well-written statement of ideas, Sevareid never attempted to influence his audience by manipulating his vocal delivery or facial expressions — little tricks that are practiced by just about everybody else in the broadcast news business. And his ideas, as usual, were helpful to the viewer who was trying to make sense out of the Hawaiian meeting and the Gavin testimony. He said:

> What is really happening here, rather late in the day, since we are now in what has become a major war, is a formal and official raising of doubts by responsible men on Capitol Hill who are, after all, representative of the people — doubts concerning the justification of the war itself, its conduct, its legality and its ultimate outcome. . . . One of the great difficulties in this whole swamp is that we are trying to fight a limited war with unlimited rhetoric and an unlimited rationale. [25]

Earlier in the year, to cite another example of the network's devotion to achieving clarity over Vietnam, CBS had abandoned its *Sports Spectacular* on January 30 to give 90 minutes to congressional leaders to discuss the war. With Sevareid as moderator, those on hand were Senators John Stennis, Wayne Morse, Karl E. Mundt and Joseph S. Clark, along with Representative Hale Boggs. They were selected not so much for balance but to exhibit diverse views. All but Mundt were Democrats, but all were influential and articulate. CBS News wasn't allowing "equal-time considerations to thwart intelligent journalistic procedure." [26]

Election coverage, both at home and in Vietnam, was another source of diverse opinions for viewers. President Johnson, speaking on May 16 to a fund-raising party-gathering of Democrats in Chicago, put the war squarely into the upcoming congressional elections:

There will be some Nervous Nellies and some who'll become frustrated and bothered and break ranks under the strain, and some will turn on their leaders and on their country and on our own fighting men. There will be times of trial and tension in the days ahead that will exact the best that is in all of us. But I have not the slightest doubt that the courage and the dedication and the good sense of the wise American people will ultimately prevail.[27]

On May 21, Charles Collingwood interviewed Lord Avon, formerly Anthony Eden, who had succeeded Churchill as prime minister and had resigned in 1957 after the British Suez crisis. Twelve years earlier, at the 1954 Geneva Conference, he had tried to settle the war in Vietnam. Now, he was trying again.

(I believe) the United States and China (are) agreed on just one point: that neither of you is prepared to see the other in control of Indochina. Out of that, it seems to me that a scheme for the neutralization of what we used to call Indochina, that's Vietnam, Laos and Cambodia, is not impossible of realization.[28]

What if a negotiated peace caused the North to consume the South? Lord Avon countered that possibility by saying economic development by America of the Mekong delta would demonstrate good American intentions. He also felt calling immediately for elections wouldn't help matters, that reconstruction should take place for well over a decade so as to give everyone time to accept the new political conditions.

If there was any drift at all to the commentary and documentary programs at CBS News in 1966 regarding Vietnam, it was toward a broader understanding of what the United States was undergoing. The year before, CBS News had tried to make the war itself clearer by getting people such as Rusk, McNamara, Arthur Goldberg, and Generals Maxwell Taylor and Earle Wheeler to discuss how we could win.

Back in April, Vice President Humphrey had forecast a Great Society in Asia. In an interview on the nineteenth with Sevareid and Martin Agronsky, Humphrey said, "I think there is a tremendous new opening here for realizing the dream of the Great Society in the great area of Asia, not just here at home."[29] He argued that the Honolulu declaration was not limited to Vietnam but was, in fact, a Johnson Doctrine for Asia, "implying enormous commitments to the entire area running into the indefinite future."[30] Such hyperbole, covering aid to Asia "for a long, long time" was disturbing. Evidently, the administration's thinking was as unreal about Asia generally as it increasingly appeared to be about Indochina alone.

The interpretative emphasis placed on Asia rather than on Indochina alone continued. Eric Sevareid visited Vietnam in the late spring, then returned

to give a half-hour "Personal Report" on Tuesday, June 21, at 10:00 p.m.
EDT. It was one of the most remarkable broadcasts he ever made. In it, he
expressed "his opinions, interpretations and conclusions." Although truly personal — a marvelous accolade, in fact, to Sevareid's talents as writer and news
analyst — it was still in the expository pattern CBS News consistently followed
that year.

"I propose to sit here," Sevareid said, ". . . and talk about America in
Asia, about the war and about truth. This may set television back a long way.
We'll find out."[31]

Sevareid said the deepest forces activating Asians was neither war nor
ideological conflicts, but "the forces of the modern scientific-industrial revolution."[32] He also didn't believe the war in Vietnam was preventing the spread
of Chinese dominance throughout Asia. He said it was obvious that tensions
and covert hostilities in Korea, Laos, Thailand, and Cambodia were affected
by the war in Vietnam. All these places, he said, were potential sites for open
conflict. Yet he didn't feel our participation in the Vietnam war necessarily
quenched the chances of war between the United States and Red China, as the
administration had claimed.

> It seems to me that it is quite as logical to argue that our very
> presence in Vietnam, with this inevitable osmotic spread of hostilities
> across other borders, is just as likely to produce war with China,
> unless we are extremely careful and extremely lucky.[33]

As for the war in Vietnam, he said, "When men of the North (including
Premier Ky) are part of the government of the South, and vice versa, it is civil
war."[34] Not only was it a civil conflict between factions sprung from a common heritage, but the war didn't make sense: "Our grand strategy remains a
mystery, at least to me. We are fighting what is essentially a war of attrition,
the most disagreeable kind of war, counting progress by the number of bodies."[35] He would rather be able to report "weekly progress in terms of hamlets
restored or resettled, classrooms built, village chiefs who feel it safe to go back
and sleep in their own houses. That, after all, is what the war is about."[36]

The war, he said, was costing us about 15 billion a year, and "in terms
of last year's total expenditures for the war, each enemy soldier killed last year
cost us well over a million dollars."[37]

> Last summer began the big increase in the American fighting
> force. So this summer, tens of thousands of men will leave Vietnam,
> but they will be replaced, these veterans, by green troops. However
> good their training at home, all soldiers are green until they have
> gone through at least one real battle. And greenness costs lives.[38]

Probably because he has been given more air time than any other American commentator to express *his* evaluations of the ongoing news scene, Sevareid always has been properly diffident about displaying this unique privilege.

Thus, at several points throughout his report, he stressed the need for reportorial truth.

> It is a reporter's business to tell appearance from reality, rhetoric from fact. He often fails. In this Vietnam war, he fails unusually often because he is normally a stranger to the land, its language and its people. And because at every level — military, political, economic, psychological — the truth is fragmented in a thousand pieces. At each level, it is a jigsaw puzzle that no single man is able to piece together.[39]

Yet he went on to have his say and it was bleak: ineffectual or mysterious United States strategies; excessive costs in blood, guns and butter; the pervasive feeling that we were on the wrong course in Asia. "It is part of the duty of national leaders to speak from their faith, not from their fears. But it is part of the duty of the press to examine their faith, to raise questions that officials never publicly raise."[40]

Television critic Barbara Delatiner saw Sevareid's report as a "verbal column," "the most refreshing thing that's happened to TV journalism in ages."[41] She said, "The Sevareid column may be another gust in a good wind blowing through network news offices." Since Sevareid "just sat there at a simple circular desk and talked," only occasionally aided by "maps and other graphic aids," Delatiner felt there might be less reliance in the future "on performers" reading bulletins and more attention paid to reporters actually reporting on events they have covered and, thus, have come to understand. "The Sevareid broadcast could go a long way in convincing the television hierarchy that words are still as important as pictures."[42]

The News Special: *Inside Red China,* and Collingwood's and Safer's interview with General Westmoreland, presented in the waning months of 1966, were exercises in frustration.

The first, telecast on Tuesday, November 22 at 10:00 p.m. EST, was "a look at the daily life of the Chinese people under Communism, concentrated largely on people living in a geographical triangle formed by Peking, the Chinese capital; the industrial city of Wuhan, China's 'Pittsburgh'; and the nation's major seaport, Shanghai." A third of the country's population lives within this triangle.

Don Hewitt was executive producer; Palmer Williams, producer. The program was filmed on the Asian mainland for CBS News by a West German production team, with additional film on the Red Guards coming from unnamed sources. That was one frustration.

Another was the fact that diplomatic correspondent Marvin Kalb, who reported the program, was prevented from visiting the mainland himself. To accommodate that problem, three skilled narrators supported Kalb, who could only station himself on the Lo Wu bridge, which joins British Hong Kong and the Red mainland. They were Hans Koningsberger, Dutch-born novelist and journalist; Robert Guillan, associate foreign editor of the French newspaper *Le Monde;* and Dr. Han Suyin, physician and author of the novel. *Love is a Many Splendored Thing.*

These writers were able to provide personal observations from recent visits into China. "So what we have done," Kalb said, "is go to these three people, run the film for them in separate screenings and ask each in turn: What does this film do to your memories of China? Does this match up with your own observations? Is this the way it is?"[43] Practicing this technique certainly must have been another frustration.

Yet the broadcast offered the viewer some insights into ineffable China — where a family's human manure nourishes privately held garden plots rather than the collective ground of the commune; where flies no longer exist; where children sang:

The Red Army is not afraid of death.
It goes forward, it advances,
It combats and it wipes out the enemy.[44]

And where Koningsberger speculated:

I wonder if we are aware of how difficult it is to even express the simplest Western idea in Chinese, for instance. How this nation has for four thousand years considered itself the Middle Kingdom, the center of the earth . . . .[45]

The net result was a program completely dependent on outside sources — admittedly out of necessity — which enabled CBS News to look into China but still left the viewer, as Kalb said, "with more questions than answers about China. The problem is not merely that we cannot look in, except through the eyes of others, but the Chinese will not, or cannot look out."[46]

Filmed at General Westmoreland's Saigon headquarters the previous week, a half-hour interview, *Westmoreland on Vietnam,* was broadcast on Tuesday, December 27, in the usual 10:00 p.m. time slot. It featured Collingwood and Safer. Inevitably, the interview tried to become an accounting of American involvement in Vietnam in 1966 and of just where that involvement would lead. It only partially succeeded.

Harriet Van Horne said:

A viewer would say that Collingwood and Safer obligingly monitored the general's monologue, occasionally prodding him with a question intended to ruffle his bland, bureaucratic calm, or, at the very least, provide some fresh insight into the Vietnam war for the home folks. But the general was, as Collingwood noted drily, 'very cagey' in his responses.[47]

Westmoreland predicted a continued buildup in troop strength.

We will have a greater number of troops. Our tempo of operations will be increased. However, I predict that as a percentage of troops deployed, that there will be reduction in casualties.[48]

As for strategy, he would use a two-fisted attack: one fist swinging out at guerrillas in the populated coastal areas, the other hitting the enemy from the jungle.

He predicted the air war would continue.

Finally, when asked how long the war would last, Westmoreland said, "It will be several years. I cannot be more precise than that."[49] That statement was far from being bland and unsatisfactory. Anyone who heard it had to accept it.

A LAST LETTER HOME

A querulous note seeps into Vietnam reportage in 1967. CBS News tipped back and away from explanation and balance programs and moved toward expressing outright opinion. Emphasis and coverage migrated out of Washington across the Pacific to Vietnam. CBS News was trying, perhaps unintentionally, to stop a practice Jules Witcover said most of the press followed throughout the years of the Vietnam conflict:

> In the coverage of the war, the press corps' job narrowed down to three basic tasks — reporting whatever the government said, finding out whether it was true and assessing whether the policy enunciated worked. The group did a highly professional job on the first task. But it fell down on the second and third, and there is strong evidence the reason is that too many reporters sought the answers in all three categories from the same basic source — the government.[50]

That problem was especially serious for the Washington-based reporter. Hence the CBS effort to move whatever reportorial resources it could to Vietnam — polltakers, documentarists, correspondents — so it could more freely probe about to see what was happening.

On March 21, a CBS News Special Report: *The People of South Vietnam: How They Feel About the War,* sampled South Vietnamese public opinion (conducted by Opinion Research Corporation), wherein 48 percent of the South Vietnamese interviewed said life was worse than it was a year previously.

> One person out of five whose village had been damaged in some fight or other openly blamed the Americans. One person in nine of the whole sample could think of no reason why the Americans should be in Vietnam except to colonize it or to 'save face'.[51]

Harriet Van Horne's reaction to the broadcast in the *World-Journal-Tribune* was puissant:

In case you care, one third of the people would like to see the United States disengage itself from the fighting. Virtually nobody imagines he'd be better off under the Viet Cong. In general, the people are not so numbed by war that they no longer give a damn. They want peace — but not at any price.[52]

Earlier, on March 14, the network had carried *Saigon,* produced by Beryl Fox, who had been with the Canadian Broadcasting Corporation and who, in 1966, had stirred up considerable reaction to her prize-winning Vietnam study, *The Mill of The Gods: Vietnam.* She ignored political realities to look at social and economic realities in Saigon — how the war and the massive presence of Americans were affecting the city.

To a man, the Vietnamese interviewed — a newspaper editor, a taxi driver, dock workers — have contempt for their "saviors," blaming us for turning them into a "nation of beggars and thieves."[53]

WTIC, Hartford, did not carry the program, telling viewers that it was too onesided. "The emphasis was entirely on human values, on morality and money, disease and diversion, sex, sin and the black market."[54]

This matter of balance, of what the documentarist will say, arose in April when *Morley Safer's Vietnam: A Personal Report* was broadcast on the fourth. It came after Safer had served a long tour of duty, reporting the war as objectively as he possibly could.

Jack Gould took Safer to task for making his report too personal, saying that "his hour was wanting in balance," that we all share an intense distaste for war "but even a personal impression of the Vietnamese conflict might have been more searching in its elucidation of the Viet Cong's offenses against South Vietnam and also have included some balance sheet on the effect of United States participation." Gould found Safer's judgments superficial and concluded that, though he disagreed with United States policies in southeast Asia, "he has the obligation to report them."[55]

Safer's *Report* was another in a series of broadcasts (see Eric Sevareid's similar efforts) wherein the CBS News correspondent transcends his usual news role of offering viewers a stand-up on-camera report by stating quite candidly at the outset that he fully intends to speak his mind. Safer said "his last letter home" will be "full of prejudice and opinion," that it will be "a parade of quite vivid impressions." Thereafter, we are exposed to Americans — from Westmoreland to front-line grunts, from battle actions to rest and recreation, from Saigon to the countryside, watching on the ground or in the air aboard a helicopter gunship, hearing formal interviews or listening to intimate cassette-tape letters from home — impressions as intense, emotional and as personal as Safer can make them. He even tries to get General "Westy" to let down his hair.

Along with these successful attempts at intimacy, Safer also clearly exposes existence of a nutty duality in the Vietnam of 1967: "A kind of schizo-phrenia takes over, and you become both a believer and cynic."[56]

Time after time, Safer substantiates this absurd black comedy: "The war is always remote, never far away,"[57]

> *Lieutenant Sullivan:* It took a long time to realize it was real (fighting the VC). It seems like it's an act of some kind, not the real thing. You see a few holes in things and it gets real.[58]
>
> *Lieutenant Sullivan:* I'd be lying if I said I was glad to be here, but since I am here I'm glad I'm doing what I am doing.[59]
>
> *Helicopter Gunner:* You shoot at Cong. Anyway, when you come out on the run and then you see them and they come into your sights, it's just like a wooden dummy or something there, you thumb off a couple of rockets. Like they weren't people at all.[60]
>
> *Safer:* . . . death is the only certainty. Somehow all other truths seem fraudulent. To this reporter the dilemma is agonizing. With-drawal seems impossible. Yet persistence seems unfruitful and in a sense immoral.[61]

What was going on in Vietnam increasingly seemed to be exercises in madness. CBS News tried to elucidate, as best it could, the policies of the Johnson Administration. In some measure it succeeded, but not nearly so well as when it forsook policy explications for personal impressions and tried to tell what war was like firsthand. Nobody did that sort of thing better than Morley Safer.

TET

CBS News showed American viewers what it was like to assault a hill in Vietnam when it telecast *Hill 943* on June 4, 1968.

"The fight for Hill 943 will not appear in the history of the Vietnam war," CBS News correspondent John Lawrence said, reporting the broadcast. "It was an insignificant action near the end of what was called the battle of Dakato, and those of us reporters who were in Vietnam covering the larger campaign did not notice 943."[62]

Producer-cameraman Erik C. Durschmeid, soundman Sepp Thomas and assistant cameraman-soundman Hubert Le Campion witnessed the assault on Hill 943; it was so called by members of Alpha Company, 3rd Battalion, 12th Infantry, 4th Division, because it was 943 meters high. It was war fought close up, with cameras concentrated on three soldiers — PFC Jim Buckner, Sergeant Bruce Black and Sergeant Harry Charles Joseph ("J.C.") Coons — as they took part in a three-day assault on the hill. Acting and reacting through the three men, the camera watched an ambush, death, casualties, incoming artillery and air strikes, and the final charge of Alpha Company to the top of the hill.

But what was most unsettling was not the frightening close-ups. Why was the hill even taken? As Barbara Delatiner asked in *Newsday:*

> Why the uninhabited rise in the area of Dakato was fought for twice, taken twice and abandoned twice by Americans? . . . And why, as the final assault which the film chronicled took place, were there six-teen casualties, two men wounded by the enemy, one man killed by our own bombs, and thirteen injured by a misplaced American artil-lery barrage?[63]

CBS News attempted "close-ups" not only of our troops but of the en-emy as well. It was still trying to solve the problem it had faced in 1967: how to report the war as independently and as objectively as possible. How, in short, could it tell the American public what was happening in Vietnam without completely resorting to government news sources?

Another program, supervised by Burton Benjamin, the *CBS Reports: Viet Cong,* produced by James B. Faichney and narrated by Bernard Kalb, was telecast February 20 — just 21 days after Tet, the lunar New Year offen-sive by the North Vietnamese, struck Saigon, Hue, My Tho and Vinh Long, raiding, in fact, all major cities below the seventeenth parallel. *Viet Cong,* as a result, was hot news.

Tet was unexpected, well-planned and stunningly effective on several levels. *Viet Cong* tried to explain why. First, there were the efficient cadres of the Viet Cong. In Bernard Kalb's words:

> The Viet Cong live mostly in a jungle-camouflaged world that is bounded by tanks, air strikes and napalm. They have been at-tacked, assaulted, ambushed, bombarded, rocketed, mortared. The arsenal of the strongest military power in the world has been directed against them — with the greatest concentration of firepower in his-tory . . . and yet they have found a way of outwitting United States strategy.[64]

The Communist party in the North controlled the Viet Cong in the South by means of a People's Revolutionary Party. The Viet Cong had two arms: The National Liberation Front, an administrative group prepared to take over the South Vietnamese government, and the National Liberation Army, the forceful means for overthrowing the southern regime. Thus, the Viet Cong was an administrative corps and an army of guerrillas, capable of exacting obedi-ence from South Vietnamese through terror or patriotic supplication, whichever worked best.

According to Robert Shaplen, a senior Vietnam correspondent who wrote *The Long Revolution* and appeared on *Viet Cong:*

> One of the tragedies of the American commitment — of the American Establishment, if you will — has been we've always had

good people out there. . . . I have papers in my file showing a really clear, clear, understanding of what the problem was of meeting a revolutionary situation with a true counter-revolutionary thrust. But the nature of the American Establishment, of bureaucracy, is such that these things get sent home, get pigeonholed. Nothing gets done. . . .[65]

The lightning thrusts of the Viet Cong during Tet, despite accepting heavy casualties from the Allies, were to give the initiative to the guerrillas in over 26 urban centers located not only in the demilitarized zone but also below it along the South Vietnamese coast, extending as far as Quan Long. Many of these centers had earlier been declared pacified as a result of Allied search-and-destroy missions against the Viet Cong. Yet, as the fighting during Tet for the American Embassy in Saigon so graphically demonstrated, the VC could harass and terrify any portion of any city almost at will. The net effect of these unexpected raids was the forced recall of pacification teams from the rural areas to come to the aid of the stricken cities, which always had been considered "pacified." But this once again left the surrounding countryside helpless.

During Tet, if we discount the separate but vital action at Khesanh — where some 40,000 northern troops were trying to surround the Marine bastion — 540,000 United States troops were still contending elsewhere with 12 full-strength North Vietnamese divisions, which included 110,000 raiders operating throughout the South as part of Tet.

By now, Vietnam had become the longest military action in United States history. Yet, despite our involvement since 1961, the year the first United States soldier died in combat, the Allied effort was woefully caught off guard by Tet. CBS News Paris correspondent Peter Kalischer later was to say:

Tet offensive . . . killed once and for all in the minds of the people of America and also in the Johnson Administration the idea that a military victory was possible in Vietnam. . . . It was directly responsible . . . for President Johnson calling a partial bombing halt over North Vietnam in March and eliminating himself as a candidate for reelection.[66]

CBS News, taking advantage of the North's desire to talk directly to the American public, sent Charles Collingwood to Hanoi, the North Vietnamese capital. He was the first American broadcast journalist to see it in wartime.

His first *Report from Hanoi,* broadcast on April 6, in a half-hour program via satellite from Tokyo, revealed that Premier Pham Van Dong was willing to hold talks on the ambassadorial level in Phnom Penh, Cambodia. Collingwood said, "It's my strong impression that . . . Hanoi wanted to make a move and decided to make it through CBS News and me."[67]

In a later telecast, on April 16, he revealed other aspects of his eight-day tour of Hanoi:

One may not like North Vietnam's kind of government. 'I'm quite sure I wouldn't like to live under it. But there is no doubt that in wartime conditions it is effective.[68]

   This broadcast also was especially informative about the effects of American bombing raids over Hanoi:

On the morning of August 22, 1967, at 7:17 in the morning, a very busy time in this part of Hanoi, two large bombs were dropped by American aircraft. In this area . . . were seven houses of about three stories each. On the ground floor . . . was a drugstore, a market, a bicycle repair shop, a little restaurant. Five hundred and sixty-five people lived on the floors above. The bombs resulted in thirteen deaths and thirty-three persons injured. Now this site is kept open and a large placard has been put up . . . and the sign says, "The American aggressors must pay for their crimes."[69]

IRELAND AND KISSINGER: 1975

   The CBS News team that produced *The Palestinians* and *The Rockefellers* — Howard Stringer and Perry Wolff — presented a News Special on March 20, 1975, at 10:00 p.m. entitled *A Tale of Two Irelands*. It considered four broad areas: the protagonists, Catholic and Protestant, in their respective districts, clubs, pubs and meeting places; a history of Ireland from its earliest days of conflict with Britain; the leaders of the two camps, both of Northern Irish and English and of Republican Ireland; and, finally, the program looked at possible outcomes.[70]

   The production, another ethnic study by CBS News, used Jack Lawrence as its reporter. But rather than describe the delights of being Irish, the program revealed a people ridden with fear, hatred, violence and strife.

   Far different in scope and treatment was *The Ups and Downs of Henry Kissinger,* narrated by Charles Collingwood and broadcast on May 25 from 7:30–8:30 p.m. EDT; it was produced by Hal Haley and Bernard Birnbaum under Les Midgley's supervision. As usual, the CBS News staff was using a highly placed news source, possessing considerable power, through which to talk. Earlier, on April 21, Cronkite, Sevareid and Bob Schieffer had interviewed President Ford in much the same manner. If the Kissinger production differed in any way, it was in the attempt to trace the Secretary of State's transition from "German-Jewish immigrant" to teacher at Harvard to "a post traditionally reserved for white Anglo-Saxon Protestant types."[71]

   As for power, Kissinger had served two presidents and had retained "the most formidable concentration of foreign policy control ever put in the hands of any government official other than the President himself."[72] Harvard professor Stanley Hoffman said it was difficult to assess Kissinger's negotiating skill.[73]

Using a series of talking heads to flesh out Kissinger's portrait, Collingwood asked how it was that a former-Harvard-professor-turned-foreign-policy-architect ever picked up the title "secret swinger"?

Secretary Henry Kissinger: Well, as often in — in Washington, the truth is really less dramatic. I was at a party and a young lady came up to me and said, "Are you a swinger?" And I said, "I'm too busy to do any — any public swinging, and I don't want you to think that I don't do any swinging, so why don't you just assume I'm a secret swinger." It turned out she was a society reporter, and this is how the reputation started, and she printed it. . . .

Roger Morris (former staff aide, National Security Council): This is a man whose — whose personal vibrations are — are as complex as his diplomacy: very mercurial — very much on and off; can be very charming; has, as you know, a charming wit; can poke fun at himself and at those around him; can also be very cold, very distant, very angry, very stern and authoritarian.

William Watts (former Secretary, National Security Council): There is . . . a certain sense of the immigrant who made good, who has found in the United States a land of principles that he believes in, and (he) is more dedicated to these perhaps than sometimes others who grew up with them and took them for granted might be.

Senator Lloyd Bentsen (Democrat, Texas): One of his problems is — is ego . . . feeling that he can do everything better than anyone else, and therefore refusing to delegate. . . .

Stanley Hoffman: I have the sense of a man who always walked with a feeling of tragedy, a feeling that this is not a happy world. After all, the experiences he went through as a child were drastic ones.

Fred Bergsten (former aide, National Security Council): Excessively secretive, paranoid, excessively concerned about self-image; insensitive to personal relationships with those other than his superiors or those from who (sic) he is seeking some advantage.[74]

The documentary then considered Kissinger as a powerbroker, a man believing, Collingwood pointed out, "in the persuasive power of bombs." Both he and Nixon failed to comprehend Hanoi's fierce independence and will to win. For Kissinger, Vietnam was a nightmare.

Another albatross Kissinger found transferred automatically to the neck of whoever was Secretary of State was the Middle East where, in October, 1973, the fourth Arab-Israeli war erupted, destroying a cease-fire. Even though Israel kept winning victory after victory, the Big Powers eventually reconsti-

tuted another cease-fire. Then, that too collapsed, forcing Kissinger to undertake a personal shuttle to win a new peace in the Middle East. Over the next
17 months, he traveled more than 250,000 miles between Jerusalem and the
Arab capitals, trying to nail down an agreement. His efforts ultimately brought
him worldwide personal prestige.[75]

The program was exceptionally forthright and fair about handling Kissinger's so-called "ups and downs." At the time of the broadcast, some of the
bitterest criticisms were being leveled at him. Calls from Capitol Hill, where
he once had stood like a god, and elsewhere were demanding that he resign.
He didn't of course, but stayed on to help President Ford complete Nixon's
truncated term in the Oval Office.

VIETNAM: A WAR THAT IS FINISHED

It could never have been done on commercial television. But the best
way to have summarized the ending of the Vietnam war on CBS, NBC and
ABC would have been to have rerun financial backer Bert Schneider's and
producer-writer Peter Davis' *Hearts and Minds,* a made-for-theater documentary, on April 29, 1975 — and not the two-and-a-half hour retrospective portrait CBS News ran entitled *Vietnam: A War That Is Finished;* nor NBC News'
hour-long instant news special: *Special Report: Seven Thousand, Three
Hundred Eighty-Two Days in Vietnam;* nor the ABC News Special: *Vietnam:
Lessons Learned, Prices Paid,* which was broadcast for an hour-and-a-half
from 11:30 p.m. to 1:00 a.m.

Shown widely in movie houses throughout the country in 1974 and thereafter, *Hearts and Minds* received its title from President Johnson's observation,
"The ultimate victory (in Vietnam) will depend on the hearts and minds of the
people who actually live out there."[76]

Why was *Hearts and Minds* better than the three accounts that concentrated so directly on the collapse of the South Vietnam armies and air force?
Why was it better than CBS News' tremendous effort, which not only described current happenings in Vietnam but tried to portray events leading up to
the South's defeat? For answers, we must look both at *Hearts and Minds* and
at what CBS News prepared for that fateful day. But before doing so, we
should keep in mind that *Hearts and Minds* appeared on a medium that was
unlicensed theater. It was not prepared for commercial television, a medium
with which Davis was fully familiar. Davis realized that television was licensed
broadcasting, selling time segments for profit in order to support its entertainment, sports and news programs. After his experiences with *The Selling of the
Pentagon,* he, of all people, knew that to retain this privilege, commercial
broadcasting is beholden to the federal government, to program sponsors and
to its audiences in numerous overt and subtle ways that can inhibit what it says
and how it says it. Public service, ratings and advertising effectiveness were

but three influences permeating relations between government and the commercial network-local affiliate axis.

Other reasons are more obvious. Television is a home medium, for example. *Hearts and Minds* required no such disclaimers as the one given by Walter Cronkite after he was well into the CBS News Vietnam retrospective:

> Before we continue with the events of 1967, we should warn you that this next report contains some very ugly scenes. They're certainly not suitable for viewing by young children. Many adults, including this one, will find them difficult to watch, but we felt it was important to include them.[77]

Another consideration is the matter of an identifiable product. Much of this study has dwelt on this proclivity of television news producers to develop a predictable program identity that suits government regulators, sponsors and the general audience. A theater film doesn't have to fool around with such restrictions. A commercial network documentary does. CBS News, for example, emphasizes information and presentation. It always has tried to offer coherent news stories and documentaries, produced and narrated by competent, knowledgeable personnel. Davis, as we know, is an alumnus of this news organization, which through the years has been populated with so many outstanding news craftsmen. From CBS, an audience expects class.

Consequently, when we come to look at *Vietnam: A War That Is Finished*, we will again see that news programming precepts, which were first set down in 1965 by Dr. Frank Stanton, Sig Michelson and Fred Friendly, were still in effect in 1975. Maybe the subtle pressures mentioned above helped retain these precepts. Still, one of the "hardest" stories of the decade broke on April 29. CBS News gave it plenty of attention in a predictable, well-tested format.

HEARTS AND MINDS

Peter Davis made this outstanding nonfiction film to say something about Vietnam that hadn't already been said (nor, I might add, ever would be said) on network television news. He wanted to do three things that would make his production different from all other visual statements about Vietnam: "what elements in our own history had led us into the war, what we actually did there, and 'what the doing of it did to us'."[78]

Davis claimed to have shown his motion picture, which consists of nearly two hours of new and old color footage, "assembled with such skill and subtlety that we see the war on film as we seemed never able to see it in real life, either on TV, in the Pentagon or . . . on the battlefield or in the POW camps."[79]

Exactly so. Numerous theater and television documentaries have been made about war. Most of them, at best, are strident propaganda. But *Hearts and Minds* ranks near the top for honesty because it never was slipshod — even while looking at a Saigon coffin-factory carpenter, a company commander, a Buddhist monk, a Saigon whore, Saigon's national police chief-executioner, the United States Defense Secretary, General Westmoreland and LBJ. On hearing Westmoreland, combat veterans in theater audiences, according to Davis, "can't believe that their leaders really believe the same things they'd been taught in basic training. They thought that stuff was only to get them to kill."[80]

This full expression of a wide range of viewpoints is important in the war documentary. It counteracts the tendency to oversimplify complex causes and effects. It tends to water down emotional colorings of stressful situations. It respects scenic particularities.

Hearts and Minds has such range. Davis' production was similar to Marcel Ophul's four-and-a-half-hour *The Sorrow and the Pity,* a saga of World War II France under the Nazis, which also especially "realized the value of every point of view, of letting truth emerge." The interview with Fascist Christian de la Maziere, for instance, "has been rightly acclaimed as one of the high points of this film."[81]

Hearts and Minds avoided another pitfall which has confronted and overcome quite a few war documentaries: the question of perspective. When one is dealing with war footage, one has a choice: to either handle it as compilation, stitching sequences together according to topic or chronology, then treating them collectively as possessing some kind of overall meaning; or to accept particular instances that have occurred accidentally and organize them without paying detailed attention as to their sequence or to their collective coherence. One presents happenings that have taken place yet mean very little except — let us say — in that someone is hurting and/or trying to kill someone else. Terrible as they are, it's these brutal moments that make war such a compelling subject for documentary. They simply afford superb actualities.

As a result, a producer of a war documentary can use the first approach, which seems relatively remote and apparently sensible and rational to the audience, or he can opt for the more intimate look, which is open-ended and apparently senseless. The first approach was used in *The Anderson Platoon* (1966) when the narrator of this French documentary introduced the platoon to viewers, then predicted who soon would be wounded as artillery-in-action scenes were intercut with a Mass taking place in the field. An example of the second approach was Davis' depiction of the Viet Cong prisoner's execution by the Saigon national police chief, General Loan. Standing on a Saigon street, hands tied behind his back the young VC rigidly awaits death as a small pistol is raised to his temple and fired. Blood gushes forth as if his mortal head wound had been previously stopped up by a cork.

Both methods obviously have their drawbacks. The problem is not to allow one or the other to dominate an entire production. Although Davis didn't allow this to happen in *Hearts and Minds,* it frequently does in most war documentaries.

COLLAPSE AND SURRENDER

What brought about the exceptional coverage CBS News gave to Vietnam throughout an evening of prime time on April 29 was the unexpected abandonment of the Central Highlands in March by President Thieu. He had suddenly ordered all his troops out of that mountainous area, which, up to then, had always been considered by his American advisors as extremely difficult to defend. Yet, no one expected such an abrupt withdrawal. As a result, the South Vietnamese forces panicked and fled while, to the north, the North Vietnamese continued a coordinated, orderly offensive directed at both the Highlands and the coastal provinces.

The South Vietnamese Air Force, aided by hundreds of American civilian mechanics who were helping keep the South's planes in the air, was still flying two missions a day out of Bien Hoa, 20 miles from Saigon. But morale was high only among the air men; they were literally above the chaos and turmoil going on below, especially the refugee-glutted highways along the coast.

Soldiers and refugees alike flooded the roads south, impeded by police roadblocks, which were set up to prevent enemy sappers from getting into Saigon. Government civil servants fled the coastal areas and Highlands right alongside the Army. Most were Thieu loyalists. Thieu could only watch his followers desert him. Having made his decision to abruptly quit the Highlands, he did nothing as South Vietnam gradually fell apart, province by province, town by town.[82]

Thus the network knew the end was not too far off. Cronkite removed himself from the Evening News to begin work on an extensive retrospective that would highlight CBS News' coverage of the war between 1964 and 1975. He was suffering from a bad back, but he didn't let it stop him appearing on the history-making show. Besides Cronkite, it featured Collingwood, Morton Dean, Jack Laurence, Bruce Morton, Dan Rather, Morley Safer, Robert Schakne, Bob Schieffer and Mike Wallace.

Others to appear were Ed Bradley, Bruce Dunning, Jed Duvall, Murray Fromson, Bernard Kalb, Peter Kalischer, Charles Kuralt, Phil Jones, Ike Pappas, Bill Plante, Bert Quint, Eric Sevareid, Gary Shepherd, Richard Threlkeld and Don Webster.

Each had served in Vietnam at one time or another; each had been asked to concentrate on a particular time period, say one or two years, then highlight what had happened, then introduce appropriate stories for that period. Finally, to conclude each correspondent's appearance, he would offer a personal assessment of the war.

In the closing minutes of the program, interpretation also was to be provided, using the talents of several foreign affairs experts, including former Under Secretary of State George Ball; Dr. John K. Fairbank, director of the East Asia Research Center at Harvard; W. Averill Harriman, former Ambassador to the Soviet Union and representative of the President at the Vietnam talks in Paris from 1968 to 1969; the Reverend Theodore Hesburgh, president of Notre Dame University; Senator Barry Goldwater, unsuccessful Republican presidential standard bearer in 1964; anthropologist Dr. Margaret Mead; Daniel Moynihan, former Ambassador to India; and former Secretary of State Dean Rusk.[83]

In his review for *Film Comment,* broadcast historian Larry Lichty said, "It was the first time any network had given such a comprehensive, introspective summary." He believed the section on the correspondents' reports "was a balanced, important review of the fighting."[84]

Variety's Bill Greeley noted:

> CBS in reprise spent more time on the dissent at home, which served to remind that it was CBS News that called the other networks and arranged for a blackout of any live or special coverage of the biggest political demonstration in the nation's history — the march on the Pentagon.[85]

John J. O'Connor, of the New York *Times,* described the CBS effort as "an extremely polished slab of television." He said:

> Instead of fully exploring the sources and many dimensions of the biggest blunder in American history, CBS News generally continued to treat the Vietnam scenario as almost logical and reasonable. "We" somehow became involved and now "we" are not involved.[86]

O'Connor believed television became anti-war as American public opinion became blatantly anti-war. He felt, as did Lichty, that the end of the war, television's so-called first war, demanded more interpretation and insight, while, at the same time, acknowledging (as I have above) the almost complete impossibility of such action taking place. "The failure of accurate communication: that problem, admittedly is complex, perhaps insoluble within the context of a medium structured for selling entertainment and products."[87]

The big broadcast consisted of 30 minutes of news summary, 90 minutes of film stories from the front and 30 minutes of "reactions" from guest experts: "what the Vietnam war had done to us as a nation; what did it prove to us; what did we learn?"[88]

Its bathetic title, *Vietnam: A War That Is Finished,* was taken from President Ford's Tulane University speech, announcing the end of American involvement in Vietnam.

After setting the scene, Cronkite led into an update on the evacuation of Americans, which was based on reports by Schieffer and Plante. Plante, talking from Hong Kong, then discussed the mood in Saigon and the unruly evacuation efforts. Cronkite then turned to Bruce Dunning at Guam, where more than

31,000 evacuees had landed; then he moved on to Terry Drinkwater at Camp Pendleton, California, one of three military bases designated as temporary homes for the 56,000 evacuees expected in from Indochina. The first segment ended with Cronkite citing the American and Vietnamese dead and wounded figures and then presenting Secretary of State Henry Kissinger, who urged the nation to put Vietnam behind "us and move ahead."

Thereafter, except for Cronkite's announcement at 10:40 p.m. of South Vietnam President Duong Van Minh's unconditional surrender to the North (President Thieu had resigned two days earlier), the war footage was largely historical in nature: a monumental replay of past Vietnam war scenes; a lengthy compilation of actualities about destruction, violence and death. It proceeded to acknowledge Vietnam as "the first televised war: the first war shown night after night in your living room. So many pictures, so many sounds."[89] Cronkite asked rhetorically what did it mean? "Tonight we shall try at least to answer that question."

Nothing in print (the archive broadcast script for *A War That Is Finished* runs 45 pages) really gets across the power of some of the film footage from the war-years segment. But here is an attempt to do so:

> *Dan Rather:* . . . one unforgettable walk — "A walk in the sun," the infantrymen called it — a march in from a forward area during one of the so-called truces; a march in for a scheduled Christmas dinner of turkey from a can. One mother's son from Tennessee — his name isn't important — stepped on a mine. There was a muffled brrrooom — and the kid's legs were gone. In that instant, many of us on that walk lost forever the essence of youth, the belief that there is always a tomorrow and that if one simply believes what he is doing is right, cares enough and tries hard enough, everything somehow will turn out all right. Nice thought and very American; sometimes it is even true. But the message from that green jungle hell was: It isn't always so.[90]
>
> *Bernard Kalb:* . . . The VC do not use their terror indiscriminately. . . . They terrorize selectively to isolate the rural population from Saigon, and to control the people, whether by allegiance or by intimidation. Their victims include village officials, administrators, school teachers, revolutionary development workers. Since 1958, the VC have been charged with more than fourteen thousand civilian assassinations and more than forty-five thousand kidnappings. . . . They used flamethrowers against people who only recently learned to use matches. The Montagnard village of Dak Song was turned to ashes. It was the VC way of trying to recruit other Montagnards into helping VC units in the mountains.[91]
>
> *Robert Schakne:* . . . The year 1968 was the turning point of the American part of the war in Vietnam. The Tet offensive shattered a

lot of illusions, illusions about pacification and body count, and about computer printouts that were telling us we were winning the war when we were not. A lot of soldiers, including General Westmoreland will still argue that the Communists lost, that we won, at Tet; that the Communists captured none of their objectives, or could not hold on to what they captured; that they suffered severe casualties. But to those of us who were there, Tet suggested something else: that all . . . of those years of search and destroy, of defoliation, of secret bombings of Laos, of pacification had not meant a thing; that the other side could launch a major attack all over Vietnam with total surprise; that nothing American armed forces had done had really changed anything.[92]

In footage taken back in 1971, Morton Dean talked to Mrs. Errol Kubiga, a physical therapist at a Quaker rehabilitation center in Quang Ngai with four years of experience in Vietnam:

Dean: What will happen, do you think, to Trah and Chan, two little girls we've seen here?

Mrs. Kubiga: Chan will probably be fine, because she has just one leg below the knee — lost one leg below the knee. So, I think she'll just lead a fairly normal life, be able to go to market and do all the things that — that she would expect to do. The sad thing may be that her marriage prospects may be affected by being a disabled person, and that of course will be sad for her when she's older. The other little one will have a much harder time. Walking for her will always be difficult. She should walk normally, but she won't be able to walk very far. And so, she'll manage all right, but she won't do as well as — as Chan.[93]

Finally, 1975. Bruce Dunning described the last flights out of the crowded Da Nang airport:

As soon as the rear stairway was lowered, the stampede of terorized people tried to storm the plane. From the cockpit, the pilots reported by radio that the situation was out of control.

Several times the pilots moved the plane, hoping to break the crowds around the ladder. There was no control. . . . CBS News cameramen Mike Marriott and soundman Mai Van Duc dared not leave the plane, aware they might not be able to get back on. The stewardesses dragged people on and rushed them to seats, screaming all the while, "Where are the women and children?" They piled four, five and six men into seats intended for three. Finally, there was room for no more. The plane began to move as people still clambered up the ladder. . . . As the plane strained laboriously into the air, people were still clinging to the wheels and the rear stairs. Seven men fell off as the plane reached heights of a thousand feet or more. As the plane reached six thousand feet, one man was still stuck in the ladder.[94]

After he had announced the unconditional surrender near the close of the broadcast, Cronkite asked his fellow correspondents what was ahead for Vietnam and America. Bob Schieffer said President Ford would continue feeling the war is over and done with, that the country should move on "to something else." Roger Mudd said Congress would be much more wary: "They're not going to believe any more the patriotic cover of national security or those slogans of the past." Marvin Kalb said the State Department would push to strengthen "all . . . the various alliances that continue to exist for the United States."[95]

But, after seeing the roll of actualities and film reports in the middle portions of the program, viewers could only treat such remarks as discursive and paltry. At that particular time, there wasn't any means at hand for CBS News to "explain" what was going to come about — just because the war was over.

The documentary closed with a roll of credits naming all those who had served CBS News in Vietnam.

20 / Washington

POLITICS: 1968

RAMIFICATIONS OF TET, of President Johnson's unwillingness to run again for the Presidency, of the limited halt to the bombing in March, 1968, and of the complete halt of air strikes in Vietnam in October, were being felt at home, especially in the political sphere. Robert McNamara was out as Secretary of Defense, and Clark Clifford was in; General Creighton Abrams had replaced General Westmoreland as supreme commander in Vietnam; President Johnson's popularity was waning while Senators Eugene McCarthy and Robert F. Kennedy were doing well in the Democratic presidential primaries.

All these domestic effects were heightened by TV. Television was giving Americans views of war never before experienced. It also would illuminate the 1968 presidential campaign with a series of broadcasts extending from the New Hampshire primaries to Nixon's inaugural. For the first time, everything about the campaign was oriented toward TV coverage. Spending was twice the levels of 1964. At year's end, the FCC reported that network TV alone took in $8.9-million for over 36 hours of broadcast time by the Republicans and Democrats.[1]

Richard M. Nixon was nominated on August 8 in Miami; Hubert H. Humphrey, on August 28 in Chicago; and George Wallace, the American Independent Party candidate, on October 3. The election was extremely close. Nixon won 43.4 percent of the popular vote; Humphrey, 42.7 percent; and Wallace, running stronger than any third-party candidate since 1924, 13.5 percent.

Television stories both of the Democratic Convention on August 26–29 at the Amphitheatre on Chicago's South Side and of the confrontations between demonstrators and police in Lincoln Park were important factors in the election because they showed viewers how Mayor Richard Daley, both inside and outside the convention, tried to control events. Security inside the Amphitheatre was tight and several reporters were manhandled while roaming the convention floor doing interviews. Outside, police worked 12-hour shifts aided by stand-by forces totaling 7,000 Army troops and 5,000 National Guardsmen. Up against these forces were 10,000 to 15,000 demonstrators, mostly young people. According to the President's Commission on Violence's 343-page report about the confrontation that took place between police and protesters that week, the "police were the targets of mounting provocation by both word and act. It took the form of obscene epithets, of rocks, sticks, bathroom tiles and even human excrement (being) hurled at police by demonstrators."[2]

In response, police reacted with "unrestrained and indiscriminate" violence, hurting people who had broken no law, disobeyed no order, made no threat.

Wednesday, August 28, the night Humphrey was nominated, was also the time police and protesters clashed and were photographed and telecast doing so near the Hilton Hotel convention headquarters. Even more brutal police behavior happened on Sunday and Monday nights on streets unmonitored by TV. In the days that followed, letters, telegrams and phone calls poured into the media. Yet, most of them blamed the press, not the police, for slanting their coverage of the riots in favor of the demonstrators.

This Business of Fairness: 1972

Now assuredly the most popular news medium in the nation, television in 1972 headed into its best year in terms of volume of business, revenues and profits. Business for the industry would top $3-billion, up 10 percent from 1971.

But along with financial success came problems. The industry always had had to consider the sensibilities of the FCC. The latter already existed as a supervising agency of the older parent, radio. It had helped bring the child, television, along, not only by assigning licenses and controlling technical advancements such as channel allocations and color systems selection, but it too had found itself evolving in importance, just as its subject industry had. Some of this accretion was inevitable, mandated by public interest. Some of it came about simply because network news and public affairs programs came to be accepted so uncritically by viewers. Some of it resulted from government officials being critical of television.

The power to license stations gave the FCC broad discretionary powers which, under Chairman Dean Burch, often were directed toward TV news people. Soon after President Nixon delivered a TV speech on Vietnam in November, 1969, Burch asked for transcripts of the network discussion programs that had followed Nixon's talk. Later, Burch said Vice President Agnew's earlier attack on network news was "thoughtful" and "provocative."[3]

The Nixon White House, meantime, with its Office of Telecommunications Policy, directed by Clay T. Whitehead, had still another network news watchdog. For the first time, broadcast journalism was being formally observed by two arms of government — Congress and the Executive Branch — and either could produce havoc. (LBJ used to watch all network nightly news programs and often would phone a miscreant reporter before the program was off the air.)

Whitehead, for example, had announced in December that a White House proposed law would "make local TV stations accountable for the content of all network programs that they broadcast, including news, entertainment and paid spots. The proposed law, Whitehead said, would cause individual stations to lose their licenses if they failed to "act to correct imbalance or consistent bias from the networks." The Nixon Administration was determined to get strong powers to control news and documentary programming.[4]

This conflict between government and broadcast journalism about news and public affairs programming had been growing ever since leading politicians such as Kennedy and Nixon, during their 1960 debates, saw the power of television to influence public feelings of favor or disfavor toward one candidate or the other.

Concern over this power was well-founded. TV *is* the most powerful means of public communications ever conceived. It also is a marvelous "democratic" means of public communications as long as it is free to tell us what people in public life are saying about the public business.

But this condition hasn't always been met. A problem with TV is that it intimidates those very politicians who cannot use it most consummately to win our favors because for a variety of reasons, they lack the requisite skills (e.g., President Nixon).

One can see how TV contributed to Watergate by making foul play necessary on the part of the marginal candidate who lacked the personality to use TV well — despite the fact that he already held the presidency — especially if he were in a contest with a rival who, on TV at least, appeared charismatic.

Senator Edmund S. Muskie of Maine could be personally quite testy and difficult, but when he gave an election eve speech over nationwide TV during the 1970 congressional campaign, speaking for the Democratic party both as that party's recent vice presidential candidate and as a potential presidential candidate in 1972, he was extremely effective. Sporting a thick head of hair and a long, mobile face, the senator spoke in a liquid Maine accent as he ticked off point after point. He was cool, knowledgeable, persuasive and acceptable, even though his rather dull assignment meant embellishing the Democratic record and disparaging that of Nixon's GOP. His performance contrasted strongly with Nixon's recent on-camera efforts, in which the President again displayed receding hair, perspiring jowls and mock sincerity.

Yet Nixon was President, Muskie, his mere opponent. In terms of being effective on television, their roles could have been reversed — one reason perhaps why Muskie later was "discredited" by means of a series of political dirty tricks which, for their effectiveness, did not use TV.

NBC News would soon face a bitter test with the FCC over whether or not it had acted fairly when it broadcast *Pensions: The Broken Promise* on September 12, 1972. It was produced by Eliot Frankel, who, along with his staff, had begun work on the program in June, "eventually shooting 40 hours of film and interviewing 300 people." All this was supervised either by Frankel or by his assistant, producer David Schmerler. A rough cut had been shown to Reuven Frank, then president of NBC News, while he was directing coverage of the political conventions in Miami. The program cost $200,000 but only two-and-a-half of its six minutes of spot time were sold. It ran against *Marcus Welby, M.D.* on ABC and *The Family Rico* on CBS, attracting only 16 percent of the potential viewers, or an audience of about 15 million people.[5]

The program was the opening show of a new prime-time documentary series, *NBC Reports*. Its prime point was expressed early in the show when a woman said, "There must be thousands, maybe millions of them that's getting the same song and dance my husband got. When they reached their time for retirement, there is no funds left to pay them."

Nothing was done to balance negative comment with positive comment. However, the program contained no personal attacks, even though its premise was a bias against pension plans that did not deliver what they promised. As Fred R. Friendly has said:

> Although *Pensions* received both an American Bar Association and Peabody award, the strong remedial action that Congress applied to the problem in the pensions-reform law of 1974 could be NBC's most enduring prize. It was an example of tough investigative reporting, and its coverage did not pretend to be fastidiously fair to all concerned. Its makers were muckrakers with their eyes and ears open, not blind disciples of the goddess of justice.[6]

On May 2, 1973, *Pensions* won its Peabody as "broadcast journalism at its best . . . a shining example of constructive and superlative investigative reporting."[7] On the same day, the FCC cited *Pensions* as "a one-sided documentary that created the impression that injustice and inequity were widespread in the administration of private pension plans."[8]

The FCC also claimed that the program appeared to violate the Fairness Doctrine obligation "for affording reasonable opportunity" to present contrasting views. Another party in the matter was AIM (Accuracy in Media), a self-styled news surveillance group, which originally had alerted the FCC to act against *Pensions*, "since legislation to regulate private pension funds was pending in Congress when the program was shown." AIM felt that *Pensions* supported the need for such legislation and it would only be fair for NBC and its affiliated stations to grant broadcast time for presenting opposing views.[9]

NBC went to court, and the die was cast: the federal government finally was directly and overtly questioning the fairness of a network television news documentary.

Thirty-four months later, after innumerable opinions, decisions and appeals, the case ended in compromise, with NBC the de facto winner, since it never had to provide additional time for airing opposing views. The case was returned from a Court of Appeals panel to the FCC, which no longer was seeking compliance.[10] The Fairness Doctrine might apply to personal attacks (see the Red Lion Decision), but it certainly had no effect — if the *Pensions* saga means anything — on the rights of networks and local stations to broadcast a news documentary that presents a distinct bias.

Other NBC News documentaries to appear in 1972 were: Frankel's *Growing Up in Prison;* Gerald Green's *NBC Reports* production, *The Cave People of Mindanao,* which was about the recently discovered Tasaday aborigines in a Philippine rain forest; George Murray's *China Lost and Found,* a report on Sino-American relations, narrated by John Chancellor; Pamela Hill's *NBC Reports: The Media and the Campaign.* Its "first half . . . consisted of a mixture of homilies and special pleading. The second half dealt with Senator Thomas Eagleton's aborted Veep nomination."[11]

Fred Freed won an Emmy for *The Blue-Collar Trap,* which revealed "the dehumanizing effects of contemporary technology on industrial workers" as told by four assembly-line men (all in their thirties) while at work at the Ford Pinto plant in Milpatas, California.[12] *Variety,* however, said the production told the viewer more than he cared or needed to know about specific workers, that it neglected to give important information about employment, such as wages and shifts.[13]

Lucy Jarvis produced two health documentaries: *Pain! Where Does It Hurt Most?* and *What Price Health?* The latter was narrated by Edwin Newman, directed by the talented Tom Priestley and had an exceptionally well-written script by George Lefferts. Broadcast on December 19, the program attacked the high cost of medical care, showed persons mauled by these costs and came out for a broad national-health-insurance package. The documentary was tough enough, in fact, to enlist a vehement protest from the powerful American Medical Association, which sent NBC president Julian Goodman 29 instances of distortions it felt were in the program and demanded equal time for rebuttal. In reply, NBC submitted a 39-page refutation. The AMA then formally applied to the FCC for an investigation.

One AMA objection centered around the case of Kristen Knapp, 5, whom the documentary had showed as being denied needed corrective heart surgery because her unemployed father couldn't afford it. The AMA said the girl had had heart surgery five weeks before the Jarvis program was even telecast. Moreover, she always had qualified for expense-paid medical service via Ohio's crippled children program.

By mid-1973, the contestants agreed to compromise, with NBC offering 15 minutes of the *Today* program for AMA president Russell B. Roth to be interviewed and to express his group's views. NBC also would allot some time to the AMA on the Eliot Frankel documentary to be telecast on August 28, 1973 — *Hospitals, Doctors and Patients.* NBC also "gave the AMA a list of organizations that have shown *What Price Health?* so that the AMA can offer them its president's interview as an addendum."[14] In return, the medical organization agreed to forego its protest now lodged with the FCC.

COPING WITH CHINA: 1972

On the surface at least, 1972 was fortuitous for Richard M. Nixon. His public postures were impeccable. After his *Conversation* with Dan Rather on January 2, he was described as "a most convincing advocate of his decisions on foreign and domestic issues."[15] At one point, he discussed himself, as Presidents are wont to do:

> My strong point, if I have a strong point, is performance. I always do more than I said. I always produce more than I promised, though I don't mean that from time to time I may not have made promises that I was unable to keep. But generally speaking, whether it's in the foreign field or in the domestic field, I believe that actions are what count. And also, I think that's what the country needs at this particular point.[16]

In spite of such temerity, the President, "an old hand at the perils of television . . . spent all Sunday afternoon" war-gaming possible questions in his hideaway office in the Executive Office Building.[17] He used 7–N makeup (a light pancake for swarthy types) and the Oval office by air time had a temperature of 35 degrees, so that the President's tendency to perspire on camera would be minimized. Still, he displayed "some nervousness" and "when Mr. Rather asked him whether his trips to Moscow and China and his withdrawal strategy in Vietnam were timed to enrich his political prospects," the President "clenched his fist (unseen by viewers) and looked Mr. Rather in the eye; on all other questions, he seemed to be addressing Mr. Rather's shirt collar."[18] He was never at ease in the give-and-take of the usual interview situation. But his testiness with the press was obscured by a stubborn determination to orchestrate the public relations necessities of his office.

Before the month was out, the President was on the air on the twenty-fifth outlining a plan to end the war in Indochina: Withdrawal of all United States forces within six months and new South Vietnamese elections in exchange for a ceasefire and the return of all American prisoners. Speaking from the Oval office, he said:

> For thirty months, whenever Secretary Rogers, Dr. Kissinger or I were asked about negotiations, we would only say we were pursuing every possible channel in our search for peace. There was never

a leak, because we were determined not to jeopardize the secret negotiations.

Until recently, this course showed signs of yielding some progress. Now, however, it is my judgment that the purposes of peace will best be served by bringing out publicly the proposals we have been making in private. . . .

The time has come to lay the record of our secret negotiations on the table. Just as secret negotiations can sometimes break a public deadlock, public disclosure may help to break a secret deadlock.[19]

Since this was an election year, the program also included Nixon's potential Democratic rivals for the presidency. One of these, George McGovern, South Dakota's junior Senator, who would ultimately face and lose to Nixon, gave his reactions to the speech to Bruce Morton in the studios of CBS Chicago affiliate WBBM-TV:

Morton: What the President said, Senator, is that in the secret talks — where there was a nine-point North Vietnamese plan, instead of the seven-point plan which had been made public — that in these secret talks, the price for getting the prisoners back was that the United States had to overthrow the Thieu Government. Is that a reasonable request?

McGovern: I find that hard to believe, Mr. Morton. . . . . I would like to make a small wager that when the full history of this exchange is known, that what they've said is that we should withdraw support from General Thieu. And that's quite different from saying they're asking us to overthrow him.

Morton: Well, that is quite different. And I assume the President knows the differences, sir. You're saying he's lying to the country?

McGovern: Well, let me say this, Mr. Morton. The President himself recognizes what I believe to be the most serious problem in American politics today — when he said that many Americans no longer believe their own government. I wonder why they don't.

Morton: Are you saying, though, to go back to what I was asking, the President is not telling the truth about these facts?

McGovern: I'm saying, Mr. Morton, that we've been misled so many times on this that I have serious doubts about the interpretation that was given here tonight.[20]

In February came the surprising trip to China. Avowed anti-Communist Richard Nixon went his precedent-breaking way to Peking — the latest ruler to pay homage to the Middle Kingdom — accompanied by 87 news people and 40 tons of equipment in 1,000 cases.[21] It was a scenario that, if it had occurred a few years earlier, people just wouldn't have believed: Nixon meeting Premier

Chou En-lai and Chairman Mao Tse-tung! Roger Mudd said, "For many people, the live color pictures coming back from China were more mysterious than watching the first pictures from the moon."[22]

To alleviate American anxieties about the China trip and its portents for the future, CBS News leaped at the chance to explain the Chinese. It promptly put producer-writer Irv Drasnin's *Misunderstanding China* on the air on February 20. Beautifully structured and extremely coherent, the program had a field day exposing ill-conceived American ideas about the Chinese. One minute it was trenchant; the next minute, plain funny. In the words of Charles Kuralt, "up to that time, anybody could immigrate to America. After 1882, anybody still could, except for imbeciles, paupers, prostitutes — and Orientals."[23]

> *"Charlie Chan":* Person who throw this knife also kill Alan Colby when he return to claim estate, place body behind secret panel. . . .
>
> *Kuralt:* Some Chinese, to be sure, possessed the wisdom of the East. One was a smart detective — Charlie Chan.
>
> *"Chan":* . . . then use ultraviolet ray device to make body appear as apparition at séance. Same murderer. . . .
>
> *Kuralt:* He was no more a real Chinese than the actors who played him. For twenty-five years, in forty-eight films made by four studios, there were six Charlie Chans — none of them Chinese. All of them spoke as if they had discovered English in a fortune cookie.
>
> *Woman:* . . . how can I thank you?
>
> *"Chan":* Justice, like virtue, brings its own reward. . . . Suspicion is only toy of fools. . . . Motive like end of string — tied in many knots.[24]

My Sensitivities Had Been Annealed: 1972

The President addressed the nation again on May 9, describing his counter-measures to North Vietnam's major attack on the South. Haiphong harbor — for the first time — was ordered mined, and air and naval strikes were stepped up against military targets. At the same time, he offered major concessions: stopping all acts of force, including bombings, and withdrawing all allied troops just prior to reaching an agreement about Saigon's future government — in return for an exchange of prisoners and a ceasefire.[25]

Nixon had called his policies in Vietnam "Vietnamization," a peculiarly American expression that was based on the conviction that South Vietnamese forces, if properly trained, equipped and supported by America's remaining air power in Vietnam, could hold their own against the North.

Before May was over, Nixon had been to Moscow (which Walter Cronkite reported was cleaner than New York), where he had signed a strategic nuclear-arms-limitation agreement and helped bolster Kissinger's policy of détente. Kissinger, although not yet Secretary of State, was rapidly becoming a power in the administration. Alternately serious and witty, he once summed up his attitude toward American civilization, as reported by *Life*'s Hugh Sidey:

> We live in a world in which some countries pursue ruthless policies. . . . We are in a period which someday may be compared to one of the religious ages, when whole values change. . . . We are a warmhearted people, concerning ourselves with a lot that is superficial, not willing to believe that we can make irrevocable errors, not willing to trust the judgment of leaders until all the facts are in and it is usually too late, absorbed in bureaucratic infighting and indulging in various forms of debilitating nostalgia."[26]

Nixon's campaign consisted of the foregoing overt acts of statecraft: frequent addresses to the nation explaining policy and actions, plus the heavily reported trips to China and Russia. Thus, he came into the Miami national GOP convention wearing the presidential mantle of power with a flair not seen since the days of J.F.K. As a result, the convention seemed anti-climactic, a not unsorry situation for Nixon, and he and Vice President Agnew were duly renominated. (Earlier, in July, Senator McGovern also had been nominated in Miami, where the facilities for one convention were quickly used again for the other.)

These national conventions, together with numerous predecessors, had been consistently covered by the networks (thoroughly by CBS and NBC and sporadically by ABC) since 1948. By 1972, the logistics for producing a televised national convention were pretty well delineated. A pool provided basic coverage from the podium and major sites in the convention hall, including cameras aimed at the podium, at delegates and at audience. Other cameras monitored the gallery and rostrum from the hall's two sides. Pool microphones and cameras were controlled by network personnel who, in turn, worked at the behest of the party's leadership. Pool coverage, then, was sent to all three networks, who could run it live or tape it for later use or intercut it with materials from other sources — for example, the cameras staked out at the headquarters of various candidates or party leaders in nearby hotels. Robert Wussler, then head of the CBS Special Events Unit, said there were "great similarities" between coverage of space (Apollo 16 had landed in the lunar highlands in April; the final Apollo flight would bring back bright orange soil from the moon in December), conventions, primaries, election nights and assassinations: "They're all live things." Still, the tape machines were banked with correspondents' reports and interviews so that they could be aired when needed.

"People ask me," Wussler said, "how can I format anything as complicated as a convention, how can I plan ahead? But I never plan more than five or six minutes in advance. They pay me for my judgment, and for my reaction time."[27]

For 19 days in July, the vice presidential fortunes of Senator Thomas Eagleton of Missouri preoccupied the nation until, finally, McGovern dumped him, replacing him with Sargent Shriver. According to Eagleton, on three occasions in his life he had voluntarily been hospitalized for what he called "nervous exhaustion and fatigue" but what turned out to be shock treatments and other therapy for severe depression. News of all this broke in mid-July, after Eagleton had been named to the Democratic ticket. Columnist Jack Anderson then ran a story about the senator having been arrested a number of times in Missouri; this account proved to be false and Anderson apologized on July 30.

Since Nixon was playing at being above the fray, most of the campaign centered on McGovern who, after the Eagleton-Shriver debacle and the lacklustre Miami convention, failed to find any issue with which he could really clobber the President.[28]

Unimpeded, Nixon proceeded to run up a tremendous landslide victory. McGovern lost every state but Massachusetts and the District of Columbia. By year's end, McGovern's brief fling with the political big time was over.

Although he had won big, President Nixon was increasingly frustrated by his failure to bring the war to an end. Angered by the North Vietnamese leaders' refusal to meet and discuss what he considered fair terms, he kept up the bombing. For the first time, scores of big B-52s hit the North's heavily defended population centers. In four days, 75 to 100 B-52s struck the environs of Hanoi daily. Later, they worked over Haiphong, each plane carrying 25 tons of bombs.[29]

Charles Collingwood said there were at least three main issues standing in the way of the agreement that so nearly was reached in October then aborted in November:

1. Should the release of American POWs be tied to the release of political prisoners now being held in the South by the Thieu regime?
2. Should America and South Vietnam insist some sort of recognition of the latter's separate sovereignty be made clear?
3. Should a proposed international supervisory truce force have any teeth, as the United States wants and the North does not?[30]

On December 16, Kissinger confessed that a settlement which always seemed "just within our reach . . . was always pulled just beyond our reach when we attempted to grasp it."[31]

John Hart, then with CBS News and the first American broadcast journalist to visit Hanoi in a long time, was debriefed after his three-week visit by Morley Safer and Mike Wallace in the News Special: *Hanoi: An Uncensored Report,* broadcast on October 13. Hart had films of Hanoi, which he showed — some were taken while American bombing planes were overhead. But what came through more directly were the trials that a correspondent undergoes, real or imaginary, in trying to send film and tapes back home.

Safer: John, this broadcast is called *An Uncensored Report*. Watching your pieces from Hanoi and from the North, I never had the feeling that you were being censored, in fact, while you were there.

Hart: The best that I can tell, I wasn't. The North Vietnamese insisted on shipping my film — taking it to the airport, shepherding it through customs. First time they did that, I was at their mercy: I had no way of getting to the airport without them and I didn't speak the language; I didn't know the road to the airport and I couldn't have gone by myself anyway. So: "Okay, here's the film." Now they had to fill out a customs form: "What's in it? What's in your shipment?" And I became very nervous. They said, "Well, how many feet of film? We don't want to know the contents of the film; we want to know how many feet." That surprised me. The only censoring that I'm aware of is when I cabled CBS to tell them, three or four days in advance, the route the three pilots were going to take out, through China, Moscow and Copenhagen. They said, "We're worried about the safety of the pilots." I said, "I have to let my company know." And they said, "Well, send the telegram after the plane goes off. The telegram goes faster than the plane." But that's the only tampering that I'm aware of.

Safer: They never said, "No, you can't say that; it's not true"?

Hart: No. They never argued with me. But of course, I was in a different position than someone cabling an account, because I would go to my room and I would tape it and they were not around when I taped, so they couldn't tell what I was saying. Although they were very interested in the reaction in the United States. They would ask me, "Is it favorable or is it unfavorable"?

Wallace: Reaction to what you sent back?

Hart: Yeah. Fortunately, I was able to say I don't know, you know, what the reaction is. But they were very pleased to know that the first story of the pilots' release took up a third of the Evening News and they liked that.[32]

Hart also saw leveled buildings, special cement cubicles set up for bomb shelters and masses of trees hiding ammunition and antiaircraft guns.

I was surfeited with the propaganda, with what I felt was arranged and sometimes staged meetings with wounded people. In fact, that feeling of force — of forced information — was so strong that when I finally saw a woman whose leg was lost and who was stitched in a cross, from her chest to below her navel and across her chest, that I could not feel what a normal human being would feel. My sensitivities had been annealed. And I'm ashamed to say that. But my sensitivities had been annealed by this insulting stream of propaganda by these very nice, warm people.[33]

WATERGATE: DIVERSIONS, 1973

When 1973 at CBS News is studied in terms of its documentaries — in this instance, the opinion reporting as well as the enormous amount of television reporting done outside the purview of the regular newscasts, such as the News Specials, correspondents' reports and live coverage dealing with the most consuming news subject of the year, Watergate — one is struck by how commonplace documentary methods have become in all forms of television news. This widespread acceptance of high standards of actuality, interviewing, camera work and narration, in turn, helped sprinkle the year with several really good productions. *Conversations with Kissinger* and *LBJ: The Last Interview* ran back to back on February 1, a new trend in programming at CBS, the strategy being once you have won over the audience for a news program, keep it by offering something equally interesting. On March 9, the *CBS Reports: What Are We Doing to Our Children?* with Daniel Schorr was aired. April 26 saw two quality productions: the News Special: *Five Presidents on the Presidency,* with Eric Sevareid reflecting with the last five presidents about the responsibilities, powers and influence of the highest federal office; and *You and the Commercial,* a *CBS Reports* examining the spinal column of American television, the TV spot. Both documentaries were produced under the aegis of Perry Wolff, with direct production for *Presidents* handled by Peter Poor and for *You* by producer-writer-director Irv Drasnin.

The *Presidents* show was a collage of film clips of Truman, Eisenhower, Kennedy, Johnson and Nixon, "with perceptive bridges supplied" by Sevareid, who said at one point:

> TV interviews with politicians have a kind of false folksiness to them; the muscle is often concealed under the homespun. . . . All American politicians worth their history always conceal the full extent of the forces they command.[34]

Poor dealt with the presidency in its seven entities: its power, selection of its occupants, its relations with the press, foreign policy and politics generally and in retrospect. The program's appearance, of course, coincided with the widespread powers then being proclaimed for the Nixon Presidency, the so-called Imperial Presidency. It is another example of how television could employ documentary to sharpen past memories, revivify history and relate it to similar present-day preoccupations.

The hour about TV spots showed how audience reactions were tested, how the $22-billion spent that year was necessary to "introduce the nation's new products to the public" and how, finally, commercials shouldn't be taken too seriously. It gave a behind-the-scenes look at the agencies and clients involved with television, even though the nation's six largest advertisers refused to be interviewed for Drasnin's program.[35]

CBS News returned to the subject of families on May 31 with *Two Family Portraits,* which absorbed the 9–11:00 p.m. EDT slot. Part I was "We're

Okay in Brick, N.J." After eight years in Jersey City, New Jersey, Tom and
Betty Hussennetter and their five children cut their ties and moved to Brick
Township, a community of 144,000 some 60 miles south of New York City
that seemed to offer the chance to flee the problems of the cities for a safer
place to live.

Part II, ". . . But What If the Dream Comes True?," originally telecast
in November of 1971, was the story of a family who had arrived at a place
with beautiful homes, good schools and safe streets — Sam and Jan Greenawalt and their three children had left Grand Rapids, Michigan, for the affluent
Detroit suburb, Birmingham.

Robert Markowitz, who produced both studies, spent close to four
months with the Hussennetters and six months with the Greenawalts, "observing not only how each family worked and played, but how they felt about who
they were, what they were doing and where they were going."[36]

Counteracting the heavy sociological angles in the Hussennetter hour,
with its "damp and gloomy images of winter," with its impression that "the
family's life is continuous struggle and pressure, relieved by an occasional
party at home or a blast at the Knights of Columbus club or cheering the local
football team," is its closing shot:

> I'm Betty Hussennetter. I'm thirty-three years old, a housewife and
> a mother. And I live in Bricktown and I'm complacent right now and
> very happy where I am. I have no desire to leave my community and
> to me it is mine because I am part of it.[37]

Charles Kuralt reported both programs, with Perry Wolff as executive
producer. William Wagner, Jr., filmed most of both shows, with some additional help by Walter Dombrow on "Dream."

Among the clutter of summer reruns, which were often encased next to
vivid live specials on Watergate emanating from the Senate Erwin Committee,
was a special 12-week segment of some of CBS News' best-known, most influential documentaries produced during the 1950s and 1960s. It ran Sundays
at 6:00 p.m. from July 8 to September 30. Called *CBS News Retrospective* and
hosted by John Hart, who put in one of his busiest years in 1973, the series
included: *See It Now:* "Milo Radulovich" (1953), "McCarthy" (1954) and
"Harvest of Shame" (1960); *The Silent Spring of Rachel Carson* (1963); *The
Mystery of Stonehenge* (1965); *Stravinsky* (1966); *Don't Count the Candles* and
The Tenement (1967); *Of Black America:* "Black History: Lost, Stolen or
Strayed" and *The Great American Novel:* "Babbitt" and "The Grapes of
Wrath" (1968).

This series obviously was inspired by the highly successful retrospective
of CBS broadcasts held in Lincoln Center in New York in November of 1971
under the sponsorship of The Film Society of Lincoln Center, Inc.*

* Discussed in Chapter 7.

In June, Peter Ustinov and Eric Sevareid teamed up again to present insights about the American Revolution with *The Last King in America,* an "interview" with George III. This wasn't the only historical re-creation. CBS News still was carrying the *You Are There* series. It also had a young people's newscast on Saturday mornings, and occasionally ran news specials — utilizing the talents of Walter Cronkite — that dealt with news of interest to the young and on which the young participated. CBS News always was diligent in pursuing an idea; in this case, doing what amounted to historical reenactments seemed like the easiest way to dramatize and resurrect the often misunderstood or forgotten past.

This same compulsion to look at the past in solely broadcast journalistic terms was a characteristic that was easily applied to current stories as well. Before June was over, *CBS Reports* did exactly that with a program very similar to the earlier one on TV commercials called *Anatomy of a News Story: TV Covers Itself,* the brainchild of John Sharnik, the urbane, articulate producer of the three-part *Justice in America, The Germans,* and *A Night in Jail, a Day in Court.* With Les Midgely, he had originated and co-produced *Eyewitness,* an earlier series of which he said:

> I had a half hour to get something more than just headlines; to get some feeling of the event, the tone of the meeting, some background of the issues being dealt with. I was never interested in the quick headline story; I was interested in the background of the thing. And I framed this thing with a model in mind, the model being the way television covered the political convention. That was an example of imposing a kind of dramatic form on an event that was just kind of amorphous.[38]

Sharnik tried to do the same with *Anatomy.*

Anatomy followed the *CBS Reports: You'll Get Yours When You're 65,* which described the 1938 Social Security Act and what it was and was not. Supervised by Burton Benjamin, it boasted Sharnik as its producer and Dan Rather as its reporter, and it took a look at CBS News looking at the GOP Miami Convention in 1972. It had all the ingredients Sharnik liked. TV was the American people's chief and most available source for news. All the flights of Apollo, totaling 17, were, in large measure, shown on TV. Since that time, what Eric Sevareid has called "the only truly new form of journalism in generations" had grown more vigorous and popular.

Yet, just as television news became increasingly more fulminating, apprehensions about its power also increased among governmental and political leaders. Vice President Agnew had attacked it; even the public was dismayed by what was broadcast at the 1968 Democratic Convention in Chicago; unless a candidate continually won primary after primary, he or she would quickly fall out of the public's notice when the TV cameras moved on to cover only the winners. TV news was like a powerful beacon: it was all right when it drenched you in light and attention, but it was terrible when it moved off and away, leaving you in the dark. Politicians didn't like that.

So when an opportunity very similar in nature presented itself in 1972 at the Republican National Convention in Miami, Sharnik was ready to do a story never before seen on the home screen. When finally completed, *Anatomy* revealed the razzle-dazzle of TV cameramen in action, the inside of the control room where the TV decision makers — executives, producers, correspondents, reporters — decided what the viewer will see or hear and why.

Not only were there insights about news gatekeeping by network personnel, but the viewers got a long look at broadcast journalism looking at its technology, its achievements, its shortcomings and its obligations and responsibilities, especially in regard to the FCC and the regulatory aspects between the government and the broadcast press. *Anatomy* was an unusual documentary. It has been underestimated. But it will, I believe, earn a much higher reputation from future screenings than it ever received in 1973.[39]

CBS News had an unerring touch in 1973. With so much Watergate coverage, it knew, it seems now, just when to spring a program on the public that would have "a clean, tangy, tonic effect." Such a show was Kuralt's *On the Road,* made up of his mini-documentaries that were first shown on CBS' regular evening newscasts. It should be noted again that documentary quality was deeply stamped on many multi-part stories, interviews and features that frequently appeared on both the morning and evening newscasts.

The year closed with several powerful broadcasts in October: the *CBS Reports: A Boy Named Terry Egan,* the story of the battle of a nine-year-old boy and his family against infantile autism, and *The Israelis,* another in the series of studies of national character, whose presentation was speeded up to coincide with the war then burgeoning in the Middle East between Israel and Egypt. Amos Elon, author of *The Israelis: Founders and Sons,* narrated with unpretentious candor. The program was a bittersweet, sensible, warmhearted tribute to a beleaguered people.

In December, the diversions in opinion reporting were two *CBS Reports: The Corporation* and *The Rockefellers.* The latter, although essentially a family portrait, just like the earlier productions about the Hussennetters and the Greenawalts, differed in dimension and concentration. Each Rockefeller — John D. III, Nelson, David, Laurence, Winthrop and the less-known sister, Abby Rockefeller Manze — talked candidly about childhood, family and wealth. What differed from the other "family" documentaries was this broadcast's emphasis on the Rockefellers as a dynasty. Their power, money, lifestyle, influence and roots were represented, sometimes from family archives such as never-before-televised home movies. And the CBS camera eye, under the direction of the talented Howard Stringer, laid open their unique privileges: the offices of the governor of New York State in Albany; Rockefeller-owned hotels at Dix Bay and Caneel Bay in the Virgin Islands, and at Mauna Kea beach in Hawaii; the family compound in Pocantico Hills, with its private golf course, playhouse, sculpture gallery and subterranean gallery.[40]

WATERGATE: NIXON

A big victory at the polls, increased prospects for peace in Vietnam, an apparent period of one-party dominance — his party — looming ahead, an affluent America still months away from the ravages of a post-Vietnam recession and worldwide inflation, a stubborn adherence to the powers and prerogatives of the presidency — all these full-blown sails carried President Nixon smoothly along the high seas of American public opinion in early 1973.

However, storm clouds were forming. There was that matter of a burglary at Democratic National Headquarters in the Watergate building in Washington, where, in the early morning hours of June 17, 1972, the first storms the President was to encounter were brewed. Gordon Liddy's break-in experts were returning to the Watergate because the wire tap on Democratic Chairman Lawrence O'Brien's phone wasn't working. But they got caught, and soon accounts of secret tactics, dirty tricks, laundered funds, conspiracies, lying, perjury, corruption and cover-up widened like an oil slick over the public's confidence in the Nixon Administration, at first engulfing the lesser occupants in the White House but finally lapping upward to the very portals of the Oval Office itself. From the time the Watergate burglars first were apprehended on throughout the whole sorry mess, one constant compass bearing remained fixed and steady: the President, once besmirched, never managed to rid himself of the suspicion that he, too, was in on it all.[41]

The cornerstone of the Nixon defense was national security. As he told the returning POWs from Vietnam:

> Had we not had secrecy, had we not had secret negotiations with the North Vietnamese, had we not had secret negotiations prior to the Soviet summit, had we not had secret negotiations over a period of time with the Chinese leaders . . . there would have been no China initiative, there would have been no limitation of arms with the Soviet Union and no summit.[42]

To correspondent Dan Rather, who was increasingly pictured by the President and his supporters — some of whom owned or worked for CBS-affiliated TV stations — as a dark nemesis, the President's use of national security "amounted to a plea to treat the irregularities committed in the name of national security as separate from irregularities committed for the sake of reelecting President Nixon . . . ."[43]

In the same broadcast, *The Watergate Year: Crisis for the President,* correspondent Daniel Schorr said five grand juries, other than the one operating in Washington for Judge Sirica, were working on abuses connected with the presidential campaign.

Of course, Watergate accommodated CBS News beautifully. Perhaps not quite so much dedication was manifested by its rivals even though, in toto, 319 hours of broadcasting about Watergate up to August 7 cost the three networks somewhere between $7- and $10-million.[44] Bob Williams of the New York *Post* reflected a general attitude when he said in November:

> It was to the credit of CBS yesterday that it invested an hour in the interest of rounding up the troubles of the Nixon Administration through the Watergate scandals, and questioned whether the President was in a position to govern the nation.[45]

He concluded that the broadcast hour itself was a distinction for CBS amid the less strenuous ABC and NBC journalistic competition. He added:

> The White House story, of course, belongs on the networks in special documentary form in the prime audience viewing hour of 9:00 p.m., Monday through Thursday, the same time any President, including Nixon, commandeers for talking to the nation.[46]

This evident edge in favor of CBS, of course, was due to a brilliant series of Special Reports put out throughout the year by Executive Producer Les Midgeley and producers Bernard Birnbaum and Hal Haley. CBS News broke no investigative coups during Watergate, but it did do what it always had done well: namely, clarify and objectify what *Time* magazine columnist Hugh Sidey called, "a long, ghastly civics lesson."[47]

In November, CBS, which had given up "instant analysis" in June, supposedly at the request of the White House, returned to it, signalizing the end of any kind of receptivity to Nixon Administration pressures against it. Another factor in CBS's intensified attentions toward Watergate was the announcement by Clay T. Whitehead, director of the President's Office of Telecommunications Policy, that he would resign in 1974.[48]

Opportunities for instant documentary presented themselves continually to Midgeley and his staff. The Watergate cast of characters was extensive, colorful and ripe with marvelous lines. For example, the President said:

> (On May) twenty-second, I stated in very specific terms — and I state again to every one of you listening tonight — these facts: I had no prior knowledge of the Watergate break-in. I neither took part in nor knew about any of the subsequent cover-up activities. I neither authorized nor encouraged subordinates to engage in illegal or improper campaign tactics.
>
> That was and that is the simple truth.[49]

Next, L. Patrick Gray, then FBI head: Gray was trying to run that law enforcement agency when he told the Senate Committee that he and assistant

CIA Director Vernon Walters thought some White House staffers were trying to confuse the FBI and the CIA. Gray said he warned the President about this but that Nixon didn't press him. Testifying in July, Gray said:

> At 11:28 a.m. on Thursday, July 6, 1972, the President called me. He expressed his congratulations to the FBI, and asked that I express his congratulations to the agents in San Francisco who successfully terminated a hijacking there the previous day.
> I thanked the President and then said . . . "Mr. President, there is something I want to speak to you about. Dick Walters and I feel that people on your staff are trying to mortally wound you by using the CIA and the FBI and by confusing the question of CIA interest in, or not in, people the FBI wishes to interview. I have just talked to Clark McGregor and asked him to speak to you about this."
> There was a slight pause, and the President said, "Pat, you just continue to conduct your aggressive and thorough investigation."
> Following this conversation I experienced further concerns of this kind. I believed that if there was anything to the concerns I expressed to the President or to Mr. McGregor that I would hear further in the matter. I did not. Frankly, I came to the conclusion that General Walters and I had been alarmists.
> . . . Throughout the summer of 1972, I continued to press the question and I continued to get the same answer. I was told again and again there was no indication that any persons were involved other than the seven who were known to have planned and carried out the operation and who were subsequently indicted and convicted.[50]

John Dean, the President's counsel, said:

> I began by telling the President that there was a cancer growing on the presidency and if the cancer were not removed, the President himself would be killed by it. I also told him that it was important that this cancer be removed immediately because it was growing more deadly every day.
> . . . Toward the end of the conversation, the President recalled the fact that at one point we had discussed the difficulty of — in raising money and that he said that one million dollars was nothing to raise to pay to maintain the silence of the defendants. He said that he — he had, of course, only been joking when he made that comment.
> As the conversation went on — and it is impossible for me to recall anything other than the high points of it — I became more convinced that the President was seeking to elicit testimony from me and put it in perspective — put his perspective on the record and get me to agree with it.

The most interesting thing that happened during the conversation came very near the end: He got up out of his chair, went behind the chair to the corner of the Executive Office Building office and in a nearly audible tone said to me he was probably foolish to have discussed Hunt's clemency with Colson. I do not recall that I responded. The conversation ended thereafter.

As I was on my way out of the office after exchanging parting pleasantries, I told the President that I hoped that my going to the prosecutors and telling the truth would not result in impeachment of the President. He jokingly said, "I certainly hope so also."[51]

Dean had told the Senate Committee that Ehrlichman, among others, was in on the Watergate cover-up for payoffs to the burglars, and that the White House was fearful for domestic security.

Ehrlichman, testifying in July, called Dean a liar.

The problems of leaks, demonstrations, bombings and terrorism, public opinion and congressional support were understandably on the President's mind, he said.[52]

Ehrlichman's attitude was made clear when he expressed the view that whatever happened in California (where the break-in into Ellsberg's psychiatrist's office had occurred) "was well within the President's powers to deal with national security."[53]

Haldeman, in his testimony, according to correspondent John Hart, insisted on defining the difference between "cover-up" and "containment." The former was illegal activities by others; the latter, legal efforts to keep the Watergate investigation from turning up something harmful to national security.[54]

Washington *Star-News* columnist Mary McGrory saw the witnesses brought before the Erwin Committee as falling into three categories. The first were shorn lambs, or the junior people, the front men on the campaign committee who did things because they wanted to be team players but later were sorry when it was pointed out to them that they had broken the law. Next were porcupines, men such as Mitchell, Ehrlichman and Haldeman. "They all had quills. The committee couldn't lay a hand on any of them. They, like the President, so far, denied everything, admitted nothing." The last category were the professionals, career servants doing a job, such as the men caught in the Watergate. To McGrory, this last group was "the most impressive because they had loyalty other than to the narrow idea of Richard Nixon's reelection and they had a concept of what their jobs ought to be."[55]

At a press conference on August 22, the President got into the matter of the tapes, recordings made in the Oval Office, where numerous conferences were held about people Nixon and his men feared and people anxious to help him and them weather his rising tide of troubles.

Question: Mr. President, one of the lingering doubts about your denial of any involvement in — is concerning your failure to make the tapes available, either to the senate committee or the special prose-cutor. You've made it perfectly clear you don't intend to release those tapes.

Nixon: Perfectly clear? (Laughter)

Reporter: Perfectly clear. But is there any way that you could have some group listen to tapes and give a report so that that might satisfy the public mind?[56]

Nixon: . . . whether it is a paper or whether it is a tape, what we have to bear in mind is that for a President to conduct the affairs of this office and conduct them effectively, he must be able to do so with the principle of confidentiality intact. Otherwise, the individuals who come to talk to him — whether it's his advisers or whether it's a visitor in the domestic field or whether it's someone in a foreign field — will always be speaking in a eunuch-like way, rather than laying it on the line. It has to be laid on the line if you're going to have the creative kind of discussions that we have often had and (that) have been responsible for some of our successes in the foreign policy period, particularly in the past few years.[57]

Correspondent Barry Serafin then led a discussion of the President's press conference in the closing moments of the News Special, trying to summarize Nixon's remarks; he was aided by correspondents Dan Rather and Robert Pierpoint and then reporter Leslie Stahl. Turning to Rather, Serafin asked him whether one important question asked that day dealt with Acting FBI Director Pat Gray's warning to the President last summer that he was being "mortally wounded" by some of his aides, and why the President did not act on that warning. Serafin asked whether the President had filled in that blank. Rather replied:

No, I can't honestly say that I think he filled it in completely. I do think that he answered the question in much more detail than he ever has before, that his defense sounded much stronger and much more believable today than ever before. He still has not explained the crucial question as to why he didn't — when Pat Gray said that "Walters and I believe that some of your aides are out to mortally wound you" — why the President simply didn't say to him at that time: "Who?"[58]

By November, Roger Mudd was reporting that the President's future as President was now apparently moving at a pace well beyond his control. Despite the ample powers of Nixon's high office, Mudd said Nixon's future as President of the United States now was in the hands of the other two branches of government, the courts and the Congress. The federal courts had uncovered the slapdash methods used to handle the Oval Office tape recordings at just the moment the White House admitted two of the tapes never existed. Mudd said the House Judiciary Committee had started a formal inquiry into "whether it would approve the impeachment of the President." As he said, the Senate Judiciary Committee was considering proposals that would take control of the Watergate investigation away from the White House and give it to a court-appointed prosecutor, "who would investigate the President himself." Meanwhile, the Senate Rules Committee was questioning House Republican Leader Gerald Ford as if he would soon be President, carefully scrutinizing his attitudes and opinions about executive privilege, releasing documents and obstructing justice as well as checking out his finances, his medical and health records.[59]

By year's end, the President and his men faced serious formal charges. What really had brought to light the circumstances for facing such charges came about in testimony during the long, hot days of the summer at the senate hearings. Mary McGrory. was asked how she felt about these hearings by correspondent George Herman during the News Special: *A Watergate Spectrum,* which was broadcast on Sunday, August 12. She responded:

> Well, they were perfectly dreadful in that they were messy and incoherent, and the same question was asked twenty times, and people made speeches and made faces and made points and did all sorts of other things. But I think they were very useful, because *I don't know how otherwise we would have learned about life in the Nixon Administration. We wouldn't have learned about their attitude toward each other and toward their fellow man and toward government.*
>
> As I say, *the scandal to me was their priorities and their interests — that they were trying to create a police state when there were so many other things to be done in this country:* unfortunate people to be assisted, the poor to be helped, the sick to be cured. There were all sorts of things to be done. And they chose to concentrate on — Heaven forbid — getting somebody who took the Pentagon papers.
>
> Now, I say there's a reason for all that, which has come out since the hearings began, which is that it turns out that we — the — *this administration was secretly bombing Cambodia for fourteen months — three thousand six hundred and seventy air strikes while we were supposedly respecting the neutrality of that country — three thousand six hundred seventy false reports that went right up the line to the top of the Pentagon and (one assumes) the Oval Office.* (Italics, author's)
>
> So that the ferocity with which they fell upon Ellsberg is now clear. An example had to be made of anyone who told war secrets, because they were sitting on the biggest secret of them all.[60]

On December 30, in still another News Special: *1973: A Television Album,* Fred Graham, CBS News specialist on the law and the courts, sheared through the thicket of testimony, claims and counterclaims to report that twelve persons associated with the Nixon Administration had been convicted of crimes related to Watergate, and five more were awaiting trial. Moreover, the new prosecutor, Leon Jaworski, who had obtained scores of White House tapes and documents after hinting that he would subpoena President Nixon again, was expected to obtain batches of new indictments early in the new year. Graham said that now it was established that the courts may order a President to obey the law as the courts interpret it; and if he refuses, it would be taken as grounds for impeachment.[61]

The strain on everyone had been incalculable. Much of the government's business was at a standstill. Since the center didn't appear to be holding, not much else was. The presidency, always potentially the source for national moral vision, was nothing of the sort in 1973. Nobody knew that better than Senator Barry Goldwater, GOP presidential standard bearer in 1964:

> The thing that bothers me is: here, I have spent over a third of my life trying to build the Republican Party, adding my little bit to it, having been successful in the South and in the Southwest, and then all of a sudden, as I near the end of my time in politics, I wonder: "What the hell has it all been for?" Here we are, just drifting around, more Independents than Democrats or Republicans, and we need a two-party system. I feel terribly let down, frankly. It's a feeling that prevails over every other feeling. I just — I get up in the mornings and I think: Oh, well, what the hell! I — What can you do?[62]

FINAL CRISIS

CBS News had a tough time producing *The Seventh Crisis: Nixon on Nixon,* which was broadcast on January 10, because the program tried to examine the President's first twelve months of his second term in his own words.

"No one is in a better position to explain the bizarre events of the past year than Richard Nixon," John Sharnik, producer of the program, pointed out. Inevitably *Nixon on Nixon* revealed the President to be noticeably altered by Watergate and its attendant anxieties. In the early part of the year he appeared youthful and confident of his mandate. In the later months, age and strain were obvious.[63]

Also in January, the news division presented *The Mysterious Alert,* about the day of October 25, 1973, during Middle East negotiations, when American forces throughout the world were put on the ready. Secretary of State Kissinger promised a full explanation would be made public when "you will be able to judge whether the decisions were taken . . . hastily or improperly."[64]

"One week has passed, twelve weeks have passed and the full information . . . still remains a mystery," Dan Rather reported. Nor did the CBS News correspondent provide answers during the telecast, since no one involved with the incident consented to be interviewed. Still, by piecing together its disparate parts, we could witness the awesome power Kissinger possessed on that night of October 25, when an urgent cable from Leonid L. Brezhnev, chairman of the Soviet Communist Party, was read by Soviet Ambassador Anatoly F. Dobrynin directly over the phone to Mr. Kissinger, as a secretary listened on an extension and took down the words. Only later was a copy dispatched to the White House.[65]

Although absent from the meeting, where only a few officials attended, including Kissinger and James R. Schlesinger, Secretary of Defense, President Nixon later ratified their joint decision to call the alert.

"Senior defense officials" speculated that the alert was the need to make clear to the Soviets that America viewed the immediate situation in the Middle East as serious and to show moreover that, despite Watergate, the government was at work.[66]

Largely because of Watergate, live television coverage was extraordinary in 1974. The ultimate television event was the unadulterated breaking story, unedited and aimless, meandering haphazardly across the screen: the Watergate indictments; the White House transcripts debacle; the cover-up indictments; the House Judiciary Committee Impeachment Hearings; President Nixon ending his two thousand days of power, walking on a red carpet spread upon the White House south lawn to the helicopter, Army One, amid an enveloping cadre of officialdom breaking forth with hugs, handshakes, kisses and tears; President Ford's succession, and a series of public statements anxiously attended for clues as to what the new, non-elected regime would do; newly appointed Vice President Nelson A. Rockefeller's emergence nationally; the Nixon pardon, and his poor health; and Election '74. All were live, all were demanding the public's attention.

A Special Report broadcast on Friday, March 1, at 11:30 p.m. was typical of what news producers, such as Russ Bensley, and correspondents, such as Dan Rather, had to piece together from the day's live and rambling accounts. *The Watergate Indictments* was about the Watergate scandal cover-up. John Mitchell and John Ehrlichman already had been indicted in other Watergate-related cases. For the first time, H. R. Haldeman and Charles Colson — along with Gordon Strachan, a Haldeman aide; Robert Mardian, a Mitchell Justice Department official; and Kenneth Parkinson, chief attorney for the President's reelection committee — were indicted. Still, the grand jury issuing these indictments couldn't clearly say who ordered the break-in and bugging at the Watergate. Daniel Schorr reported that although evidence implied the President's involvement, the grand jury decided it couldn't indict a sitting President.

"This whole thing," Lesley Stahl said of Judge John Sirica's court, "was handled in a classical sense in that the prosecutors went after the lower echelon people in the conspiracy to get the higher-ups."[67]

By May, CBS News had shifted Walter Cronkite from New York down to Washington to anchor a series of fast-breaking programs about the White House transcripts. In July, Cronkite announced that "a unanimous Supreme Court told the President of the United States that he has no right to withhold White House tapes subpoenaed for the Watergate cover-up trial."[68] The President agreed to obey. But he still maintained, through his attorney, James St. Clair, that there was a need to preserve the confidentiality of presidential conversations. Chief Justice Burger, in turn, agreed and instructed Judge Sirica to listen to the tapes but to keep secret all conversations except those required for the trial.[69]

Roger Mudd reported that it was difficult to imagine a more memorable day in the history of constitutional law than that particular Wednesday. At 11:00 a.m., the high court told the President he was wrong to withhold the tapes; at 7:00 p.m., Nixon agreed to obey; at 8:00 p.m., the House Judiciary Committee allowed a national television audience to witness its final impeachment debate. Mudd concluded, "No one has any doubt any longer that the House Committee will approve a bill of impeachment."[70] Bruce Morton echoed Mudd, saying that in the whole House, the impeachment issue was one that a representative could vote for and still survive.[71]

It now was practical politics to ditch the President.

On August 8, at 1:31 p.m., CBS News announced that the President had resigned. He thereby avoided the oncoming impeachment. But St. Clair, his attorney, and Alexander Haig, Haldeman's successor as presidential chief of staff, finally had learned what Nixon had known and kept secret from everybody — namely, that the tapes (three June recordings) revealed his active role in the cover-up from its earliest days.[72] His support quickly fell apart, including that of the ten GOP House Judiciary members who had just defended him on TV. The tapes revealed that he had tried to keep the FBI away by "limiting public exposure" of what his supporters had done.[73]

Only one final step remained. On September 8, President Ford pardoned Nixon, "cutting his losses," as Eric Sevareid called it, ridding himself of the "Nixon albatross" on his back by making his first onerous decision and thereby ending the honeymoon he had enjoyed with public and press. Defending this action, Ford said, "It could go on and on and on, or someone must write the end of it. I have concluded that only I can do that, and if I can I must."[74]

Accepting the new President's action, Nixon, speaking through an aide from his San Clemente compound in California, said that the way he had tried to deal with Watergate had been wrong. It was "a burden I shall bear for every day of the life that is left for me."[75]

Elsewhere, Herbert Kalmbach, John Dean and Charles Colson already were in prison. Others would follow. And although the future lot of the former President remained uncertain, one thing was sure: the national nightmare called

Watergate was over, even though it continued to rankle CBS News president Richard S. Salant. Speaking to CBS-Radio network affiliates on October 2 at a Phoenix, Arizona, convention, he said:

> We ourselves should examine ourselves. . . . If we assume something went wrong with the late administration, one can fairly ask whether the press — print and electronic — must not have failed somewhere along the pre-August 8, 1974, way.
>
> It would seem reasonable to conclude that the Richard Nixon who in 1972 got more votes than, and the largest plurality of, any candidate for the presidency in history was not the Nixon of the Senate and House Committee hearings and reports and the transcripts of the tapes. It was our job to cause them more nearly to coincide. We didn't do that job.[76]

ANDY ROONEY'S WASHINGTON AND — UNFORTUNATELY — OURS

One problem of living in the last quarter of the twentieth century has been our omnipresent dependence on the media to tell us exactly what is happening in places far away. But that's only the hub of the problem. They don't tell us *exactly* what's happening. Most of the time we get a capsulized statement of conditions which makes it difficult for us to comprehend those strange names and alien peoples so far away. Only occasionally does the fog roll back to disclose another figure or another place to our clear scrutiny and understanding.

Andy Rooney managed to do this for viewers when he and several CBS News cameramen spent two months in 1974 wandering around Washington, trying to come up with a documentary that would reestablish Washington, D.C., in our minds as it really is, not in the media terms we see and hear most frequently on the news: "bastion of the free world," "the nation's capital" or "this flag which has flown over the capitol of the United States of America." And certainly not the Washington, D.C., the tourist sees: spacecraft in the Smithsonian; a few congressmen vaguely attending the business of the House of Representatives; the monuments, carillons and groves dedicated to the great and near-great — Washington, Lincoln, Jefferson, Taft and Johnson; the spacious avenues and streets downtown encompassing fortresslike buildings.

No, Rooney chose to show us Washington's reason for being: its bureaucracy. As Washington *Post* critic John Carmody said, "With his upper-register, non-TV voice and the dance of his thick eyebrows, Rooney adds just the right fey tone to the sometimes puzzling proceedings."[77]

Mr. Rooney Goes to Washington was funny. Broadcast on January 26, from 9:30–10:30 p.m. EST, and written and produced by Rooney, it made its points:

On government departments: a government department devotes itself to advising other departments on how to save on paper work; on titles: assistant to the assistant of the deputy secretary, associate deputy administrator, deputy associate administrator; on beekeepers: for whom the government set aside some half million dollars in case any bees got accidentally killed by insecticides; on bureaucratic growth—Rooney found it alarming: between 1930 and 1973, while our birth rate increased 70 percent, the highest ever, the rate of government employees hired expanded by 460 percent.[78]

Nothing got across that feeling of being on the inside in Washington better than Rooney's meeting with a Selective Service official:

Rooney: With the draft over, I thought our government might be saving money by closing the Selective Service Agency. We talked to the director, Byron Pepitone, a retired Air Force Colonel. We asked him what the Selective Service was doing now that it wasn't selecting anyone any more.

Pepitone: We have become an organization in standby — much as an organization in the sense of insurance against an emergency. We're not inducting anyone, you see. The authority to do so has expired. But our staff and our officers have been reduced by a quarter — by three-quarters.

Rooney: How much is your budget?

Pepitone: In the spring of 1973, before inductions stopped, we were operating on — on a budget of approximately a hundred million dollars. Our request to the Congress for the fiscal year of seventy-five forthcoming will be for forty-seven million dollars.

Rooney: Is that the absolute minimum that it costs to do nothing — not to draft anyone?

Pepitone: Forty-seven million dollars is a very small amount to guarantee that, should you have to augment that force, you have the capacity to do it in a timely fashion.

Rooney: What would happen to your operation if you spent only twenty million?

Pepitone: Well, my personal opinion is that if it gets much below the present level, we might just as well decide that we don't need it.[79]

We are more familiar with the necessary machinations congressmen indulge in on behalf of their respective districts back home, even though one representative's pet project may be another's pet peeve:

Rooney: We can't get cameras into the House of Representatives, so we don't have film of a little argument that we saw break out one day between Congressman James Cleveland of New Hampshire and Congressman Pierre duPont of Delaware. We went to their offices later and talked to each of them about that.

I heard you speak on the floor of the House a few days ago. You were trying to get money for people in a ski area because they said they were in trouble because it hadn't snowed much. Is protecting business men from the elements a function of government?

Representative James Cleveland (R.-N.H.): I think so. I'm sure you're acquainted with flood insurance and disaster insurance. And I think that we have various federal programs to assist people that have been victims of some natural dis — disaster.

Rooney: Is not snowing a natural disaster?

Cleveland: Well, apparently, it didn't fall within the provisions of any existing law and that's why I got the amendment through that I did.

Representative Pierre duPont (R.-Del.): My reaction to that is that we've come to the ultimate in government now. We're paying people because it isn't snowing where they live.

Rooney: But what do you say to Congressman Cleveland, who says there are five thousand people in New Hampshire who aren't going to eat well enough because it didn't snow; they need help?

duPont: Well, you say, "Jim Cleveland, you're a good friend and you're a nice guy, but we shouldn't be paying people because it doesn't snow. If it doesn't snow, it doesn't snow, and that's one of the things we live with."[80]

Summing up the post-Watergate Washington scene, Rooney hit upon a profound truth, one concerning documentary on TV as much as the federal bureaucracy. He concluded:

Our society has become so interested in the visual aspect of everything, it's easy to forget that there are no pictures of the most interesting things that go on in the world. In Washington, it's not only hard to get pictures, it's hard to find out anything about anything.

(Washington is) not being run by evil, it's being run by people like you and me. And you know how we have to be watched.[81]

Conclusion

DON HEWITT, the best producer of television documentary in America, got permission to develop *60 Minutes* because he felt the traditional hour-long, one-topic news documentary repeatedly reached the same audience — small, homogeneous, made up of persons truly curious about the world. Hewitt wanted to test his theory that there was a more general audience for a different kind of documentary, a multi-topic program, patterned after *Life* magazine. He since has overwhelmingly proved his point. *60 Minutes* is the first documentary series to remain consistently among the top ten most-watched programs on the air. This is a unique distinction that documentary managed to earn for itself during the decade.

There were others much more parochial. 1965–1975 was a decade of news propagation exclusivity for NBC, CBS and ABC. This awkward term means that the networks, working through their affiliates, were able to control television news and opinion programming to a degree never before experienced in this country. The news operations of NBC, CBS and ABC were, in effect, three giant electronic versions of the Associated Press or United Press International — national in scope and centralized in their presentations, facilities and formats. By the seventies, most American communities were getting most of their news from TV. They were receiving equally a wide range of viewpoints and insights into what that TV news covered.

There was a tug of war on commercial network television between commercial exigencies (making a profit) and telecasting prime world and national events in terms of news from 1965 to 1975.

$2.5 billion was spent yearly on network television advertising on the average up to and including the year 1975.

Most TV spots were informational junk, telling little except how marvelous was the product being demonstrated.

The same banalities existed in programs: stereotyped characters mouthing snappy one-liners, story plots rolling endlessly day-after-day, involving characters working in a static setting.

CBS-TV dominated the ratings scene in overall programming throughout that decade. Only in 1975 did harbingers appear that signalized change was about to take place. ABC-TV saw its prime-time rating increase 17.8 percent during the first eight weeks of 1975, while equivalent ratings during the same period at NBC-TV and CBS-TV dropped 7 percent and 12 percent respectively.

What's more, ratings generally dropped in 1975 by about 1 percent — the first time in TV history that this had happened. A plethora of similar shows, the resulting apparent lack of audience interest, and introduction of the family hour by then CBS, Inc., President Arthur Taylor were blamed. The family hour limited program content in the 8 to 9 p.m. period. In effect, children decided what a family watched, at least up until 9 p.m.

Only when we look at the efforts of the news and documentary units of the three networks do we find a swing away from empty-headed show biz values.

Yet, even in these areas, the networks remained conservative. Most of the time throughout 1965–1975, network documentarists followed the Murrow-Friendly tradition of employing documentaries as cultural loss-leaders. American television documentarists were allowed to embroil themselves freely in controversy because the lion's share of programs never did. *Rhoda, Phyllis* and *The Waltons* never got into programming hot water so network managers could allow the infrequent documentary, such as *The Guns of Autumn,* to stir up acerbic debate.

Documentaries demonstrated to the government that the networks possessed the power to fry hell out of anybody they wanted. Murrow and Friendly had revealed that. They had helped break the power of a United States Senator, despite the fact that he had possessed considerable persuasive powers himself. The networks had the power to say whatever they wanted to say. They spoke out quite clearly and relevantly, I feel, from 1965 to 1968. Thereafter, confronting the harsh animosities of the Nixon Administration, they often turned tail and ran.

The networks rarely used outside producers as production sources for documentaries. All decisions affecting production were company decisions. If there were any difficulties about whether a documentary was made, whether it was broadcast, or when it was broadcast — these difficulties pretty much stayed in the family, where they were nicely worked out by the networks and their respective affiliates. As a result, news telecasting was a one-way street during the decade, with NBC, CBS and ABC controlling the traffic.

Hopefully, this traffic pattern will be changed if Congress approves proposed legislation calling for deregulation of radio, television and cable broadcasting, allowing stations to pick up programs via satellites or by cable, just as they choose, and allowing a grand proliferation of new TV channels on the UHF (Ultra High Frequency) band.

Did the public appreciate the generally excellent reporting of the decade? I'd say No. Because much of the news was literally repulsive. Because much of the news was reported live during daytime hours when audiences tended to be small. Because traditional news formats didn't excite the same interest amongst viewers as in the past. Because the public became used to the sameness of television entertainment and accepted its meaninglessness.

A news event such as the murder of Robert F. Kennedy sometimes forced networks news staffs into nearly constant coverage. In mid-June, 1968, for nearly a week, NBC devoted 55 hours to the Kennedy shooting and its aftermath, ABC 43, and CBS 42. Some of it was boring, repetitive and trivial. But NBC Executive Vice President Reuven Frank justified such coverage, saying, "This is a serious and grievous time in American history, and we think what we are doing not only emphasizes this to the people in their homes but allows them to think about it in those terms."

Thus, television news documentary regressed only after it was clearly demonstrated that its various subjects had become too heady to be taken steadily. Viewers didn't like to see too much reality. After all, most of what was being shown was fantasy, so why show what was really going on?

As a result, a trend developed toward other documentary categories — the mini-doc, the magazine format, prime-time blockbusters, theme shows. They could more easily remove viewers from bleak but realistic subjects to topics appealing to their pocketbooks, their interest in nature and adventure or their curiosity about celebrities. When hard-news documentaries became too hard to take, they often were replaced by so-called soft subjects. The horrors of Vietnam and the excesses of Watergate were diminished by dramatic reenactments of the critical days in the careers of Presidents Truman and Kennedy, as if the tragic aftermath of Vietnam and the chaos of Watergate somehow could be overcome by showcasing appropriate national icons who could demonstrate more positive national leadership qualities than those manifested during the Johnson and Nixon years.

As news and news documentary staffs at the networks moved away from the frightful headlines of the sixties toward the consumer-interest stories of the seventies (so-called "you-appeal" stories), the news mix each week settled into a softer and softer mire until, by 1975, documentary journalists found themselves moving toward the entertainment bailiwick. They really had no other place to go.

SOURCES

CHAPTER 1: EVOLUTION OF THE TELEVISION NEWS DOCUMENTARY

1. Tom Baun, NBC News Brochure: "The Invention of the Television Documentary, NBC News 1950–1975."
2. John Sharnik interview with author, June 3, 1975.
3. *CBS Reports:* "The Germans," broadcast Sept. 27, 1967, 10:00 p.m. EDT, pp. 7–9.
4. Martin Mayer, "How Television Covers the World (in 4,000 Words or Less)," *Esquire*, Jan. 19, 1972, p. 182.
5. *Ibid.*
6. Pete Axhelm, "Waiting for Glory," *Newsweek*, July 7, 1969, p. 82.
7. Kay Gardella, "TV Review," N.Y. *Daily News*, June 12, 1968.
8. Al and David Maysles and Charlotte Zwerin, *Salesman* (New York: The New American Library, 1969), p. 19.
9. *Ibid.*, pp. 102–4.
10. *Ibid.*, p. 30.
11. A. William Bluem, "TV Documentaries and the Social Order," pp. 8–11. Speech to the National Archives Conference, Thursday, Nov. 9, 1972, at the Continuing Education Center, University of Delaware, Newark, Del.

CHAPTER 2: ENVIRONMENT OF THE TELEVISION NEWS DOCUMENTARY

1. Saul Braun, "What Makes *60 Minutes* Tick?" *TV Guide*, Oct. 20, 1973, p. 16.
2. Av Westin interview with author, Aug. 5, 1975.
3. John Sharnik interview with author, June 3, 1975.
4. *Ibid.*
5. Edith Efron, "The Great Television Myth," reprint of her article in *TV Guide*, May 6, 1967.
6. *Ibid.*
7. Av Westin interview with author, Aug. 5, 1975.
8. Burton Benjamin, "The Shape of the Documentary." Remarks before the annual conference, Western Educational Society for Telecommunications, Las Vegas, Nev., Oct. 28, 1972.

9. Jean M. White, "You Still Feel It as You See It Now," Washington *Post,* July 14, 1973, p. D-5. The second part of this showing covered *Argument in Indianapolis,* describing the hassle to keep the American Civil Liberties Union from using the Indianapolis War Memorial.
10. Typescript, "A Retrospective of CBS News Broadcasts," Lincoln Center, Dec. 1, 1971, p. 10. Presented by the Film Society of Lincoln Center. McMullen's panel was chaired by CBS News Vice President Bill Leonard and included Mike Wallace, of *60 Minutes,* and Peter Davis, writer of *Hunger in America, The Selling of the Pentagon* and producer-writer of *Hearts and Minds,* a theater documentary.
11. CBS News: *60 Minutes,* Vol. III, No. 3, broadcast March 11, 1971, p. 7.
12. *Time,* Oct. 4, 1968, p. 84.
13. Saul Braun, "What Makes *60 Minutes* Tick?" *TV Guide,* Oct. 20, 1973, p. 16.
14. Typescript, "A Retrospective . . . , p. 18.
15. *Time,* Oct. 4, 1968, p. 84.
16. Steve Robinson, *"60 Minutes* vs. Wyoming," *More,* Feb. 1978, p. 8.
17. *Ibid.,* p. 7.
18. Robert Friedman, "A Lone Soldier's War Against CBS and Mike Wallace," *More,* Feb. 1977, p. 34.
19. Richard Carelli, "Ruling Defeat for Media," Syracuse *Herald-Journal,* April 18, 1979, p. 1.
20. Reuven Frank, "Balming Out in Gilead," *Television Quarterly* vol. XIV (Spring, 1977): 19.
21. *Ibid.,* p. 20.
22. *Ibid.,* p. 22.
23. *Ibid.,* p. 24.
24. Val Adams, "TV Review," N.Y. *Daily News,* July 29, 1972, p. 35.
25. *Ibid.*
26. John J. O'Connor, "TV Review," N.Y. *Times,* July 9, 1975, p. 9.
27. Martin Mayer, "How Television News Covers the World (in 4,000 Words or Less)," *Esquire,* Jan. 19, 1972, p. 182.
28. NBC News press release, June 21, 1966.
29. *Ibid.*
30. John Sharnik interview with author, June 3, 1975.
31. Alvin H. Perlmutter interview with author, May 30, 1975.
32. *Broadcasting,* Aug. 1975, p. 34.

CHAPTER 3: TELEVISION THEME DOCUMENTARY

1. Tom Baun, NBC News Brochure.
2. Jack Gould, "TV Review," N.Y. *Times,* Jan. 13, 1965.
3. *Current Biography,* 1967, p. 383.
4. *Ibid.*
5. *Ibid.*
6. N.Y. *World-Telegram-Sun,* Feb. 24, 1965.
7. N.Y. *Times,* April 10, 1965.
8. *Ibid.*
9. Robert Lewis Shayon, "Where Sociology Meets Journalism," *Saturday Review,* April 2, 1966.
10. *Ibid.*
11. CBS News Special: *Sixteen in Webster Groves,* broadcast Friday, Feb. 25, 1966, 10:00 p.m. EST, p. 1.
12. *Ibid.,* pp. 2, 4.
13. *Ibid.,* pp. 18, 19.
14. *Ibid.,* pp. 24, 25.
15. Martin Mayer, *About Television* (New York: Harper & Row, 1972), p. 253.

16. Kay Gardella, "TV Review," N.Y. *Daily News,* Feb. 26, 1966.
17. Susan Szekely, "The View from Webster Groves," in "Teen Talk," N.Y. *Post,* March 1, 1966.
18. Harriet Van Horne, "What Teens in Suburbia Ask of Life," N.Y. *World-Telegram-Sun,* Feb. 28, 1966, p. 38.
19. John Horn, "TV Review," N.Y. *Herald-Tribune,* April 9, 1966, p. 40.
20. CBS News Special: *Webster Groves Revisited,* broadcast Friday, April 8, 1966, 10:00 p.m. EST.
21. CBS News press release, July 16, 1966.
22. John Horn, "TV Review," N.Y. *Herald-Tribune,* Feb. 16, 1965.
23. CBS News press release, Sept. 27, 1966.
24. Harriet Van Horne, "TV Review," N.Y. *World-Journal-Tribune,* Oct. 11, 1966.
25. CBS News press release, July 23, 1965.
26. CBS News Special: *An Essay on Hotels,* broadcast Tuesday, June 28, 1966, 10:00 p.m. EDT, p. 7.
27. *Ibid.,* p. 14.
28. *Ibid.,* p. 23.
29. *Ibid.,* p. 28.
30. Kay Gardella, "TV Review," N.Y. *Daily News,* June 29, 1966.
31. *Broadcasting,* May 23, 1966, p. 64.
32. *Newsweek,* Sept. 11, 1967, p. 59.
33. Jack Gould, "TV Review," N.Y. *Times,* Sept. 11, 1967.
34. *Ibid.*
35. *Broadcasting, loc. cit.*
36. *Ibid.*
37. Richard K. Doan, "The Doan Report," *TV Guide,* June 21–27, 1975, p. A-1.
38. CBS-TV Memo: "Specials," about *Benjamin Franklin,* Oct. 1, 1973; extremely paraphrased in this segment.
39. *Variety,* Nov. 27, 1974, p. 64.
40. *Variety,* Dec. 25, 1974, p. 26.
41. CBS-TV Memo: "Specials."
42. *Variety, loc. cit.*
43. "Docu on Chicago Trial, Brushed off by TV Webs, Gets Academic Time," *Variety,* Oct. 9, 1974, p. 54.
44. John J. O'Connor, "TV Review," N.Y. *Times,* Jan. 26, 1972, p. 75.
45. *Ibid.*

PART TWO: INTRODUCTION

1. Interview with author, August 5, 1975.
2. *Ibid.*
3. *Ibid.*

CHAPTER 4: PRODUCERS AT NBC NEWS

1. Tom Baun, NBC News Brochure.
2. David G. Yellin, *Special: Fred Freed and the Television Documentary* (New York: The MacMillan Company, 1972), pp. 131–133.
3. David G. Yellin, "What Needs to Be Done; the Memoranda of Fred Freed," *Television Quarterly* XI (Summer, 1974): 44.
4. Jack Gould, "TV Review," N.Y. *Times,* Jan. 6, 1965.
5. Jack Gould, "TV Review," N.Y. *Times,* Sept. 8, 1965.
6. Yellin, *Special: Fred Freed . . . ,* p. 133.
7. Jack Gould, "TV Review," N.Y. *Times,* June 10, 1966.
8. Yellin, *Special: Fred Freed . . . ,* p. 252–53.

9. *Newsweek,* June 17, 1968, p. 112.
10. *Newsweek,* Dec. 23, 1968, p. 76.
11. *Ibid.*
12. Jack Gould, "TV Review," N.Y. *Times,* Dec. 10, 1970.
13. *Ibid.*
14. *Ibid.*
15. *Variety,* Jan. 27, 1971.
16. John J. O'Connor, "TV Review," N.Y. *Times,* Jan. 31, 1973, p. 83.
17. *Ibid.*
18. John J. O'Connor, "TV Review," N.Y. *Times,* June 14, 1973, p. 95.
19. *Ibid.*
20. *Ibid.*
21. NBC News press release, June 7, 1973.
22. *Ibid.*
23. *Ibid.*
24. John J. O'Connor, "TV Review," N.Y. *Times,* Sept. 5, 1973, p. 83.
25. *Ibid.*
26. NBC News press release, Aug. 15, 1973.
27. *Ibid.*
28. N.Y. *Times,* Biographical Edition, April, 1974.
29. Tom Baun, NBC News Brochure.
30. *Time,* July 17, 1967, p. 100.
31. *Variety,* Sept. 2, 1970, p. 54.
32. *Current Biography,* 1972, p. 243.
33. John J. O'Connor, "TV Review," N.Y. *Times,* May 31, 1974, p. 67.
34. Les Brown, "NBC Gun Program, Never Shown, Attracts Letters," N.Y. *Times,* April 4, 1975, p. 57.
35. NBC News documentary script: *A Shooting Gallery Called America,* broadcast April 27, 1975, p. 2.
36. *Ibid.,* p. 20.
37. NBC News press release, Feb. 18, 1975.
38. *Variety,* Feb. 3, 1971, p. 38.
39. *Variety,* Aug. 11, 1971, p. 44.
40. *Variety,* Sept. 15, 1971.
41. NBC News *White Paper: Suffer the Little Children,* broadcast Jan. 11, 1972, p. 1. Producer: Northshield; associate producer: John Lord; director: Fred Flamenhaft; camera: Chris Callery; editors: John Teeple and Jean Venable.
42. *Ibid.,* pp. 5, 32–34.
43. *Variety,* June 27, 1973.
44. John J. O'Connor, "TV Review," N.Y. *Times,* Oct. 23, 1973, p. 95.
45. *Ibid.*
46. *Ibid.*
47. John J. O'Connor, "TV Review," N.Y. *Times,* Nov. 26, 1974, p. 79.
48. Tom Baun, NBC News Brochure.
49. Robert Northshield, "The Healing of Robert Lee," *Smithsonian* V, 76.
50. John J. O'Connor, "TV Review" N.Y. *Times,* Oct. 28, 1975.
51. *Ibid.*

CHAPTER 5: PRODUCERS AT CBS NEWS

1. CBS News press release, May 29, 1969.
2. Bill Leonard," *CBS Reports:* Fifteen Years of Sweat, Toil and Glory," *Television Quarterly* XII (Fall, 1974): 21.
3. CBS News Press Information: *"CBS Reports,* 1959–1964," p. 5.

4. "Did You Know *CBS Reports* Never Stops Trying to Open America's Eyes?" *TV Guide,* Feb. 19–25, 1965, p. 12.
5. N.Y. *Times,* June 3, 1971, obituary page.
6. *Ibid.*
7. John Horn, *"CBS Reports* Plans for 1965–66," N.Y. *Herald-Tribune,* Jan. 9, 1965.
8. CBS News Brochure, 1965, p. 5.
9. Leonard, *op. cit.,* p. 5.
10. CBS News press release, April 21, 1964.
11. George Maksian, "Mitgang Quits CBS News," N.Y. *Daily News,* July 10, 1967.
12. CBS News Brochure, 1965, pp. 34–36.
13. *Newsweek,* March 27, 1967, p. 92.
14. *Current Biography,* 1961, p. 405.
15. Tom Snyder interview with Hewitt, NBC-TV *Tomorrow* program, April 26, 1976.
16. Les Brown, "TV Notes: How *60 Minutes* Stumbled into Prime Time," N.Y. *Times,* Nov. 23, 1975, Sunday TV page.
17. Richard Zoglin, "What Makes *60 Minutes* Tick?" N.Y. *Times,* Sept. 11, 1977, Sunday TV page.
18. Jack Gould, "TV Review," N.Y. *Times,* March 27, 1968.
19. Harriet Van Horne, "TV Review," N.Y. *Post,* April 27, 1968.
20. CBS News press release, March 25, 1968.
21. *Ibid.*
22. "TV Review," *Variety,* April 11, 1968.
23. N.Y. *Post,* April 10, 1968.
24. *Newsday,* April 10, 1968.
25. Lawrence Laurent, "TV Review," Washington *Post,* April 11, 1968.
26. George Gent, "TV Review," N.Y. *Times,* April 10, 1968.
27. Ted Lewis, "Hugo Black Gives Lift to a Troubled Nation," N.Y. *Daily News,* Dec. 4, 1968.
28. CBS News Special: *Justice Black and the Bill of Rights,* broadcast Tuesday, Dec. 3, 1968, 10:00 p.m. EST, p. 2.
29. *Ibid.,* p. 4.
30. *Ibid.,* pp. 11, 12.
31. *Ibid.,* p. 14.

CHAPTER 6: TWO-TON PENCIL: CBS NEWS, 1970

1. Les Brown, *The Encyclopedia of Television* (New York: New York Times Books, 1977), p. 10.
2. *Americana Annual,* 1969 (New York: Americana Corp., 1969), p. 664.
3. Kay Gardella, "TV Review," N.Y. *Daily News,* May 6, 1970.
4. Bob Williams, "TV Review," N.Y. *Post,* April 23, 1970.
5. Jack Gould, "TV Review," N.Y. *Times,* April 14, 1970.
6. Fred Ferretti, "CBS Schedules Expo '70 Special," N.Y. *Times,* Mar. 7, 1970.
7. Brown, *op. cit.,* p. 379.
8. Jack Gould, "TV Review," N.Y. *Times,* April 23, 1970.
9. Kay Gardella, "TV Review," N.Y. *Daily News,* May 20, 1970.
10. Harriet Van Horne, "TV Review," N.Y. *Post,* May 23, 1970.
11. R. Chandler and P. Lynch, *The National Environment Test* (New York: Pocket Books, Inc., 1970), pp. 7–9.
12. CBS News press release, May 19, 1970.
13. *The Christian Science Monitor,* Aug. 7, 1970 (TCSM Mirror of Opinion quotes the London *Times*).
14. Diana Loercher, "TV Review," *The Christian Science Monitor,* July 31, 1970.
15. Paul Wohl, "TV Review," *The Christian Science Monitor,* Aug. 12, 1970.

16. Chalmers M. Roberts, "Secretly Made Tape Proves One Can Fight Inside Russia," Washington *Post,* Aug. 12, 1970.
17. "Amalrik's Trial Set in USSR," N.Y. *Post,* Sept. 12, 1970.
18. N.Y. *Post,* Sept. 12, 1970.
19. Diana Loercher, "TV Review," *The Christian Science Monitor,* Sept. 11, 1970.
20. Rosemary Armmia Kent, "TV Review," *Women's Wear Daily,* Sept. 8, 1970.
21. Kay Gardella, "TV Review," N.Y. *Daily News,* Sept. 9, 1970.
22. Lawrence Laurent, "TV Review," Washington *Post,* Sept. 8, 1970.
23. Kent, *op. cit.*
24. Jack Gould, "TV Review," N.Y. *Times,* Sept. 9, 1970.
25. *Iibd.*

CHAPTER 7: RETROSPECTIVE AT LINCOLN CENTER

1. CBS News press release, May 28, 1971.
2. Panel discussion transcript, Dec. 2, 1971, p. 6.
3. *Ibid.,* p. 10.
4. *Ibid.,* p. 11.
5. *Ibid.,* pp. 11–14.
6. Panel discussion transcript, Dec. 3, 1971, p. 42.

CHAPTER 8: CBS NEWS, 1974

1. *Variety,* Oct. 9, 1974.
2. *Variety,* Oct. 30, 1974.
3. *Variety,* Sept. 4, 1974.
4. *Variety,* Oct. 30, 1974.
5. CBS News Special: *Walter Lippmann, 1889–1974,* broadcast Saturday, Dec. 14, 1974, 7:30 p.m. EST.
6. *Variety,* Nov. 27, 1974.
7. Carol Burton, "Solzhenitsyn Speaks," *Newsday,* June 21, 1974.
8. Arthur Unger, "TV Review," *The Christian Science Monitor,* Feb. 1, 1974.
9. *Ibid.*
10. Grace Lichtenstein, "CBS News Talks of Payola on Records," N.Y. *Times,* Aug. 10, 1974.
11. *Ibid.*
12. *Ibid.*
13. Kay Gardella, "TV Review," N.Y. *Daily News,* Aug. 6, 1974, p. 29.
14. Les Brown, "CBS to Show Report of Inquiry into Payola in Record Industry," N.Y. *Times,* Aug. 6, 1974.
15. CBS News Special: *The Trouble with Rock,* broadcast Sunday, Aug. 11, 1974, 6:00 p.m. EST, p. 1.
16. *Ibid.,* p. 3.
17. *Ibid.,* p. 4.
18. *Ibid.,* p. 5.
19. *Ibid.*
20. *Ibid.,* p. 6.
21. *Ibid.,* pp. 6–7.
22. *Ibid.,* p. 9.
23. Kay Gardella, "TV Review," N.Y. *Daily News,* Aug. 12, 1974.
24. *The Trouble with Rock,* p. 12.
25. *Ibid.,* p. 13.
26. *Ibid.*
27. *Ibid.,* p. 14.
28. *Ibid.*
29. *Ibid.*

30. *Ibid.*, p. 17.
31. *Ibid.*, p. 18.
32. Gardella, *op. cit.*
33. Tom Zito, "Money Under the Table," Washington *Post,* Aug. 10, 1974.

CHAPTER 9: CBS NEWS, 1975

1. CBS News Special: *Haldeman: The Nixon Years, Conversations with Mike Wallace,* broadcast Sunday, March 23, 1975, 6:00 p.m. EST, pp. 8, 9.
2. "Haldeman: Part 2," *Newsday,* March 31, 1975.
3. Cyclops, "Should TV Pay for Interviews?" N.Y. *Times,* April 13, 1975, p. D-25.
4. *Ibid.*
5. Alvin H. Perlmutter interview with author, May 30, 1975.
6. Les Brown, "Haldeman Said to Get $25,000 for CBS Interviews by Wallace," N.Y. *Times,* March 6, 1975.
7. *Ibid.*
8. Les Brown, "Networks Reviewing Policies on Paying for Exclusive Interviews," N.Y. *Times,* April 2, 1975.
9. Les Brown, "TV Interview Payments," N.Y. *Times,* May 24, 1975.
10. "Television and Radio," *American Encyclopaedia,* 1975, p. 536.

CHAPTER 10: PRODUCERS AT ABC NEWS

1. "ABC: The 25th Year," *Television-Radio Age,* May 9, 1977, p. A-45.
2. American Broadcasting Companies, Inc., Brochure: "The First Twenty-Five Years: 1953–1977."
3. Interview with author, New York City, Aug. 4, 1975. The remainder of this section largely is based on this discussion.
4. *Ibid.*
5. *Ibid.*
6. *Ibid.*
7. *Ibid.*
8. *Ibid.*
9. *Ibid.*
10. *Ibid.*
11. *Ibid.*

CHAPTER 11: AV WESTIN

1. Av Westin, "The ABC Evening News Chapter," written March 12, 1971, for use by the ABC News staff.
2. *Ibid.*
3. *Ibid.*
4. *Ibid.*
5. Av Westin interview with author, New York City, Aug. 4, 1975.
6. Kay Gardella, "Exec Av Westin Discusses ABC-TV News *Close-up,*" N.Y. *Daily News,* July 18, 1973, p. 75.
7. *Ibid.*
8. *Ibid.*
9. *Ibid.*
10. Cyclops, "On Being Buffaloed by the News," N.Y. *Times,* March 16, 1975, p. D-19.
11. ABC News *Close-up: IRS: A Question of Power,* broadcast Friday, March 21, 1975, 10:00 p.m. EDT.
12. *Time,* March 24, 1975, pp. 74, 75.
13. *Ibid.*
14. *Ibid.*

15. Av Westin interview with author, Aug. 4, 1975.
16. Richard Zoglin, "Is Av Westin Shaping the Future of TV News?" N.Y. *Times,* April 13, 1975, Arts & Leisure Section, p. 1.
17. *Ibid.,* p. 25.
18. Les Brown, "Westin and TV News," N.Y. *Times,* Jan. 28, 1976.
19. *Ibid.*
20. *Ibid.*
21. *Ibid.*
22. Les Brown, "Leading Lady," N.Y. *Times,* Feb. 8, 1976.
23. Bill Greeley, "Up Close, ABC Docus Are Growing Softer and Softer," *Variety,* April 21, 1976, p. 82.
24. *Ibid.*
25. Les Brown, "ABC News Cuts Its Documentary Schedule in Half," N.Y. *Times,* Nov. 4, 1975.

CHAPTER 12: THE REASONER REPORT

1. John J. O'Connor, "TV Review," N.Y. *Times,* June 27, 1975.
2. *Ibid.*

CHAPTER 13: MARTIN CARR

1. CBS News Special: *The Search for Ulysses,* broadcast Tuesday, Jan. 11, 1966, 10:00 p.m. EST, pp. 7, 8.
2. Tom Baun, NBC News Brochure.
3. Martin Carr, "Charisma . . . Ban or Blessing? Does the Camera See Through the Hearts of Men?" *Television Quarterly* XII, 2 (1975): 2.
4. *Variety,* May 5, 1971.

PART THREE: INTRODUCTION

1. John J. O'Connor, "TV Review," N.Y. *Times,* Dec. 22, 1971.
2. Leonard Probst, "People Are Generally Skeptical of Us . . . and Indeed They Should Be," *TV Guide,* Nov. 29, 1975, p. 4.
3. Karl E. Meyer, "Candy Telegrams to Kiddyland," *More,* Feb. 1975, p. 10.
4. Interview with author, June 3, 1975.
5. Kay Gardella, "TV Review," N.Y. *Daily News,* Jan. 14, 1974.
6. *Ibid.*

CHAPTER 14: NBC NEWS, 1966–1975: MORE ON TV NEWS MAGAZINES

1. Les Brown, *The Business Behind the Box* (New York: Harcourt Brace Jovanovich, Inc., 1971), pp. 331, 332.
2. *Broadcasting,* April 12, 1976, p. 81.
3. Tom Baun, NBC News Brochure.
4. *Newsweek,* Jan. 20, 1969, p. 95.
5. *Time,* April 11, 1969, p. 86.
6. Interview with author, May 30, 1975.

CHAPTER 15: *ABC SCOPE:* 1965–1970

1. ABC News Program Summary, 1965.

CHAPTER 16: CBS NEWS, 1971: INTERVIEWING

1. N.Y. *Post,* Sept. 25, 1971, p. 4.
2. *Ibid.,* pp. 4, 5.
3. *Newsday,* June 24, 1971.
4. *Ibid.*

5. N.Y. *Times,* June 24, 1971. Ellsberg interview transcript.
6. *Newsday,* June 24, 1971.
7. Walter Cronkite, "Such Interesting People," in *Eye on the World* (New York: Cowles Book Co., Inc., 1971), p. 291.
8. *Ibid.,* p. 292.
9. *Ibid.,* p. 295.
10. John J. O'Connor, "TV Review," N.Y. *Times,* Sept. 7, 1971.

CHAPTER 17: CBS NEWS, 1971: CLASHES WITH NEWS SOURCES

1. John Chancellor, "News Media: Is That All There Is? Electronic Journalism," *Playboy,* Vol. XIX, No. 1, Jan. 1972, pp. 120; 216–17.
2. *Film 71/72,* David Denby, ed. New York. Simon & Schuster, 1972, p. 195.
3. Daniel Bell, "Teletext and Technology," *Encounter,* No. 285 (June, 1977): 26.
4. Eugene McCarthy, "The Fourth Estate, 'Sins of Omission'," *Harper's Magazine,* June, 1977.
5. *Broadcasting,* June 6, 1977, p. 24.
6. *Ibid.*
7. Richard Doan, "CBS Concern for IBM Costs $250,000," N.Y. *Tribune,* April 15, 1966.
8. Val Adams, *"The Volga* Shown: Moscow Angry," N.Y. *Times,* Jan. 5, 1966.
9. Val Adams, "CBS Confesses It Erred on Show," N.Y. *Times,* June 16, 1966.
10. Robert E. Dallos, "CBS Hartford Station Scored for Canceling Vietnam Program," N.Y. *Times,* March 21, 1967.
11. Robert Sherrill, "The Happy Ending (Maybe) of *The Selling of the Pentagon,"* N.Y. *Times,* May 16, 1971, p. 26.
12. *Ibid.,* p. 25.
13. *Ibid.* See also Martin Mayer, *About Television* (New York: Harper & Row, 1972), pp. 254–68.
14. CBS News press release, March 25, 1971.
15. CBS News press release, March 19, 1971.
16. CBS News press release, April 12, 1971.
17. Harriet Van Horne, "An Agnew Dud," N.Y. *Post,* March 22, 1971.
18. Sherrill, *op. cit.,* p. 78.
19. *Ibid.,* p. 87.

CHAPTER 18: THE DESPAIRING EYE

1. CBS News Memo, 1967, regarding subjects for future broadcast.
2. Variety, Mar. 8, 1967, p. 38.
3. CBS News Special: *The Tenement,* broadcast Tuesday, Feb. 28, 1967, 10:00 p.m. EST.
4. *Ibid.,* p. 3.
5. *Ibid.,* p. 2.
6. *Ibid.,* pp. 12, 13.
7. *Ibid.,* p. 15.
8. Jack Gould, "TV: Stark Despair in a Chicago Tenement," N.Y. *Times,* Mar. 1, 1967.
9. CBS News Special: *The Correspondents Report,* Part I: "America and the World," broadcast Tuesday, Dec. 31, 1968, 10:00 p.m. EST, p. 4.
10.. Letter from Secretary of Agriculture Orville L. Freeman to Congressman Carl Perkins, Chairman, House of Representatives Education and Labor Committee, May 27, 1968, p. 7.
11. "FCC Drops Complaints Alleging CBS Slanted News on Documentary," *Wall Street Journal,* Oct. 20, 1969.
12. *Newsweek,* July 8, 1968, p. 76.
13. Ben Gross, "The British *Royal Family* an Engrossing Special," N.Y. *Daily News,* Sept. 22, 1969. Also, "BBC Film Shows Queen's Private World," N.Y. *Times,* June 20, 1969.
14. Kay Gardella, *"Battle of East St. Louis* Sounds a Positive Note," N.Y. *Daily News,* Dec. 31, 1969.

15. CBS News Special: *The Battle of East St. Louis*, broadcast Tuesday, Dec. 30, 1969, 10:00 p.m. EST, p. 14.
16. *Ibid.*, pp. 4–5.
17. *Ibid.*
18. *Ibid.*, p. 20.
19. *Ibid.*, pp. 15, 16.
20. *Variety*, Feb. 3, 1971.
21. John J. O'Connor, "TV: CBS Views an American Family's Discontent," N.Y. *Times*, Nov. 24, 1971.
22. *Ibid.*
23. *Ibid.*
24. *Ibid.*
25. Val Adams, "CBS to Televise Report on Mafia," N.Y. *Daily News*, June 6, 1976.
26. CBS News Special: *An Essay on the Mafia*, broadcast June 25, 1972, 8:30 p.m. EDT, p. 6.
27. *Ibid.*
28. *Ibid.*, p. 9.
29. *Ibid.*, p. 3.
30. *Ibid.*, pp. 11–12.
31. *Ibid.*, p. 16.
32. Joel Dreyfuss, "Four Portraits in Black," Washington *Post*, April 26, 1974.
33. N.Y. *Post*, April 26, 1974.
34. CBS News press release, April 10, 1974.
35. Bob Williams, "On the Air," N.Y. *Post*, April 27, 1974.
36. *Ibid.*
37. CBS News Memo: "Four Portraits in Black," April 9, 1974, pp. 1, 2.

CHAPTER 19: WAR

1. Albert R. Leventhal, *War* (Chicago: Playboy Press, 1969), pp. 226–28.
2. CBS News Special Report: *Vietnam: The Hawks and The Doves*, broadcast Monday, March 8, 1965, 10:00 p.m. EST, paraphrased from p. 2.
3. *Ibid.*, p. 24.
4. CBS News Special: *Vietnam Perspective*, Part I: "The Decisions," broadcast Aug. 9, 1965, 10:00 p.m. EDT, pp. 4, 5.
5. Jules Witcover, "Where Washington Reporting Failed," *Columbia Journalism Review*, Winter, 1970–71, p. 8.
6. Don Stillman, "Tonkin: What Should Have Been Asked," *Columbia Journalism Review*, Winter, 1970–71, p. 21.
7. Frances Fitzgerald, *Fire in the Lake* (Boston: Little Brown & Co., 1972), p. 142.
8. CBS News Special: *Where We Stand in Vietnam*, broadcast Tuesday, Dec. 14, 1965, 10:00 p.m. EST, p. 9.
9. *Ibid.*, Roger Mudd, p. 2.
10. Harriet Van Horne, "TV Review," N.Y. *World-Journal-Sun*, Dec. 29, 1965.
11. *Ibid.*
12. CBS News Special: *Christmas in Vietnam*, broadcast Tuesday Dec. 28, 1965, 10: p.m. EST, pp. 12, 13.
13. N.Y. *Herald-Tribune*, Dec. 15, 1965.
14. Barbara Delatiner, "TV Review," *Newsday*, Dec. 1, 1965.
15. CBS News Special: *The Battle for The Ia Drang Valley*, broadcast Tuesday, Nov. 30, 1965, 10:00 p.m. EST, p. 1.
16. *Ibid.*, p. 2.
17. *Ibid.*
18. *Ibid.*, pp. 2, 3.
19. *Ibid.*, p. 5.

20. *Ibid.*
21. Delatiner, *op. cit.*
22. CBS News Special: *The Anti-Americans,* broadcast June 7, 1966, 10:00 p.m. EDT, pp. 8, 9.
23. CBS News press release, Aug. 11, 1966.
24. Jack Gould, "TV Review," N.Y. *Times,* Aug. 26, 1965.
25. CBS News Special: *The Councils of War,* broadcast Tuesday, Feb. 8, 1966, 10:00 p.m. EST, p. 31.
26. Jack Gould, "TV Review," N.Y. *Times,* Jan. 31, 1966.
27. CBS News Special Report: *Campaign '66, Vietnam and the Elections,* broadcast Friday, May 20, 1966, 10:00 p.m. EDT, p. 30.
28. CBS News Special Report: *The Anthony Eden Proposals,* broadcast Tuesday, May 31, 1966, 10:00 p.m. EDT, p. 2.
29. "Review and Outlook: The Great Society in Asia," *The Wall Street Journal,* April 22, 1966.
30. *Ibid.*
31. CBS News Special Report: *Vietnam: Eric Sevareid's Personal Report,* broadcast June 21, 1966, 10:00 p.m. EDT, p. 1.
32. *Ibid.,* p. 15.
33. *Ibid.,* pp. 6, 7,
34. *Ibid.,* p. 7.
35. *Ibid.,* p. 9.
36. *Ibid.*
37. *Ibid.,* p. 10.
38. *Ibid.,* p. 12.
39. *Ibid.,* p. 1.
40. *Ibid.,* p. 14.
41. Barbara Delatiner, "TV Review," *Newsday,* June 22, 1966.
42. *Ibid.*
43. CBS News press release, Nov. 11, 1966.
44. CBS News Special Report: *Inside Red China,* broadcast Tuesday, Nov. 22, 1966, 10:00 p.m. EST, pp. 12, 14.
45. *Ibid.,* p. 14.
46. *Ibid.,* p. 16.
47. Harriet Van Horne, "TV Review," N.Y. *World-Journal-Tribune,* Dec. 28, 1966.
48. CBS News Special Report: *Westmoreland on Vietnam,* Dec. 27, 1966, 10:00 p.m. EST, p. 3.
49. *Ibid.,* p. 7.
50. Jules Witcover, "Where Washington Reporting Failed," *Columbia Journalism Review,* Winter, 1970–71, p. 8.
51. Murray Kempton, "Our Peace Victims," N.Y. *Post,* May 5, 1967.
52. Harriet Van Horne, TV news item, N.Y. *World-Journal-Tribune,* March 22, 1967.
53. Barbara Delatiner, "Brutal Picture of Saigon Emerges on CBS Tour," *Newsday,* March 15, 1967.
54. Harriet Van Horne, "A Woman's View of the Vietnam War," N.Y. *World-Journal-Tribune,* March 16, 1967.
55. Jack Gould, "TV Review," N.Y. *Times,* April 5, 1967.
56. CBS News Special Report,: *Morley Safer's Vietnam: A Personal Report,* broadcast Tuesday, April 4, 1967, 10:00 p.m. EST, p. 1.
57. *Ibid.,* p. 2.
58. *Ibid.,* p. 3.
59. *Ibid.,* p. 4.
60. *Ibid.,* p. 11.
61. *Ibid.,* p. 13.
62. CBS News press release, May 16, 1968.
63. Barbara Delatiner, "Studies Contrast Vietnam, World War II," *Newsday,* June 5, 1968.

64. *CBS Reports: Viet Cong,* broadcast Tuesday, Feb. 20, 1968, 10:00 p.m. EST, p. 1.
65. *Ibid.,* p. 12.
66. CBS News Special: *The Correspondents Report,* Part I: "America and the World," broadcast Tuesday, Dec. 31, 1968, 10:00 p.m. EST, p. 1.
67. CBS News press release, April 8, 1962, p. 2.
68. CBS News Special: *Hanoi: A Report by Charles Collingwood,* broadcast Tuesday, April 16, 1968, 10:00 p.m. EST, p. 3.
69. *Ibid.,* p. 7.
70. CBS News program memo, Mar, 17, 1975.
71. CBS News Special Report: *The Ups and Downs of Henry Kissinger,* broadcast May 25, 1975, 7:30 EDT, p. 1.
72. *Ibid.,* p. 2.
73. *Ibid.,* p. 3.
74. *Ibid.*
75. *Ibid.,* p. 7.
76. Shana Alexander, "Season's Greetings," *Newsweek,* Dec. 23, 1974, p. 80.
77. *CBS News Special: Vietnam: A War That Is Finished,* broadcast April 29, 1975, 8:30 EDT, p. 16.
78. Alexander, *loc. cit.*
79. *Ibid.*
80. *Ibid.*
81. Phillip Whitehead, "TV Review," *The Listener,* September 16, 1971.
82. CBS Special Report: *Indo China 1975: The End of the Road?,* broadcast April 8, 1975, 10:00 p.m. EDT, p. 1.
83. CBS News press release, April 30, 1975.
84. Larry Lichty, "The Night at the End of the Tunnel," *Film Comment,* July–August, 1975, p. 33.
85. Bill Greeley, "Wrap-up on Vietnam," *Variety,* Sept. 3, 1975, p. 33.
86. John J. O'Connor, "TV Review," N.Y. *Times,* May 11, 1975, p. 1.
87. *Ibid.,* p. 25.
88. *Vietnam: A War That Is Finished,* p. 40.
89. *Ibid.,* p. 7.
90. *Ibid.,* p. 19.
91. *Ibid.,* p. 22.
92. *Ibid.,* p. 23.
93. *Ibid.,* p. 32.
94. *Ibid.,* pp. 36, 37.
95. *Ibid.,* p. 43.

CHAPTER 20: WASHINGTON

1. *Americana Annual,* 1969 (New York: Americana Corp., 1969), p. 672.
2. CBS News Special Report: *That Week in Chicago,* broadcast Sunday, Dec. 1, 1968, 11:30 p.m. EST.
3. *Time,* Nov. 21, 1969, p. 22.
4. *Americana Annual,* 1973 (New York: Americana Corp., 1973), p. 660.
5. Ben Bagdikian, "Pensions, The FCC's Dangerous Decision Against NBC," *Columbia Journalism Review,* March–April, 1974, p. 18.
6. Fred W. Friendly, *The Good Guys, The Bad Guys, and The First Amendment: Free Speech vs. Fairness in Broadcasting* (New York: Vintage Books, 1977), p. 150.
7. Bagdikian, *op. cit.,* p. 16.
8. *Ibid.*
9. *Ibid.,* p. 18.

10. Friendly, *op. cit.,* pp. 157–66; Chapter 10 presents a complete account of this vital confrontation between press and state.
11. *Variety,* Oct. 15, 1972.
12. David G. Yellin, *Special: Fred Freed and the Television Documentary* (New York: Macmillan, 1973), pp. 143–44.
13. *Variety,* July 5, 1972.
14. *Time,* Aug. 27, 1973, p. 59.
15. Ben Lupanello, "Nixon Registers Strongly in Telecast Conversation," N.Y. Daily News, Jan. 3, 1972.
16. CBS News Special: *A Conversation with President Nixon,* broadcast Jan. 2, 1972, 9:30 p.m. EST, p. 12.
17. Robert B. Semple, Jr., "Nixon Shows He Is an Old Hand at TV Techniques," N.Y. *Times,* Jan 5, 1972.
18. *Ibid.*
19. CBS News Special Report: *Vietnam: A Plan for Peace,* broadcast Jan. 25, 1972, 11:30 p.m. EST, p. 2.
20. *Ibid.,* p. 4.
21. Alan Bunce, "TV's View of a View: China Misunderstood," *The Christian Science Monitor,* Feb. 18, 1972.
22. CBS News Special for Young People: *Whatever Happened to '72?,* broadcast Dec. 28, 1972, 8:00 p.m. EST, p. 1.
23. CBS News Special: *Misunderstanding China,* broadcast Feb. 20, 1972, 6:00 p.m. EST, p. 2.
24. *Ibid.,* p. 3.
25. CBS News Special: *Escalation in Vietnam: Reasons, Risks and Reactions,* broadcast May 9, 1972, 10:30 p.m. EDT, p. 3.
26. Hugh Sidey, "Henry Kissinger, the Top No. 2 Man," *Life* 72 (Feb. 11, 1972): 41.
27. Martin Mayer, "Televising the Conventions," *Harper's Magazine* 244 (May, 1972): 68–71.
28. CBS News Special: *The Eagleton Case,* broadcast July 30, 1972, 6:00 p.m. EDT, p. 2.
29. CBS News Special: *The Elusive Peace,* broadcast Dec. 28, 1972, 10:00 p.m. EST, pp. 1, 2.
30. *Ibid.,* p. 7.
31. *Ibid.,* p. 5.
32. CBS News Special: *Hanoi: An Uncensored Report,* broadcast Friday, Oct. 13, 1972, 11:30 p.m. EDT, p. 4.
33. *Ibid.,* p. 9.
34. Kay Gardella, "TV Review," N.Y. *Daily News,* April 26, 1973.
35. *Ibid.*
36. CBS News press release, May 23, 1973.
37. John J. O'Connor, "TV Review," N.Y. *Times,* May 31, 1973.
38. Interview with author, June 3, 1975.
39. CBS News Memo: "Television and the News," May 31, 1973.
40. CBS News Memo: *The Rockefellers,* Dec. 28, 1973.
41. CBS News Special Report: *The Watergate Year — Crisis for the President,* broadcast Sunday, June 17, 1973, 6:00 p.m. EDT, pp. 1, 2.
42. *Ibid.,* p. 3.
43. *Ibid.*
44. *Americana Annual,* 1974 (New York, Americana Corp. 1974), p. 579.
45. Bob Williams, "On the Air," N.Y. *Post,* Nov. 5, 1973.
46. *Ibid.*
47. CBS News Special Report: *A Watergate Spectrum,* broadcast Sunday, Aug. 12, 1973, 6:00 p.m. EDT, p. 2.
48. *Americana Annual,* 1974, p. 580.
49. CBS News Special Report: *Watergate and the President,* broadcast Aug. 16, 1973, 8:00 p.m. EDT, p. 1.

50. *Ibid.*, pp. 2, 3.
51. *Ibid.*, p. 11.
52. CBS News Special Report: *The Watergate Hearings* — "The Erlichman Testimony," broadcast Tuesday, July 24, 1973, 10:00 p.m. EDT, p. 3.
53. *Ibid.*, p. 6.
54. CBS News Special Report: *The Watergate Hearings* — "The Haldeman Testimony," broadcast Wednesday, Aug. 1, 1973, 8:00 p.m. EDT, p. 10.
55. *A Watergate Spectrum,* p. 3.
56. CBS News Special Report: *Watergate: The President's News Conference,* broadcast Wednesday, Aug. 22, 1973, 9:00 p.m. EDT, p. 3.
57. *Ibid.*, p. 4.
58. *Ibid.*, p. 18.
59. CBS News Special Report: *The Embattled President,* broadcast Sunday, Nov. 4, 1973, 7:30 p.m. EST, p. 1.
60. *A Watergate Spectrum,* p. 20.
61. CBS News Special Report: *1973: A Television Album,* broadcast Dec. 30, 1973, 6:00 p.m. EST, p. 7.
62. *The Watergate Year — Crisis for the President,* p. 18.
63. Val Adams, "What's on: CBS Books Show on Nixon Quoting Nixon on 2nd Term," N.Y. *Times,* Jan. 10, 1974.
64. John J. O'Connor, "TV: CBS Examines October 25 Alert on Middle East," N.Y. *Times,* Jan. 17, 1974.
65. *Ibid.*
66. *Ibid.*
67. CBS News Special Report: *The Watergate Indictments,* broadcast Friday, March 1, 1974, 11:30 p.m. EST, p. 9.
68. CBS News Special Report: *Impeachment: The Court and the Committee,* broadcast Wednesday, July 24, 1974, 11:30 p.m. EDT, p. 1.
69. *Ibid.*, p. 4.
70. *Ibid.*, p. 9.
71. *Ibid.*, p. 18.
72. *Newsweek,* Aug. 19, 1974, p. 15.
73. *Ibid.*, p. 19.
74. CBS News Special Report: *Nixon: A Full, Free and Absolute Pardon,* broadcast Sunday, Sept. 8, 1974, 6:00 p.m. EDT, p. 2.
75. *Ibid.*, p. 3.
76. "Salant Re-Examines Press' Role in the Aftermath of Watergate," *Variety,* Oct. 2, 1974, p. 44.
77. John Carmody, "CBS: Rooney . . . ," Washington *Post,* Jan. 25, 1975, p. E-1.
78. CBS News internal memo, Jan. 17, 1975.
79. CBS News Special: *Mr. Rooney Goes to Washington,* broadcast Jan. 26, 1975, 9:30 p.m. EST, p. 3.
80. *Ibid.*, p. 13.
81. *Ibid.*, p. 21.

BIBLIOGRAPHY

Arlen, Michael J. *The Living Room War*. New York: Viking, 1969.

Barnouw, Erik. *Documentary: A History of the Non-Fiction Film*. New York: Oxford University Press, 1974.

Barrett, Marvin. *The Politics of Broadcasting*. New York: Thomas Y. Crowell, 1973.

————. *Rich News, Poor News*. Sixth Alfred DuPont-Columbia University Survey of Broadcast Journalism. New York: Harper & Row, 1978.

————. *Survey of Broadcast Journalism*. New York: Grosset & Dunlap, 1969.

————, ed. *A Survey of Broadcast Journalism, 1970–1971: A State of Siege*. New York: Grosset & Dunlap, 1971.

Barsam, Richard Meran. *Nonfiction Film: A Critical History*. New York: E. P. Dutton, 1973.

Baun, Tom. *The Invention of the Television Documentary: NBC News 1950–1975*. NBC News Brochure, 1975.

Bluem, A. William. *Documentary in American Television: Form; Function; Method*. New York: Hastings House, 1965.

Bower, Robert T. *Television and the Public*. New York: Holt, Rinehart & Winston, 1973.

Braestrup, Peter. *Big Story*. New York: Anchor/Doubleday, 1978.

Brown, Les. *Television: The Business Behind the Box*. New York: Harcourt, Brace, Jovanovich, Inc., 1971.

Calder-Marshall, Arthur. *The Innocent Eye: The Life of Robert Flaherty*. London, W. H. Allen, 1963.

Carr, Martin. "Charisma . . . Bane or Blessing? Does the Camera See Through the Hearts of Men?" *TV Quarterly* XII, 1975.

Cole, Barry G., ed. *Television: A Selection of Readings from* TV Guide. New York: The Free Press, 1970.

Combs, James E., and Michael W. Mansfield. eds. *Drama in Life: The Uses of Communication in Society.* New York: Hastings House, 1976.

DeFleur, Melvin L., and Sandra Ball-Rokeach. *Theories of Mass Communication,* 3d ed. New York: David McKay, 1975.

Diamond, Edwin. *Television, Politics and the News.* Cambridge, Mass.: MIT Press, 1975.

———. *The Tin Kazoo: Television, Politics and the News.* Boston: MIT Press, 1975.

Epstein, Edward Jay. *News from Nowhere: Television and the News.* New York: Vintage, 1974.

Fielding, Raymond. *The March of Time.* New York: Oxford University Press, 1978.

Fitzgerald, Frances. *Fire in the Lake: The Vietnamese and the Americans in Vietnam.* New York: Random House, 1972.

Friendly, Fred W. *Due to Circumstances Beyond Our Control.* New York: Random House, 1968.

———. *The Good Guys, The Bad Guys and the First Amendment: Free Speech vs. Fairness in Broadcasting.* New York: Vintage, 1977.

Gettleman, Marvin, ed. *Vietnam: History, Documents and Opinions on a Major World Crisis.* New York: Fawcett, 1965.

Gillette, Frank. *Video Process and Meta-Process.* Ed. Judson Rosebush. Syracuse, New York: Everson Museum of Art, 1973.

Ginsburg, Douglas H. *Regulation of Broadcasting.* St. Paul, Minn.: West Publishing, 1979.

Grierson, John. *Grierson on Documentary.* Ed. Hardy Forsyth. London: Faber & Faber, 1966.

Griffith, Richard. *The World of Robert Flaherty.* New York: Duell, Sloan & Pearce, 1953.

Jacobs, Lewis, ed. *The Documentary Tradition: From Nanook to Woodstock.* New York: Hopkinson & Blake, 1971.

Journal of Popular Culture, Vol. VII, No. 4, 1974. Special edition on television.

Kendrick, Alexander. *Prime Time: The Life of Edward R. Murrow.* Boston: Little, Brown, 1969.

Levin, G. Roy. *Documentary Explorations.* Garden City, New York: Doubleday, 1971.

Lichty, Lawrence W., and Malachi C. Topping. *American Broadcasting.* New York: Hastings House, 1975.

MacNeil, Robert. *The People Machine.* New York: Harper & Row, 1968.

Mamber, Stephen. *Cinema Vérité in America: Studies in Uncontrolled Documentary.* Cambridge, Mass.: MIT Press, 1974.

Manvell, Roger. *Films and the Second World War.* New York: Dell, 1974.

Mayer, Martin. *About Television.* New York: Harper & Row, 1972.

Maysles, Albert, David Maysles and Charlotte Zwerin. *Salesman.* New York: The New American Library, 1969.

Mekas, Jonas. *Movie Journal: The Rise of a New American Cinema, 1959–1971.* New York: Collier, 1972.

Newcomb, Horace. *TV: The Most Popular Art.* Garden City, New York: Anchor Press/Doubleday, 1974.

———, ed. *Television: The Critical View.* New York: Oxford University Press, 1976.

Powers, Ron. *The Newscasters: The News Business as Show Business.* New York: St. Martin's Press, 1977.

Rosenthal, Alan. *The New Documentary in Action: A Casebook in Filmmaking*. Berkeley: University of California Press, 1972.

Rotha, Paul. *Documentary Film*. New York: Hastings House, 1952.

Schwartz, Tony. *The Responsive Chord*. Garden City, New York: Anchor Press/Doubleday, 1974.

Seidle, Ronald J. *Air Time*. Boston: Holbrook Press, 1977.

Skornia, Harry J. *Television and Society*. New York: McGraw-Hill, 1965.

Small, William. *To Kill a Messenger: Television News and the Real World*. New York: Hastings House, 1970.

Steinberg, Charles S., ed. *Broadcasting: The Critical Challenges*. International Radio & Television Society's Third Annual Faculty/Industry Seminar. New York: Hastings House, 1974.

Stone, Vernon, and Bruce Hinson. *Television Newsfilm Techniques*. New York: Hastings House, 1974.

Williams, Raymond. *Communications*. London: Penguin, Cox & Wyman, 1966.

———. *Television: Technology and Cultural Form*. New York: Schocken, 1974.

Yellin, David G. *Special: Fred Freed and the Television Documentary*. New York: MacMillan, 1972.

INDEX